D1710803

Architectural
Signing and Graphics

Architectural Signing and Graphics

BY JOHN FOLLIS AND DAVE HAMMER

WHITNEY LIBRARY OF DESIGN
an imprint of Watson-Guptill Publications/New York

The Architectural Press Ltd./London

Unless otherwise credited in the captions, architectural signing and graphics
illustrated in this book were designed by John Follis and Associates, Inc.

First published 1979 in the United States and Canada by Whitney Library of Design,
an imprint of Watson-Guptill Publications,
a division of Billboard Publications, Inc.,
1515 Broadway, New York, N.Y. 10036

Library of Congress Cataloging in Publication Data
Follis, John, 1923-
   Architectural signing and graphics.
   Bibliography: p.
Includes index.
1. Signs and symbols in architecture.
2. Communication in architectural design. I. Hammer,
Dave, 1923-   joint author. II. Title.
NA2500.F63   720   79-933
ISBN 0-8230-7051-4

Published in Great Britain by The Architectural Press Ltd.,
9 Queen Anne's Gate, London SW1H 9BY
ISBN 0-85139-060-9

Manufactured in U.S.A.

First Printing, 1979

Edited by Sarah Bodine and Susan Davis

To Gyorgy Kepes for his writing and his art
DAVE HAMMER

To Alvin Lustig, my design teacher, who first introduced me to the basic need for good architectural signing
JOHN FOLLIS

Acknowledgments

To John Follis and Associates staff members:

Joseph Stoddard for the fine free-hand drawings used in the Design and Design Development chapters; and for helping to gather all the material needed for the Designers' Portfolio, including preliminary layouts of that chapter.

Mary Singleton, for typing those many draft versions, for the endless series of letters and phone calls, and for coordinating the many details.

Arno Ford Furstenberg for both writing and illustrating the Typography chapter and for assistance with many other aspects of the book.

Elizabeth Baird for assistance on drawings for the Documentation chapter and for technical advice.

Jean-Claude Muller for his expert typographic advice.

To others:

Our wives, June Follis and Eleanor Hammer, for sympathy, patient understanding, and editorial help.

The designers whose work is shown in Chapter 8, Designers' Portfolio.

John Berry for reading some of the first drafts and making valued suggestions on several chapters.

Joe Lonergan for reading the first drafts of the Fabrication and Supervision chapters.

Sarah Bodine and Susan Davis, our editors, who provided boundless advice on content and organization.

Credits:

To the Society of Environmental Graphic Designers for material excerpted from the *Environmental Graphics Sourcebook*, Part I: Materials and Techniques.

To Architectural Signing Inc. and ASI Sign Systems Inc. for the use of material excerpted from their *Architectural Signing Handbook* and for technical assistance with artwork.

Contents

Introduction

Contemporary communications take many forms—from orbiting satellites to transistor wrist watches. But the creations of modern science have not replaced one of the oldest forms of communication: the written word and symbol—the sign. Many years ago even this simple form of communication was seldom needed for public buildings. The village church and meeting house were identified by their form; entrances and exits were easily located and familiar to all. Craftsmen's shops were identified by a symbol of their trade; the few merchant signs communicated simple messages.

However, as society became increasingly complex, random signs could no longer provide the quantity of information needed. In an attempt to meet the need, signs multiplied, often creating a kind of visual pollution. Today, however, we are beginning to see a way out of the visual chaos with total signing systems.

An effective signing and graphics system functions not as a separate entity but as an integral part of its environment. Carefully planned signs communicate essential information while also enhancing the architectural environment. Graphics—in the form of murals, flags, and banners—extend the esthetic scope of the system, adding color, movement, and vitality.

Why a book on architectural signing and graphics? Various publications have touched upon aspects of the total process of designing these systems, but none has attempted a comprehensive approach. Other books have included pictorial reviews of current work in the field, but none provides a thorough survey of the best work accomplished during the last ten years. While other books have described functional signing systems, this book investigates ways to integrate signing and architecture, through an environmental approach.

Of necessity, this book is personal and selective. But it is based on broad experience—the authors' combined experience of over thirty years in signing, graphics, interior design, and architecture. This varied experience from related disciplines provides the special viewpoint needed to integrate signing with architectural spaces and the larger environment. From this vantage point, the authors have formulated methods for solving the planning and functional problems of signing, and they have established esthetic guidelines for architectural graphics.

This book has been organized to combine an explanation of the overall process of planning and designing signing systems and architectural graphics with specific methods and technical information needed in various phases of the process.

The book first explains in Chapter 1, The Need Today, why sign systems are essential, for large, complex architectural facilities and describes the psychological and physical factors related to the way people respond to signs in Chapter 2, Human Factors.

Various phases of the overall process of designing architectural signing and graphics systems are then outlined. Chapter 3, Organizing the Process, explores ways to organize design tasks and to establish time schedules for completing the various phases. Coordination problems which involve the client, architect, and other professionals are reviewed.

Chapter 4, Planning, explains in detail the methods used in analyzing requirements for specific projects and in planning a system of signs to meet them. This is followed by a general discussion of the esthetic aspects of sign systems and specific methods for solving functional problems in Chapter 5, Design.

Chapter 6, Alphabets and Symbols, discusses problems of selecting, modifying, and designing alphabets and symbols for signing applications, while Chapter 7, Typography, outlines methods of utilizing alphabets and symbols in the design of the sign's message.

Chapter 8, Designers' Portfolio, illustrates examples of outstanding work completed during the last decade by some 25 designers. A variety of projects is shown—airports, office buildings, zoos—to provide an overview of well-designed signing and graphics programs from every part of the country.

Chapter 9, Graphics, Flags, and Banners, shows how the architectural environment can be enhanced by the use of decorative designs.

Chapters 10 through 13—Design Development, Documentation and Bidding, Fabrication, and Supervision, respectively—describe the more technical aspects of the process, including the preparation of working drawings and specifications and the supervision of sign fabrication and installation.

Chapter 14, Compensation and Agreements, provides criteria for writing agreements that clearly define the scope of services to be provided by the designer and the compensation to be paid by the client. Various fee arrangements are outlined and pertinent contract forms are shown.

In an area of design which is growing and changing swiftly, there is a need to provide guidelines where none now exist. The intent is to establish these guidelines in the form of a process and methods which have been found to be successful and which are sufficiently flexible to be applicable to any project. Design is not art, nor is it science; it involves aspects of both. Design should be an effective blending of creative intuition, logical analysis, and technical knowhow. The result of this synthesis can be signing and graphics programs that communicate efficiently while enhancing the architectural environment.

1
The Need Today

In the last two decades there has been an explosive growth in the field of communications. Of all the media, television is often singled out for top billing in the communications fight for our attention, but FM radio, records, paperback books, and other media have grown rapidly too. Never before has there been such a deluge of information, and it becomes increasingly difficult to select what is needed to live sane, satisfying lives.

Cities have also grown in size, and with people's increased mobility, our lives have become increasingly complex. To cope with the growing need for the kind of visual information that helps make a city work, enlightened planners and shapers of the physical environment have given increasing importance to well-designed signs that identify, direct, and warn.

Still, useless and unattractive signs abound, causing visual clutter. Pedestrian and auto traffic control signs often add to the visual confusion at street intersections. With proper planning, pedestrians and vehicles can be separated on different levels, eliminating the need for many of these signs. Proper architectural planning can reduce the need for signs around and within buildings. To be most effective, signing should be a system of interrelated elements, planned at the same time the project is planned, and not an afterthought. If treated as part of the total environmental design problem, signing systems can communicate necessary information without clutter.

Some retailers believe that the bigger the storefront signs, the more auto and pedestrian traffic they will attract. This may be true of some shoppers in certain areas of the city where sale signs are plastered across store windows. But other shoppers find such signs offensive and are turned off by them, even when the merchandise they advertise may be of good quality. Most cities have ordinances to help control the size and clutter of storefront signs, but code restrictions are not enough. Design criteria are needed to encourage the use of well-designed signing.

Modern shopping centers exert strong controls on the quality of tenant signing by having design criteria written into lease agreements. Criteria may or may not impose limitations on size and shape, but quality materials and craftsmanship are always insisted upon. The best of these centers may establish a design review committee empowered to accept or reject a design on esthetic grounds. Under this system, the designer can interpret broad criteria in a more imaginative way, so long as the committee finds his solution appropriate.

Shopping centers are specifically designed to shut out the noise and confusion of auto traffic; with stores facing comfortable malls, they make shopping leisurely and pleasant. Oriented to the pedestrian, signing within these centers (Figure 1) is scaled down in size, placed parallel to storefronts, and can be made of a wide range of more subtle, richer interior materials than signs along city streets.

Compared with the casual pace of shopping centers, airports and other transportation facilities that serve the city are often hectic. The need for effective sign programs there is acute because they serve large masses of people pressed for time. This is particularly true in large cities where an accelerated sense of time is most keenly felt. Major cities like New York, Chicago, and Los Angeles are crossroads for business people and travelers whose time is often in short supply. These cities all have airport (Figure 2), bus, and rail terminals where time is the critical factor in making travel connections. Travelers must plan ahead, know exactly where to go and how to get there in order to arrive on time. Sign systems point the way quickly and clearly, playing a crucial role in accelerated lives.

The overwhelming size of large building complexes—office buildings, government centers, sports arenas, with their mixture of pedestrians and vehicles—creates a need for coordinated sign systems. Such a system is one that communicates equally well with people, whether walking slowly or moving more rapidly in vehicles. The typical visitor to an office building usually arrives by auto (Figures 3–10); and after parking, he walks through the building to his appointment. Sign copy must be adjusted in size as the viewer changes from driver to pedestrian.

Owners, architects, and building managers are increasingly aware that well-designed sign systems are the only effective way to communicate directional information. They are not equally aware that signing can be integrated with building design to help establish a specific architectural character and enliven public spaces. The Cannery and Ghirardelli Square in San Francisco are two projects where signs help create character or an ambience appropriate to the setting and function of these revitalized complexes. Colorful design elements are particularly useful in old and new projects where there is a rich mixture of shops and restaurants (Figure 11).

The boundary between signing and architectural graphics (wall treatments, flags, and banners, for example) is often subtle, at times nonexistent. Some wall graphics can serve the dual function of displaying information and providing large areas of color. But architectural graphics as abstract wall designs are most often used to enliven large public spaces which otherwise would be very dull. Designs can involve recognizable motifs appropriate to the facility or may be completely abstract. With office workers increasingly housed in windowless areas, painted wall graphics are a relatively inexpensive way to make large spaces more livable, and they can be easily changed when they grow tiresome.

Signs have always been used to identify, direct, and inform. But today there is a broader need than ever before for signs to identify territories. The territory may be a civic center (Figure 12), a project site, a special section of street turned into a shopping mall, or a small department within some corporate office. Each of these has a different form and function; each can be best identified by a sign system tailored to its needs. These territories may overlap in a very complex way within the urban environment, making for difficult problems where various systems interface. The designer must often coordinate his work with city agencies to solve these problems and bridge the gap between project signs and city sign systems. This will often give him the challenge of participating in the process of designing city signs.

New highrise buildings have made dramatic changes in the skylines of our cities. More subtle changes have come from older institutions like hospitals and universities, both of which have expanded horizontally. Hospitals have significantly increased their outpatient care facilities and sophisticated treatment centers—generating a need for new sign systems to handle increased patient loads (Figure 13). Old and new parts of many hospitals are interrelated like parts of a puzzle. Sign systems decode this puzzle and help patients, employees, and visitors all find their way around. According to Rupert Jensen & Associates' "Building Research Survey," in a typical 800-bed hospital without adequate signs, an average of 8,000 hours is spent each year by staff members giving directions to visitors. The cost of installing a system to stop this inefficiency is recovered in a short period of time.

Sign systems provide many other economic benefits. They are an essential part of the overall advertising and identity programs of any corporation (Figure 14). They help create an easily recognized and distinctive public image necessary for the corporation to survive in a competitive market. As an extension of their public image, service-oriented corporations such as banks and savings and loan associations use interior signs to identify various departments which serve the public (Figure 15). They reduce operating costs by using directories and signs in main lobbies and on upper floors to replace receptionists.

Inflation and competitive pressures force many merchants to cut operating costs. Interior signs are a key element in the self-service concept of merchandising. By clearly identifying goods displayed in a supermarket or drugstore, for example, signs reduce the need for salespeople, which lowers operating costs. Many gasoline stations have been converted to automated operations, and more will be in the future. Some can operate with only one employee—the cashier—because signs provide necessary information to the customer. When combined into a coordinated system, signs can direct the flow of vehicles and pedestrians in a parking garage that otherwise would require many parking attendants. In this age of technological sophistication, most signs, when well designed, are relatively simple devices which can continue providing information for years unaided by complex electronic gadgetry—and unattended.

In sophisticated manufacturing plants, each skilled employee is an essential part of a team and is increasingly important to its smooth operation. To help prevent injuries and downtime resulting from hospitalization of employees, these plants adopt sign and graphics programs that far exceed Occupational Health and Safety Administration requirements (Figure 16). Enlightened managements also install wall graphics and special

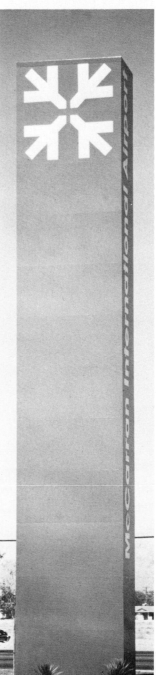

Figure 1. Identification sign for clothing store, Al's Garage, Fashion Island, Newport Center, California.

Figure 2. Project identification sign, McCarran International Airport, Las Vegas, Nevada.

Figure 3. This sign has large copy that is easily read by the approaching driver. Identification of parking facility, Security Pacific Plaza, Los Angeles.

Figure 4. Illuminated sign identifies entrances and exit of the parking facility.

Figure 5. Within the parking facility, the visitor follows auto directional signs which have large copy.

Figure 6. After parking his car, the visitor follows pedestrian-oriented signs, like this one.

Figure 7. This part of the sign system can have smaller copy, adjusted for closer reading distances.

Figure 8. This illuminated directory located in the main lobby lists corporate offices, tenants, and their floor location.

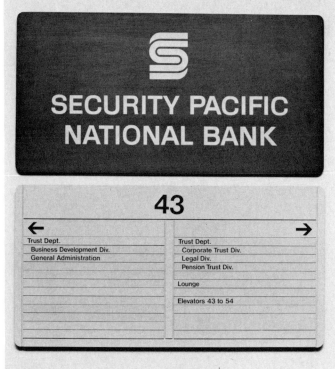

Figure 9. (left) Cast bronze numbers on the lobby wall indicate the floors served by these elevators.

Figure 10. (above) This wall-mounted sign on the 43rd floor indicates directions to various departments.

Figure 11. Sign of carved wood with gold leaf identifies the Willows Restaurant, Security Pacific Plaza, Los Angeles.

Figure 12. This sign helps to identify the civic center of Pasadena, California.

Figure 13. Directional signs, with changeable message panels, St. Joseph Medical Center, Burbank, California.

color schemes to boost morale and increase productivity.

Government officials are also aware of employee morale and are slowly responding to other changing needs. As a result of pressure from the public or their own planning departments, city councils are adopting stricter sign ordinances in an attempt to reduce the amount of visual pollution. By way of setting a good example, they are starting to have sign systems installed in government buildings which serve the public. If a majority of those served are not English-speaking, then signs have bilingual copy (Figure 17). By using signs to communicate information to those who need it most, fewer public employees can serve more people efficiently.

Current needs for good signing are widespread and most critical in airports, government facilities, highrise office buildings, and hospitals—or wherever masses of people need directional information. Sign systems communicate information to people quickly and at relatively low cost. The economic benefits of signing, in terms of time savings alone, can far outweigh the cost of providing the signs. The contribution of architectural graphics in creating more colorful, lively public spaces and more livable, productive workspaces is immeasurable. Together, architectural signing and graphics can make any city an easier and more enjoyable place to be.

Figure 14. A directional sign utilizing the IBM symbol in Los Angeles.

Figure 15. Department sign, Bank of America, Southern California Headquarters, Los Angeles.

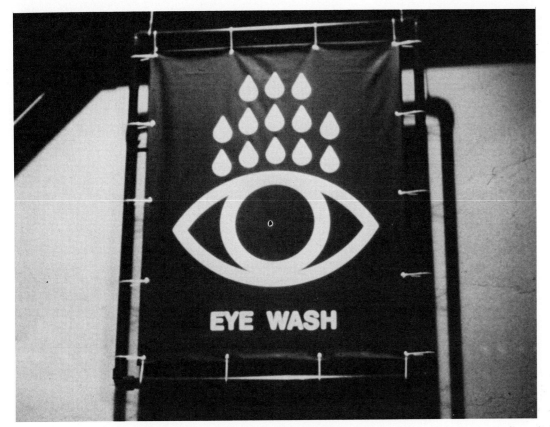

Figure 16. Signs like this help prevent injuries: a safety sign installed in a factory, designed by Smith, Henchman, Grylls for Deere & Company, Waterloo, Iowa, Engine Plant.

Figure 17. This sign combines an eye symbol with a bilingual message, designed for the New York City Health and Hospitals Corporation by E. Christopher Klumb Associates Inc.

2
Human Factors

Ask ten people to guess how many traffic control signs there are at a busy street intersection they pass every day (Figure 18) and you will probably get ten different responses. (Just for the record, the average is 20 basic electrically operated traffic and pedestrian signs.) What this example illustrates is that people vary greatly in their awareness of signs, how quickly they read them, and their ability to remember the sign message.

Perception of signs is influenced by numerous physical and psychological factors such as quality of eyesight, reading ability, memory, color sensitivity, and mental attitude. While these vary with the individual and are beyond the designer's control, he should have a general understanding of how these factors affect the viewer's response to signing.

The average city dweller has been conditioned by years of exposure to signing. Some viewers may respond negatively when exposed to many signs, but most seem to have a rather neutral attitude toward signing in general. There are many signs to which a person responds out of habit; he reacts to stop and go traffic signals and to other traffic control signs often without conscious thought. This automatic response leaves the conscious mind free for gathering information and making decisions.

As he drives or walks through the city looking for information, he scans the environment. Signs along with many other elements within his field of vision are seen in a generalized way, unless they provide some needed information—and then they are focused upon. The designer should be aware of this basic response and realize that signs compete for the viewer's attention with all other elements in the environment.

When a specific environment can be visually controlled by the designer, the viewer's awareness of the sign system and its effectiveness can be dramatically increased. A new underground parking garage, for example, can give the designer such an opportunity. By using good lighting and colorful wall graphics (Figure 19), he can create an appropriate psychological environment to enhance the message.

WHAT ARE HUMAN FACTORS?
Each viewer's perception of and response to signs are conditioned by certain physical and psychological characteristics, referred to as *human factors*.

Physical Factors

Normal Field of Vision. Studies indicate that the normal field or cone of vision suitable for signing covers an angle of about 60°. Areas outside the angle tend to be seen in much less detail. While it is true that this field of vision can be greatly

enlarged by turning the head or tilting the head, the average viewer resists this extra effort. For example, if a sign were supported from a high ceiling so that a sight line between the viewer's eye and the horizontal were more than 30°, it would probably be overlooked. Normally, viewers are not in the habit of tilting their heads to look at a sign, nor will they make any unusual head motions in order to see a sign which is not within their normal field of vision. Consistency in the height of signs in a system reduces the viewer's need to look many places for information.

Visual Acuity. Viewers differ considerably in their ability to see clearly.

Reading Rate. Among the normal reading public there is a wide variation in individual reading rates from perhaps 125 words per minute to 500 or 600. Factors like age, intelligence, and education influence reading rates; the average is about 250 words per minute. Considering this reading rate, vehicular signs, which may be seen for only a few seconds, should include no more than six short items.

Legibility. Distance studies indicate that under normal daylight when standing still a person with normal 20/20 vision can read 1-inch (25-millimeter) high letters on a standard Snellen eye chart used by optometrists at a distance of 50 feet (15 meters). However, this kind of laboratory ideal must be modified for sign design legibility.

Eye Level. The average height of a viewer's eye level, measured from the ground when the viewer is standing, is about 5 feet, 6 inches (1.7 meters); when sitting, it is about 4 feet, 3 inches (1.3 meters); when driving an auto, it is about 4 feet, 6 inches (1.4 meters). The eye level of a viewer driving a large truck is much higher than that of auto drivers and should be verified for each specialized vehicle where relevant to the design problem.

Letter Heights. Determining letter heights of copy for vehicle-oriented signs involves additional factors: primarily the speed of the vehicle and the time it takes to recognize and read the sign. For a thorough discussion of this topic, see the Case Study at the end of this chapter, and refer to the Selected Readings for sources of additional data.

Meeting Needs of Aging and Physically Disabled People. In an era of aging and disabled populations, public facilities are used by elderly and physically disabled people to an increasing extent. To meet broad public needs, then, a letter height of 1 inch for 25 feet (7.5 meters) of viewing distance, based on

Helvetica capital letters, is a more practical guide for pedestrian signs than the Snellen chart.

Psychological Factors

Figure-Ground Relationships. Psychologists refer to figure-ground relationships when they talk about how shapes or patterns are perceived against a background. Shapes are delineated by edges and edges are contours in perception. Anything which affects a clear perception of the contours may affect recognition of the object.

Figure-ground concepts also relate to how the negative spaces between letters affect perception and recognition of letters and words. In learning to read we mentally organize letters into words, learning to distinguish an entire word by its shape. Psychologists call this "perceptual filling in" or "figural organization." If letters are crowded together so that they touch or are letterspaced excessively, the negative spaces may be affected to the point where recognition of the word as a whole is destroyed.

Dark bronze letters mounted on a rough stone wall present an example of figure-ground problems. In bright sunlight, these letters cast shadows nearly as dark as the letters (Figure 20). Recognition of the letter forms is reduced or destroyed because perception of letter contours is blurred by the shadows. It follows that light colored letters on a dark background are less affected by cast shadows.

Implications of Color. Individuals seem to vary considerably in their ability to distinguish and remember colors. Probably only six different colors, not including white and black—red, yellow, blue, green, orange, brown—can be readily distinguished and remembered by normal viewers. Despite these limitations, color can be used as a secondary identification element or as a coding device in situations where the number of colors is very limited. For example, colors are used on painted columns or walls in a parking garage to help identify the different levels. This coding application does not require color memory when reinforced by numbers or letters.

Color can evoke particular moods or feelings; this positive quality of color is widely used in wall graphics, interior design, and lighting. Certain colors can be powerful reinforcing agents in signing; the viewer has been conditioned to associate red, for example, with danger or emergency because of experience with fire engines, flashing red lights, or traffic signals. Used as the background of a street stop sign in most states, the color red reinforces but could not function alone in place of the "stop." Similarly, we respond to yellow as a warning color, probably because we have seen it used in traffic signals and construction signs for so many years.

Certain applications of colors produce visual phenomena which can be exciting when applied to op-art or graphics, but troublesome when applied to signing. When two complementary colors of equal chroma are used together, as in the case of letters and background, a displeasing vibration can occur.

FACTORS AFFECTING PERCEPTION

There are a number of environmental factors which may affect how the viewer perceives a specific sign. The most important of these have to do with the quality, intensity, and color of ambient light falling on the sign; the physical obstructions of sight lines between the viewer and signs; and the visual environment behind or around signs.

For the most part, these environmental factors are beyond the

Figure 18. Few people realize how many traffic control signs there are at a typical city intersection, such as this in Pasadena, California.

Figure 19. Bands of bright color are used to emphasize this directional sign. Underground parking garage, Security Pacific Plaza, Los Angeles.

Figure 20. In sunlight, these bronze letters cast distorted shadows, which interfere with legibility. Old building at California Institute of Technology, Pasadena, California (designer unknown).

direct control of the designer, but there are closely related design factors which can be controlled. Artificial lighting can be used to increase perception of signs. Signs can be placed to improve sight lines. Most design elements of a sign can be adjusted to improve legibility of a sign, compensating for a poor visual environment.

The human factors aspects of some important environmental and design factors are outlined in the following discussion. For more detailed information related to design solutions, refer to Chapter 5, Design.

Ambient Lighting

The normal light existing in the environment, or *ambient* lighting, is a primary consideration. The minimum ambient interior light level most viewers find adequate for nonilluminated interior signs is about 25 footcandles. However, for viewing nonilluminated exterior signs at night, ambient light can be as low as 2 footcandles because of the eye's ability to adjust.

As ambient light levels decrease, contrast between copy and sign backgrounds should increase. In nonilluminated signs, this is achieved by using light copy on dark panels, or vice versa. If either copy or sign background is to be reproduced in color, the designer should, whenever possible, test samples of proposed colors in the actual space where they will be installed. White copy messages on light yellow backgrounds where ambient light is low can, for example, be unreadable because of lack of contrast. White copy on black or the reverse produces high contrast and good legibility with adequate light. Regardless of copy and background contrasts, studies indicate that visual acuity increases in general with an increase in the level of illumination. Also, the speed with which viewers recognize signs and sign copy increases as illumination increases. However, colored light falling on a colored sign can reduce legibility if it diminishes contrasts between copy and background.

If ambient light is insufficient, signs can be made legible by internal illumination. This is obviously needed for exterior signs to be read at night if no other light exists or if it is necessary to make copy very prominent or dramatic. However, excessive internal illumination can reduce legibility by creating a "halo effect" of lighted letters on a dark background. This visual phenomenon makes the letters appear larger or heavier at night than in daylight. This can be corrected by either reducing the intensity of the internal light source or modifying the weight of the letters, or a combination of the two.

Internal illumination may be used for interior signs even where ambient light is adequate to provide added emphasis. Lighted copy, when used with a dark background, is a reinforcing device to help separate a sign system from competing signs. For example, airport information signs must stand out against a background of concessionaires' advertising signs which compete for the viewer's attention.

Sight Lines

A basic human factor concerned with the placement of signs is the average eye-level height. It may seem obvious that pedestrian signs should be placed at eye level, but that would be a gross simplification of the problem. The important thing to remember is that signs should be placed to avoid obstructing normal sight lines. The designer must be empathetic, putting himself in place of the viewer when considering each sign placement problem. Some questions to ask are

1. Can the sign be seen over the heads of other people by a viewer of average height?
2. Will the sign face be at an acute angle to the normal line of vision?
3. Will the sign be outside the normal field of vision?
4. What is the background behind the sign, the environment around it, the lighting?
5. Will other signs or architectural features be in the way of the sight lines?
6. Will trees or other landscaping grow and obscure the sign?
7. Will parked vehicles obscure the sign at certain times?
8. Can the sign be seen by both vehicle drivers and pedestrians if it is a sign to be read by both? (Auto drivers' eye level is somewhat lower than that of pedestrians.)

Sign Backgrounds

There are several background conditions which can affect perception. One is the wall surface on which individual letters are mounted, as described above under "Figure-Ground Relationships." Another can be a distracting environment behind any freestanding sign panel. It too may cause visual interference with the sign message unless the sign panel is properly designed and large enough to isolate the message from visual distractions.

Shadows cast by all rough textures in sunlight produce patterns, and printed wall coverings can produce similar effects. The designer should normally avoid using cutout script letters mounted over a scroll-patterned wallpaper since letters fight with the background for attention. One should also avoid using letters of any style against certain geometric patterns (such as equally spaced black and white strips); such patterns can set up a visual vibration which interferes with the legibility of the letters. For optimum legibility of freestanding signs, which often are seen against a confusing background, a plain sign panel or wall creates an effective background for the letterforms.

SIGN MESSAGE CAN AFFECT PERCEPTION

Symbols Can Be Ambiguous

The majority of people are verbally oriented, absorbing most information through words, while the minority respond more quickly to visual devices, such as symbols. This indicates that most sign systems need verbal messages. Facilities such as international airports often use symbols to reinforce the verbal message or to stand alone. If symbols are used alone, they should be broadly accepted ones, such as the U.S. Department of Transportation symbols shown in Chapter 6, Alphabets and Symbols.

The viewer expects a sign system to be consistently worded and logically organized. For signs along an airport circulation road, for example, there are two basic ways to organize the listing of airline terminals on anticipatory signs. One way is to list them in alphabetical order; the other is according to the order in which they occur along the road. Either method works if the actual terminal buildings are well identified.

Arrows can often be used to replace words in directional signs, and we have been conditioned to respond to directional signs which utilize arrows. By convention we clearly understand a sign worded "Restrooms," accompanied by an arrow pointing toward the restrooms. But arrows can be ambiguous. A building with several floors, such as a hospital, usually requires directional signs hanging from the ceiling. At corridor intersections, arrows indicating right or left are clearly understood; the difficulty comes when the direction "ahead" is to be indicated by an arrow. When the sign is at right angles to the flow of traffic, some designers point the arrow down, while others point it up. There can be confusion about which direction is being given—down or ahead versus up or ahead—especially if there is a stairway, escalator, or elevator nearby because the viewer can infer that the destination indicated is on the next floor of the building. Apparently most sign viewers have adjusted to the fact that an arrow pointing down may indicate "down" in one situation and "ahead" in another. For additional information about the application of arrows, refer to Chapter 6, Alphabets and Symbols.

Copy Wording

Because certain phrases tend to be ambiguous or subject to personal interpretation, criteria should be established to reduce the possibility of confusion. For a sign system to be clearly understood, such criteria should include copy that is

1. Consistent
2. Short as possible in order to be read quickly
3. Mean the same thing to all viewers
4. Stated positively

With this criteria, the sign copy wording shown in Figure 21 was developed for a specific project. For another project, it might be preferable to use "Information Desk" rather than "Reception," or it might be necessary to identify the "Mechanical Room." While copy wording may vary from one project to another, it is important to maintain consistency of wording within any sign system.

Considering the broad range of the human factors outlined in this chapter, the designer will soon realize that no sign system can communicate equally well with all viewers. However, the constraints imposed by these factors and environmental limitations help define each signing problem and the specific audience the system is designed to reach.

A COMPARISON OF SIGN COPY WORDING

Application	Accepted	Rejected
Exterior vehicular	One Way (arrow)	Circulate (arrow)
	No Parking	Don't Park
		No Parking Anytime
	Slow	Drive Slowly
	Do Not Enter	One Way, Do Not Enter
		Exit, Do Not Enter
		No Entry
Parking	Vertical Clearance 8 feet	Caution! Low Overhead
	Reserved	Assigned Spaces
Pedestrian	Men	Gentlemen
	Women	Ladies
		Restrooms
	Reception	Information Desk
	No Identification	Mechanical Room
	Firehose	Fire Hose Cabinet

Figure 21.

The information and recommendations included in this chapter are not meant to be absolute, but to form rough guidelines to be further defined by the designer's own experience. Signing is a complex art, with each project providing new challenges and new information about reactions of the sign viewers.

CASE STUDY: LEGIBILITY OF VEHICLE-ORIENTED SIGNS

The legibility of signs viewed from a moving vehicle is determined by the following items listed in order of priorities:

1. Driving speed and the number of traffic lanes, both of which influence reaction time.
2. The distance from which signs should be recognizable.
3. Type of environment (commercial, industrial, residential, or agricultural).
4. Setback distance, within cone of vision and outside cone of vision.
5. Graphic design considerations, such as selected typeface; letterspacing; number of words, names, or syllables on a sign; color; number of items of information (there should be six or fewer); area of total signface; lighting and sources of illuminations; and other auxiliary and basic design elements.

The most important considerations in designing vehicle-oriented signs are

1. The distance from which a sign should be read when the vehicle is parked.
2. Reaction time when the car is moving—the time it takes a driver to see a display, read its message, and respond to that message by preparing a turn.

Field tests have shown that the reaction time which allows a driver to see a sign, read it, and respond is related to the number of lanes as follows:

2-lane road	8 seconds
4-lane road	10 seconds
6-lane road	11 seconds
Freeway	12 seconds

The faster a car is moving, the farther it travels while the driver is reacting to a message and, therefore, the larger that message must be (Figure 22). It is fairly well established that for every 50 feet (15 meters) of distance separating a viewer from an object, 1 inch (2.5 millimeters) of letter height is required. To be absolutely sure that the sign can be read, 1 inch Helvetica capital letters is recommended for every 30 feet (9 meters) of distance.

Since there is a limit to what a person may see and remember as he is driving, the number of items of information being communicated to him as he moves down the street becomes vitally important. An item of information is defined as being a symbol, word, syllable, or discontinuous shape. As a maximum, six items of information are more than adequate to help a driver find what he is seeking. Moreover, six items of information seem to be the maximum a driver can usefully and safely absorb from any one street sign. Ten items of information can be communicated from a property to an adjacent right-of-way by various signs. Figure 22 gives the size of sign needed in relation to speed reaction time/distance traveled so that the sign will be large enough to permit all six items of information to be put into one ground sign.

Number of Lanes	Speed (MPH)	Reaction Time (Seconds)	Distance Traveled during Reaction (Feet)	Letter Height (Inches)	Total Area of Sign (Square Feet)	
					Commercial Industrial	Institutional Residential Agricultural
2	15	8	176	4	8	6
	30		352	7	25	18
	45		528	10	50	36
	55		704	14	100	70
4	15	10	220	4	8	6
	30		440	9	40	28
	45		660	13	90	64
	55		880	17	150	106
6	15	11	242	5	13	10
	30		484	9	140	28
	45		726	14	100	70
	55		968	19	190	134
Freeway	55	12	1,056	21	230	162

Figure 22.

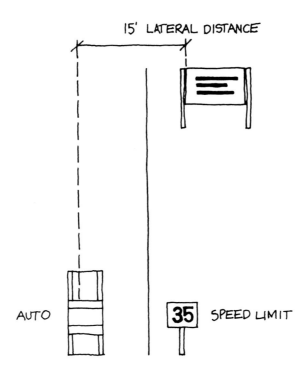

Figure 23. Here is an example of the size of sign needed in relation to speed reaction time/distance traveled.

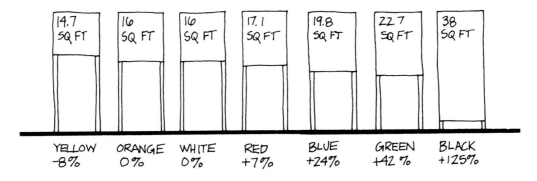

Figure 24. The percentage of area a colored sign has to exceed a white sign to be equally conspicuous is shown here.

Letter Height

In addition to the selection of letterstyle, spacing, and capitalization, the letter height is also dependent on the number of statements or lines of text, the speed at which the vehicle will be traveling, and the lateral distance between the viewer and the sign.

For this example (Figure 23) there are three lines of text, the speed limit is 35 miles per hour, and the lateral distance is 15 feet (4.6 meters). To determine the letter height, follow these steps:

1. Add 6 to the number of statements or lines of text.

$$3 + 6 = 9$$

2. Multiply the speed limit by the results of step 1.

$$35 \times 9 = 315$$

3. Divide the results of step 2 by 100.

$$315 \div 100 = 3.15$$

4. Divide the lateral distance by 10.

$$15 \div 10 = 1.5$$

5. Add the results of steps 3 and 4.

$$3.15 + 1.5 = 4.65$$

6. This is the approximate minimum letter height that should be used.

$$4.65''$$

7. If desired, the letter height can be rounded off to the nearest whole number or fraction.

$$5'' \text{ or } 4\frac{1}{2}''$$

This is an approximate number based on six factors; all factors must be considered when determining the letter height.

When possible your results should be verified by either comparing them to a similar existing sign with the same letter height or by making a full-scale mockup.

Color and Conspicuity

Various experiments and tests have been conducted to determine the amount by which signs of various colors would have to be larger or smaller than white signs to be equally conspicuous. Generally, the results in terms of the percentage of area a colored sign had to exceed a white sign are shown in Figure 24.

To be conspicuous under open conditions at 250 yards (220 meters), signs of different colors have to be of different sizes to be equally conspicuous. To be equally conspicuous in shaded areas, the colored sign areas have to be doubled.

3
Organizing the Process

Architects, industrial designers, and graphic designers develop office procedures which help them cope with large projects. It is common practice to organize the tasks to be accomplished into *phases* and to establish time schedules which vary depending on the demands of each project.

Each office that designs signing systems may have slightly different ways of organizing the work into phases and different names may be used for each phase. Some offices may prefer three phases: planning, design, and documentation. Others may prefer six: planning, programing, preliminary design, design, documentation, supervision.

In this book, the work is phased in this manner:

Phase 1: Planning
Phase 2: Design
Phase 3: Documentation and bidding
Phase 4: Supervision

To provide an overview of the entire process of developing a sign system, Figure 25, Outline of Services, is included. This is merely one method of defining the work to be accomplished during each phase.

This kind of outline is useful for presentation to the client at the beginning of a project. As discussed in Chapter 14, Compensation and Agreements, it can help define the scope of services to be provided as part of a contract agreement.

SCHEDULING THE WORK
In another form, an outline of the various tasks is necessary to organize the flow of work. Especially for large signing projects to be completed within a fixed amount of time, it is necessary to establish a time schedule at the beginning of the job. Time often becomes a critical factor affecting the process because few clients allow sufficient time to plan and design a system or to fabricate and install it. One effective method of scheduling the work is a flowchart, such as the one reproduced in Figure 26, which organizes day-to-day tasks in a horizontal fashion. Calendar dates can be shown as target dates for accomplishing important tasks. Dates should also be shown for meetings with the client to gather information and to review, approve, or coordinate the work.

CLIENT COORDINATION
In Figure 26, client approval meetings are indicated at the end of each major phase of work. These are very important and should be planned well in advance.

An orientation meeting is invariably held at the beginning of the project to determine overall requirements for signing. This involves a preliminary inspection of the buildings and the site and of any existing signs. The architect's plans should be obtained from the client and liaison should be established with the person responsible for coordinating the work with the designer.

During the planning phase, frequent meetings may be necessary to obtain information about how the facility functions. The client may have strong preferences about the appearance or location of certain signing items and these should be considered. The client should be involved in determining copy wording, which is the shared responsibility of client and designer.

A major coordination meeting occurs at the end of phase 1, when the results of planning and analysis are presented to the client. A report is presented consisting of plans showing sign location; a schedule listing all sign types and wording; schematic drawings of all items. A copy of the report is usually left with the client representative who may review it in detail with various managers or department heads. After making any necessary changes, the designer uses the report as a basis for proceeding with the design phase.

Preliminary cost estimates may be requested at this time. The designer can review the report and schematic designs with a fabricator and obtain very rough estimates, which will help in establishing an overall budget for fabrication and installation of the signs. Additional information about coordination and cost estimating is included in Chapter 4, Planning.

COORDINATION AS THE WORK PROGRESSES
The major design presentation occurs at the end of phase 2. On very large projects, it is good to present colored elevation drawings of important items. These to-scale drawings include copy messages applied with transfer lettering. A final plan showing sign locations and a graphic schedule is also presented for approval at this time.

During this major design presentation is also the most effective time to present a realistic budget of costs to fabricate and install the signs. For additional information, refer to "Budgeting for Fabrication," on page 51 in Chapter 5, Design.

Two or three meetings with the client may be required during phase 3 when working drawings and specifications are being produced. At times the client may want to review working drawings before these have been completed to check progress of the work. But the important meeting is held when all documents have been completed and are ready for issuance to bidders. A week or so should be allowed for a careful review of all documents by client staff people.

OUTLINE OF SERVICES

Phase 1. Planning

A. Analysis of project requirements for graphic communication
1. Survey existing or planned site conditions, project facilities and existing signs if any.
2. Review architect's plans of existing and/or future facilities.
3. Obtain necessary information concerning operating and functional requirements for the facility or complex.
4. Determine requirements for all code and handicapped signing.

B. Planning and schematic design
1. Develop concepts for a system of graphic elements which will communicate information effectively.
2. Provide Preliminary Graphics Schedule, a complete list of graphic elements which includes recommended wording for signs.
3. Using architect's plans, show preliminary locations for all items.
4. Provide schematic designs showing approximate size and shape of signs.
5. Review sign types, copy and locations with the client for approval.

Phase 2. Design

A. Final design
1. Using design techniques as required, develop designs for all signing and graphic items which were approved in Phase 1.
2. Design and/or select letterforms, alphabets, etc., for all items.
3. Select color and materials for all items.

B. Coordination
1. Review all designs of signs and graphics with client.
2. Coordinate final copy with client.
3. Obtain cost estimates for sign fabrication, if required.

Phase 3. Documentation and Bidding

A. Working drawings and specifications
1. Provide complete working drawings for all signing and graphic items.
2. Provide final specifications for all colors and materials.
3. Provide final location plans and Graphics Schedule of all items.

B. Competitive bids
1. Select competent bidders for the work involved.
2. Issue documents for bidding and review drawings with bidders.
3. Assist the owners, if necessary, in bid negotiations.

Phase 4. Supervision

A. Supervision of fabricator's work
1. Administer the awarding of contracts to successful bidder as required.
2. Check shop drawings provided by fabricator.
3. Inspect work in fabricator's shop.
4. Supervise installation of fabricator's work at the project site.

B. Evaluation and future implementation
1. Provide drawings of the completed sign system.
2. Develop Sign Criteria or Sign Ordering Manuals as required for the project under a separate design agreement.
3. Review and evaluate sign system after it has been operating for a period of time.
4. Make changes or additions to the sign system as required under a separate design agreement.

Figure 25.

After final documents have been approved by the client, the designer coordinates the issuance of these to various bidders. Refer to "Bidding Procedures" on page 166 in Chapter 11, Documentation and Bidding, for further information.

The designer meets again with the client about two or three weeks after issuing documents in order to review the bids which have been received. He will review the bids in detail and recommend which bidder should be awarded the contract. The actual contract is usually prepared and issued by the client.

During phase 4, supervision, the designer usually does not meet again with the client until signs are ready for installation. He usually attends initial meetings between the client representative and the fabricator to make arrangements for installing signs. As often as required during the installation period, the designer will inspect progress of the work and report any problems to the client. At the end of the supervision phase, the designer usually reviews the entire system with the client. See "Final Inspection" on page 182 in Chapter 13, Supervision, for further information.

PROJECT EVALUATION

After the signing has been in operation for a period of time (usually several months), it may be necessary to recommend changes or additions. There are several possible reasons for this: viewers do not always respond to signs in a predictable fashion; changes may have been made in the way the project operates; some signs may have been improperly designed. The designer will submit a report recommending the necessary changes.

FUTURE CHANGES AND ADDITIONS

Large facilities, whether office buildings or hospitals, have continuing internal changes, which result in changes in their signing systems. This can be handled by providing ongoing consulting design services and/or through the use of signing manuals (refer to Chapter 13, Supervision). The first method requires more coordination with the client, but is necessary if entirely new kinds of sign types are being added. Signing manuals, if properly designed, can provide a method of reordering

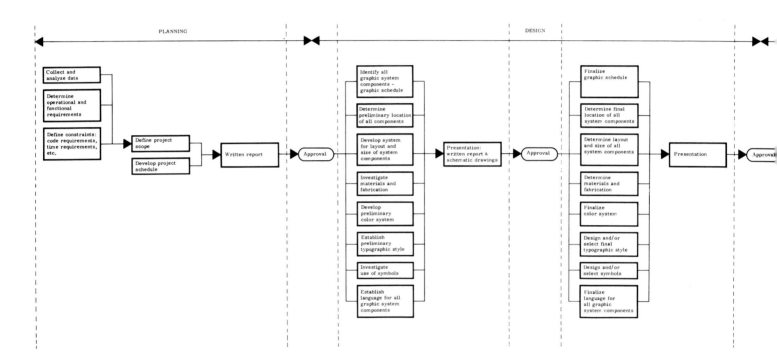

Figure 26. Flowchart showing typical work schedule needed to complete a signing project.

signs without the designer's involvement, provided that the new signs to be added are covered by criteria indicated in the manual.

COORDINATION WITH OTHER PROFESSIONALS

On most existing projects the designer coordinates all signing work with a client representative, but on new projects he may need to coordinate his work with the architect or others involved with construction. Most such coordination will occur early in the planning phase of his work. (Refer to "Orientation" on page 29 in Chapter 4, Planning.) The architect can provide plans of the project and much technical and functional information about it. Coordinating the location of power outlets for electrical signs will involve the architect's electrical engineer or contractor. Signs which affect the building structure or surface, such as a sign cast into a concrete wall, will involve the architect.

The architect should be represented at all design presentation meetings so that he can be constantly informed. Out of cour-

tesy, the architect should be shown all designs which affect the appearance of the project, particularly exterior signs. The client may give him veto power or even delegate the approval function to him. It is often wise to present major designs to him in a preview meeting before showing them to the client for final approval.

On large projects which are under construction, the designer may coordinate all his work through the architect's office. Contracts for fabrication and installation of the signs may be administered by him; in such cases, the sign fabricator may become a subcontractor of the project's general contractor. Such coordination problems will vary with each project and are best worked out with the architect's project administrators.

Regardless of what forms or methods are finally chosen, design offices cannot function without utilizing a method for organizing the overall process of developing a sign system. The process should be divided into phases of work and time schedules established which show when each phase should be finished as well as outlining the day-to-day tasks for each project.

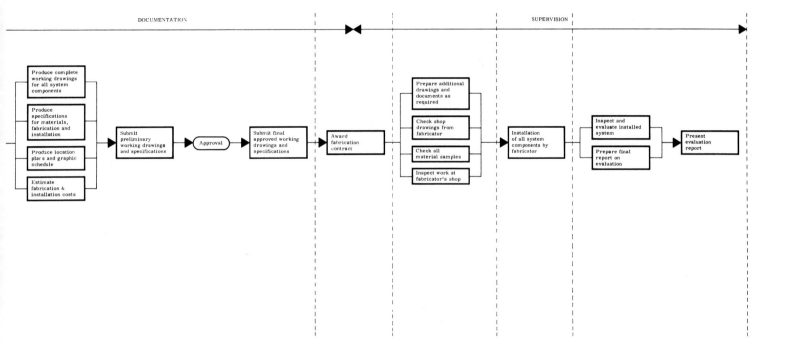

4
Planning

Airports, large bus terminals, a sports arena or stadium are all examples of facilities that have a high percentage of first-time visitors. Many of these visitors are also in a hurry to board an airplane or find their seat before the game starts. They need to have specific information in the proper time sequence—at the point of decision. For example, the airplane passenger must determine quickly the corridor or area of the terminal and the specific gate his plane will leave from. Signs directing visitors to their destination must be large, easily read from long distances, and well placed so that they can be conveniently seen above moving crowds. Directional signs must be located at every point of decision so that there is no doubt in the visitor's mind whether to turn right, left, or go straight ahead. Sign systems for these kinds of facilities should stand out clearly from the architectural environment and be bold and colorful.

Planning a system for a large office building can be approached somewhat differently. While it too has a high percentage of first-time visitors, time is not as great a factor. The internal arrangement of the building may be very complex with security or restricted areas requiring a complete system of interior directional signs; it may also have many floors, requiring a system of floor directories at elevator lobbies. Office building signs usually require flexibility; names and titles on doors and desk signs are subject to frequent change. In general, when working on an office complex the designer can plan signs that are smaller in size, with less color, and which relate more closely to the building design than when designing for an airport.

World's fairs and large amusement parks are examples of projects with long distances between areas or buildings on complicated sites. These require elaborate systems of *exterior* signs which may include map-type directories to help orient the visitors, nearly all of whom are there for the first time.

Another factor strongly influencing the planning of a system for a world's fair is that many visitors do not speak the same language as that of the host country. Some of the language problems can be resolved by using pictograms or international symbols. But the designer must also plan to supplement these symbols with copy translated into several languages.

By contrast with the large projects mentioned above, a small commercial office building will need very few signs. Most of the building users are employees and the few daily visitors are self-directed to specific offices by referring to the building directory, usually a simple alphabetical listing including room and floor numbers.

The foregoing general examples indicate how sign planning is influenced by the physical characteristics of the facility and

by human factors. While each type of facility has its own characteristic set of problems, certain key questions can be asked about any facility as a means of discovering its particular needs. The designer should have general questions in mind, however, when analyzing sign requirements for any facility as part of his orientation to it.

ANALYZING BASIC SIGNING REQUIREMENTS

It has been said that the solution to a problem is inherent in asking the right questions. The designer must ask pertinent questions, assemble information about a specific project, and organize it in a logical sequence before he can develop plans for a sign system. The following are some basic questions about the facility and about the sign viewer which will affect planning:

1. How many new viewers visit the site daily?
2. Is the viewer under duress or in a great hurry to get to his destination (as in a hospital emergency or an airport)?
3. Is the internal arrangement of the facility very complex (a large hospital, for example)?
4. Does the facility have many floors or levels stacked vertically which may not conform to the typical highrise building?
5. Do the owners of the complex want people to wander around looking for their destination (as in shopping centers) in hopes that they will find something new?
6. Is there a complex relationship between various areas of the architectural site?
7. Are there long distances between various areas of the architectural site (such as a college campus or amusement park)?
8. Are there security or safety restrictions related to the viewer and his use of the facility?
9. What are the special sign requirements for bilingual viewers or physically disabled people?
10. Are automobiles involved?

Knowing that signs are intended to communicate information to people and that people do not always behave in a predictable way, the designer may feel that planning sign systems is more of an art than a science. Often decisions will be based on his best judgment and past experience, not on any scientific principle. However, the ambiguities of human behavior should not be used as an excuse to abandon reason when planning signs. A goal of most good signing systems is to resolve the signing problems with the least number of signs possible and still answer most of the important questions.

The designer must follow certain procedures in planning signs for all facilities, regardless of how much these facilities vary in size or function. He must use a systematic method for gathering information, analyzing that information, and recording it. The balance of this chapter explains one systematic method which has been found effective in phase 1, planning, for all projects.

ORIENTATION

Meetings

For new projects, the graphic designer should meet with the project architect and/or client representatives just as soon as final building plans are firm, but prior to the completion of architectural working drawings, to familiarize himself with the project in general terms, to learn how the building functions, and to obtain names of consultants or agencies having information affecting sign planning. Questions which often arise are:

Who is the client representative in charge of this project and what are the approval procedures?

Who will be the client's liaison or coordinator on the day-to-day work?

What limitations are imposed by the client?

What look is desired? Is there a corporate image or symbol? Are there any taboos, any sacred cows?

Has a corporate alphabet or color been established?

Have building directories or exit and elevator signing been designed or specified by the architect, and what are the architect's other sign-related responsibilities?

Is any special signing necessary to identify the overall project, such as signs on the top of the building?

Will temporary signs be required during the construction phases of the project?

Review Project Plans

On new projects the architect can provide complete building plans and pertinent information about sign items which he may have included as part of the building specifications, such as exit signs and other signing required by code. For an existing facility, necessary plans and information can usually be provided by the client if no architect is involved. If the facility is old and has been remodeled, existing plans can usually be brought up to date by a drafting service rather than by the designer.

Building plans normally include all important physical features of the project (such as entrances, exits, lobbies) and name the functions of various areas or rooms. By observing the names of rooms on plans, the designer can learn much about how the project functions.

Determine Scope

A thorough study of plans and information obtained from the architect or client will enable the designer to determine the scope of the work in general terms. However, the full extent of the sign system will not be determined until planning and programing have been completed. The following questions will help define the extent of the designer's involvement. Does the scope of work include:

Development of corporate identification for the project (such as a symbol or logotype)?

Major exterior site signs identifying the overall project?

Exterior identification and directional signing that indicates parking facilities?

Exterior identification of each building?

Environmental graphics?

Interior signing of all buildings and parking structures?

Criteria for shop interior or exterior signing?

Criteria for office tenant signing?

Individual office or desk identification signs?

RESEARCH

Obtain Operational Information

The designer must ask many questions concerning the operations of the facility and its needs for signing information. Answers to these questions will supplement what he has determined by a thorough review of the building plans. Questions will vary somewhat with each project, but basic ones are as follows:

Is there a high percentage of daily visitors?

What is the visitors' socioeconomic and ethnic background?

Will a high percentage of employees have occasion to visit unfamiliar parts of the facility?

Are there special requirements for physically disabled people, such as braille signs for the blind and/or wheelchair ramp signs?

Is the ambient light sufficient for daytime viewing of all signs?

What signs should be illuminated for night viewing?

What signs should be ordered early to meet building schedules?

What signs should function on an emergency system?

What signs should be portable?

What signs should have changeable copy?

Should any sign messages be bilingual or multilingual, such as in an airport or world's fair?

Are there security checkpoints or restricted areas?

Obtain Code Information

To ensure that all signs of an existing building will satisfy code requirements, check with the local department of building and safety and/or fire department. On new projects, the architect may already have selected basic exit and fire code signs. At least, he should be familiar with code requirements and can inform the designer accordingly.

Visit the Site

If there is a physical facility, visit it and take photographs of existing signs and conditions. Polaroid 3 × 5 color prints are very helpful because they can be verified on the spot. Photograph typical public areas and any special conditions which are not adequately shown on building plans. An invaluable aid during planning, these color photographs will also be helpful during the design phase when sign colors are determined. Take dimensions where required. The following are additional questions about the site and buildings which relate to sign planning:

Are the buildings spread out over a large area, indicating a need for map-type directories?

Are there existing list-type directories or other changeable sign hardware which can be reused with new graphics?

Are there obvious landmarks, such as a bell tower, which can be used as an orientation device in the sign system?

Does the site involve hilly land, resulting in buildings with entrances on different levels which will affect floor numbering?

Does the facility have a complex layout of buildings with interconnecting corridors from one building to another?

If the visitor approaches the site in an automobile, what are the problems of getting into the parking facility, if any? Visitors are likely to have such questions as:

Am I near the place? Where do I park? How do I get in the parking lot? Can I go in my camper or bus? Do I have to pay to get in? If so, must I have correct change? Do I park in one place for several possible destinations?

Review Other Projects

If time permits, visit other facilities with similar signing problems. By observing how others have solved or failed to solve certain problems, the designer can often devise a better solution.

ANALYSIS, PROGRAMING, AND SCHEMATIC DESIGN

There are a variety of tasks during this part of the work which involve the analysis, organization, and recording of information gathered during the research phase. This information forms the basis for locating all signs on the architectural plans and determining preliminary sign shape, size, and copy message.

Analyze the Movement of Project Users

Whether planning signs for auto traffic in a parking garage or for a project involving people on foot, it is essential to analyze movements of the users. Parking consultants call this "traffic flow analysis" (Figure 27), but the methods involved can be utilized for analyzing the flow of people as well. The movement of visitors through a large project needing interior signing will be used as an example.

Architectural plans are often produced in sections for large projects, but for sign planning it is often necessary to work with an overall plan showing one entire level, including all entrances and exits. This can be done by assembling several plans and photoreducing them. Using such a plan, trace all public corridors or hallways, entrances, and elevator lobbies on a tissue overlay to make them stand out. Next, mark all points of entry and exit and the various major and minor destination points users and visitors will be moving toward. After this has been completed, make a flow diagram showing the path of an imaginary visitor through the entire facility. This will help the designer locate all points of decision (such as corridor intersections) and determine the location of all sign elements as listed below:

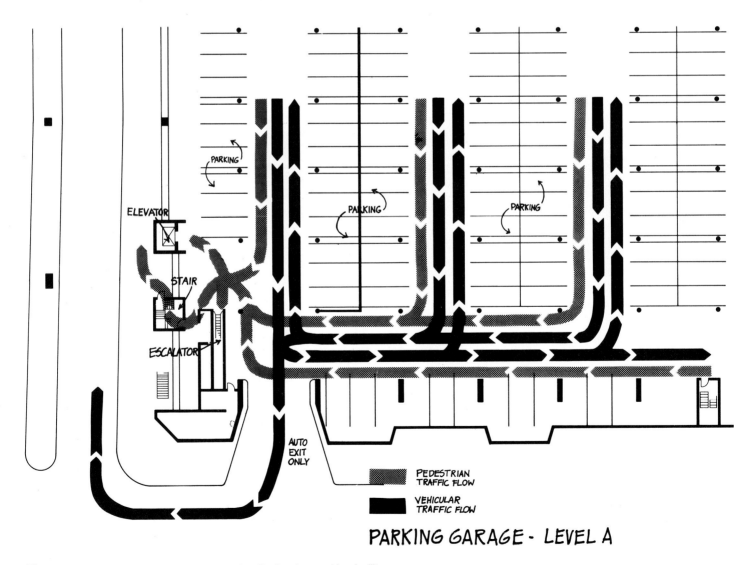

PARKING GARAGE - LEVEL A

Figure 27. This plan is a schematic analysis of traffic flow in a parking facility.

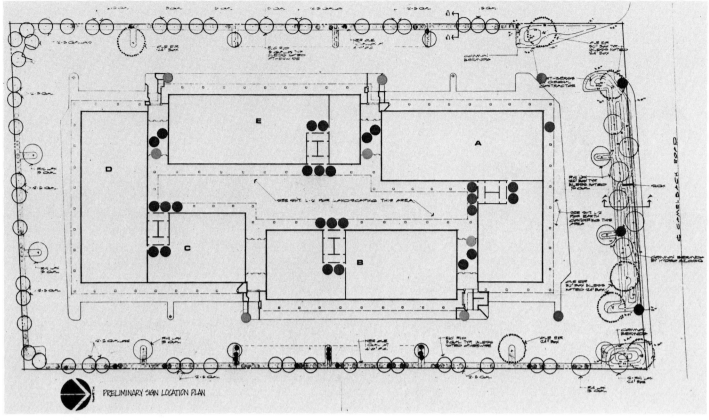

Figure 28. A plan with the preliminary location of signs indicated by color-coded dots.

Locate Sign Elements

Sign elements fall into four basic categories according to function or the information they provide:

Directional. As the term implies, these indicate directions. These may be simple signs indicating the direction to only one destination or very complex directories listing many destinations to the right, left, or straight ahead.

Identifying. These signs name a place or thing: a conference room, fire hose cabinet, or office of the president.

Informational. All signs give information, but by common usage these kinds of signs display specific, detailed information about business hours or special procedures.

Restrictive or Prohibitive. A variation of the information sign, these signs restrict the public from entering (Employees Only) or have an even stronger emphasis if there is danger (Radiation—Danger—Do Not Enter).

All these kinds of sign elements can be located on architectural plans by the designer after properly completing the work outlined under "Research" and after analyzing the movement of users. A suggested method of noting locations of these basic sign elements is to affix a color-coded adhesive-backed paper dot to the plan at each proposed sign location (Figure 28). Apply a similar dot to a 3 × 5 card and record tentative copy on the card. It is a good practice to also indicate whether the signs are single-faced or double-faced. On the graphics schedule should be noted whether the sign is illuminated or not.

Group Sign Elements into Sign Types

When designing signs for a large project, the designer's goal is to develop a *system of signs*, each element of which functions well and yet is integrated visually with all other elements. In most instances, to avoid visual clutter, the resulting system must involve the smallest number of different looking sign elements which will communicate all the necessary information. The designer must organize the large number of different signs required into manageable groups, referred to here as *sign types*. All signs in a given sign type should have the same size, shape, and method of attachment to the building. Each sign type need be drawn only once on the working drawings.

Check Copy Wording with Client

At least some of the copy wording will be tentative at this time, and it is advisable to review it with the client, consultants, government agencies, or others involved in the project. Although the message for many signs is predetermined by common usage or governmental regulation, there remains much sign copy which must be decided as the joint responsibility of client and designer. Frequently the designer, who is very sensitive to typographic layout, can suggest a shorter phrase which may communicate more rapidly than one commonly used. But the client should approve any decision affecting copy wording. Be sure to include any changes on the file cards.

Establish an Item Number System

Each sign type is assigned a number, for example, 10. To allow for the fact that not all sign types noted 10 have the same copy message, an *item number* is added, which makes a two-part number, for example, 10-1, and that number is used on the plans to identify each sign. The first number refers to the sign type and the second to the copy message it will display. One sign type may have as few as 1 or as many as 10 copy message variations. There may be as many as 80 sign types and over 2,000 separate signs within a large signing system.

Establish a File Card System

By setting up a file of 3 × 5 cards for each project and assigning an item number to each sign and corresponding card, the designer creates a flexible reference system which can be rearranged as necessary. This item number card (Figure 29),

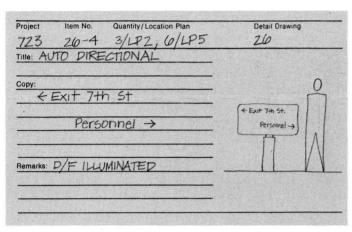

Figure 29. This is a sign item card which includes detailed information and schematic drawing of the sign.

which replaces the temporary one having colored dots, should include the following information:

Item number and title

Preliminary copy wording

Schematic drawing of sign shape (a thumbnail sketch)

Remarks, such as

SF (single-faced, message on one side only) or

DF (double-faced, message on both sides) designation and type of illumination

Assign Item Numbers

Item numbers should now be assigned to each sign and noted on the plans. These are not noted on plans until the end of the planning phase because it is often necessary to shift items from one sign type group to another as copy messages are finalized and during the production of schematic designs.

By making use of this type of documentation, planning efforts can be kept in good order and the client or architect can easily review the work at any time with the designer. Should the client wish to proceed with another designer at some point, there is a record of the work that anyone can understand. By explaining this to the client at the outset, it often calms his fears about proceeding with phase 1 before knowing the full cost of design services.

Schematic Designs

It is suggested that schematic designs of the most important sign types be drawn on 8½ × 11 paper. These can be freehand outline drawings including a person or auto to give the correct sense of scale. These are necessary to help the client visualize the basic character of the signs and thereby develop an understanding of signing. Also, many times the client doesn't understand the jargon of the designer—for example, such terms as "flush-mounted," "double-faced," "wall- or ceiling-hung"—so the drawings are helpful.

Preview Meeting

On new projects it is advisable to have a preview meeting with the project architect before presenting phase 1 report material to the client. Even though the architect usually attends the formal presentation, this preview will allow time for the designer to incorporate any late project changes and to respond to the architect's general comments or criticisms before formal meetings with the client.

REPORT PREPARATION AND PRESENTATION

Report Contents

During the initial contact with the client, the designer should describe the kind of report that will result from phase 1 services. The report should consist of plans showing the location of all sign items (Figure 30) and schematic drawings of important sign types (Figure 31). It should be called the "preliminary graphics schedule" because it is subject to client review and possible revision.

The schedule should include the following information and have item numbers typed in numerical order:

Project number and name, presentation date

Item number

Title and/or copy

Quantity

Plan drawing and schematic drawing references

Remarks: Special considerations, information needed from client, etc.

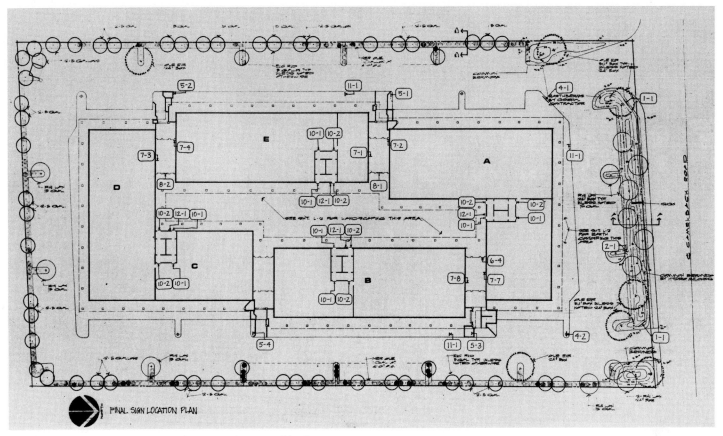

Figure 30. The final locations of sign items are shown on this plan.

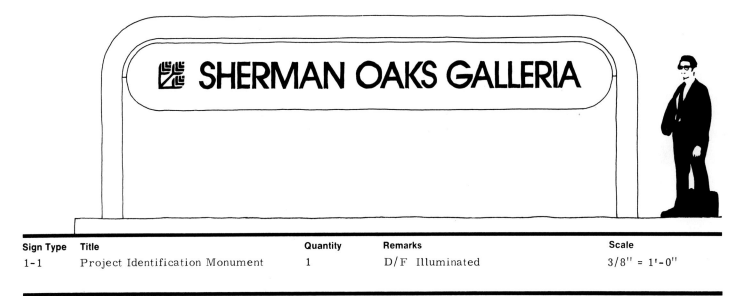

Sign Type	Title	Quantity	Remarks	Scale
1-1	Project Identification Monument	1	D/F Illuminated	3/8" = 1'-0"

Figure 31. Schematic designs, such as this freehand drawing, should be produced for all important sign types.

Item No.	Copy	Quantity	Location Plans	Remarks
9-1	← Ventura Blvd. Sepulveda Blvd. →	4	LP1	
9-2	← Sepulveda Blvd. Ventura Blvd. →	4	LP1	
9-3	↓ Exit Mall Shops, May Co & Parking →	1	LP1	
9-4	Valet Parking Park Car Leave Keys	1	LP1	
9-5	Sepulveda Blvd. Watch For Pedestrians	1	LP1	
		1	LP1	
9-7	← May Co, Mall Shops ↓ Robinson's	1	LP1	
9-8	← Robinson's ↓ Mall Shops May Co & Parking	1	LP1	
9-9	↓ Ventura Blvd.	1	LP1	
9-10	↓ Additional Parking	1	LP1	
9-11	Do Not Enter Exit →	1	LP1	
9-12	← Sepulveda Blvd. ↓ Mall Shops, Ventura Blvd.	1	LP1	
9-13	← Exit to Ventura Blvd. Sepulveda Blvd. →	1	LP1	
9-14	← May Co ↓ Parking Sepulveda Blvd. →	1	LP1	
9-15	← Mall Shops Parking →	1	LP1	
9-16	← Mall Shops, May Co ↓ Bank Parking	1	LP1	

Figure 32. This is one page from a typical preliminary graphic schedule.

Presentation of Report

It is important to have a critical review of the report material with the client's operating personnel at this point. Stress its preliminary nature and the possibility that signs may be added later as the need arises. This is especially important with newly planned projects which have never been in operation. If the client realizes that he has a joint responsibility with the designer, particularly in the area of copy wording, he will be more understanding if certain signs fail to communicate as planned. They may fail to communicate for a number of reasons based on human factors (discussed in Chapter 2), but at this point the client should be made aware that some so-called free souls do not read or pay attention to signs.

While the designer should point out the limitations of the report (it is only one part of a complete design process), he should stress its real value as a document which defines signing needs for the entire project. The preliminary graphics schedule (Figure 32), which lists the quantity of each sign, together with schematic drawings, can be used to establish a construction budget for the sign system.

PRELIMINARY COST ESTIMATES

The client may insist that the designer prepare preliminary estimates of the costs required to fabricate the signs as part of phase 1 services. By reviewing schematic drawings with a knowledgeable sign contractor and providing supplementary information about materials, the designer can produce a ballpark estimate, which can be used as a rough guide for establishing a construction budget. Realistic estimates can be made only after materials and processes have been more accurately determined during the actual design phase. Preliminary cost estimates provided by the designer, however inaccurate, are much more reliable than any budget guesstimates that an uninformed client or architect may produce without the designer's advice.

DETERMINING FEES FOR PLANNING SERVICES

The following discussion of fees is related *only to phase 1 services*. A more complete review of fee problems will be found in Chapter 14, Compensation and Agreements.

For even the most experienced designer, determining fees involves some risk unless he can proceed on a cost-plus basis.

Because it is ultimately the fairest arrangement for both client and designer, he should try for a cost-plus agreement after giving the client an estimate of the design time or cost involved. Each design office will have its own formula for determining charges under a cost-plus arrangement. One method is to charge the hourly salary paid to the employee multiplied by a factor to cover all operating expenses, employee benefits, materials used for the job, and so forth. This factor may range from a multiplier of 2.5 to 3.25 and may vary from one project to another. As an example of how a multiplier works, if a staff designer is paid $7 per hour and a multiplier of 2.5 is chosen, the client would be billed 7 × 2.5, or $17.50 per hour for his time. (See "Billed-out Rate" on page 185 in Chapter 14, Compensation and Agreements.)

Some clients may expect the fee to be based on a percentage of construction costs because of their experience with architects who often establish fees on this basis. To naive designers and clients alike this may seem like a reasonable way to determine fees, but we must wave a flag of warning here—avoid it!

If the client rejects a cost-plus fee—and the designer rejects one based on a percent of construction costs—what then? The designer must estimate his time to provide initial services based on a thorough review of the architectural plans and all other information he can obtain. Unless he has previous experience with projects very similar to one under consideration, he should add up all the hours he thinks will be needed and then double it before using the multiplier. Often phase 1 fees can range from $1,500 to $10,000 depending on the size and complexity of the project. Usually phase 1 fees are approximately 5 to 10 percent of the total fee, *assuming the phase 1 procedures outlined in this chapter*.

The designer is asked the inevitable question if the client is pleased with the report presentation: "What is your fee to complete the rest of your work?" Fortunately, having completed phase 1, the designer is now in a much better position to answer that question than when first introduced to the project. Even though the scope of work may be expanded somewhat as the design work progresses, he now knows the number of sign types to be designed. This information is central to an accurate determination of total fees covering all phases.

5
Design

Toward the end of the previous chapter, schematic designs were discussed. Like enlarged thumbnail sketches, these concept drawings are made to help establish sign types and give the client a rough idea of their size, location, and general appearance. This chapter follows the esthetic and functional aspects of the design process as these concepts are transformed into final designs. Whenever possible, solutions are given for the basic functional problems. However, sign design involves personal design judgment and therefore cannot be reduced to a few absolute rules. Rather, various esthetic approaches will be reviewed to stimulate the search for creative solutions.

Experienced designers are well aware of the constant interplay between esthetics and function in the design of any functional object; a good design achieves a synthesis of these often conflicting factors. However, for purposes of discussion they will at times be considered separately here. First, the esthetic relationship between the architectural environment and the sign system will be considered; this will include problems of sign shape, material, color, and lighting. These esthetic factors are similar for both exterior and interior signs. The functional factors for exterior signs differ somewhat from those of interior signs; each will be considered separately.

TWO APPROACHES TO DESIGN
Most designers would agree that the design of a sign system should be appropriate to its architectural environment; and this may be considered one approach to designing sign systems. Of course, designers will differ in what they think is appropriate, and they will differ in how sensitive or responsive they are to the environment. For this approach they should be sympathetic to the architecture, trying to see it, for the most part, as the architect does. For some industrial projects, signing and graphics can add more visual excitement and color than even the architect may have envisioned. But for all projects the sign system should be considered an integral part of the architecture, as visually important as light fixtures, elevators, and other vital elements. As with these other elements, signing has both functional and esthetic aspects. To communicate information, signs must be noticed; but to accomplish this in an esthetically appropriate manner requires a careful balancing of esthetics and function.

Another approach to designing sign systems considers the communicative function of signs of primary importance and the esthetics as secondary. With this approach, all elements of a system may be similar in shape, material, color, and detail. This method often requires modular copy layouts wherein the longest phrase determines the length of all signs in a group.

This approach usually results in signs which strongly contrast with the environment and seem most appropriate for transportation or industrial projects. Sign systems of this kind do a good job of communicating information, but they are seldom carefully integrated with colors and materials of the architectural environment.

ARCHITECTURALLY INTEGRATED SIGNING
The first approach considers a sign system appropriate when both its function and esthetics are tailored to the specific environment of a project and to the client's needs. The architecture of each project is unique in both appearance and function and its sign system should reflect that uniqueness. The authors favor this approach. It is more complex and more time consuming because all the relationships between the environment and the signs must be carefully considered. However, it can result in a great variety of creative solutions as indicated by the work of the many designers illustrated in Chapter 8, Designers' Portfolio.

Building Environment Can Affect Design of Signs
Designers who stress function often seem to ignore the environment, making all signs in a group identical rectangles, differing only in the length of copy. But forget for a moment that signs must present information. Think of them as design elements inside spaces of various shapes and sizes, which can therefore influence the shape and size of the design elements. If the environment is a tall space, such as an arena corridor with a very high ceiling, there is an opportunity to design tall, bannerlike elements for this space. A very low, wide corridor space in an airport terminal suggests the use of slender sign boxes that stretch across the corridor ceiling and display illuminated copy at either end. Signs can relate to the spaces they occupy.

Designing a Family of Signs
Not only do the shapes of architectural spaces suggest the need for variety in sign shape and size, but functional requirements for most projects also indicate such a need. One sign may have to be long and horizontal to accommodate a long message or to fit a restricted space; another will require a large vertical shape to be seen from a great distance. Although necessary, this variety can lead to visual chaos unless the signs are organized into families or visual groups, which include all the sign types. A square and a rectangle can be made to relate by giving square or rounded corners to both, as shown in Figures 33–37.

However, too much repetition of the same shape or very similar shapes can be monotonous. It is better to vary the shape

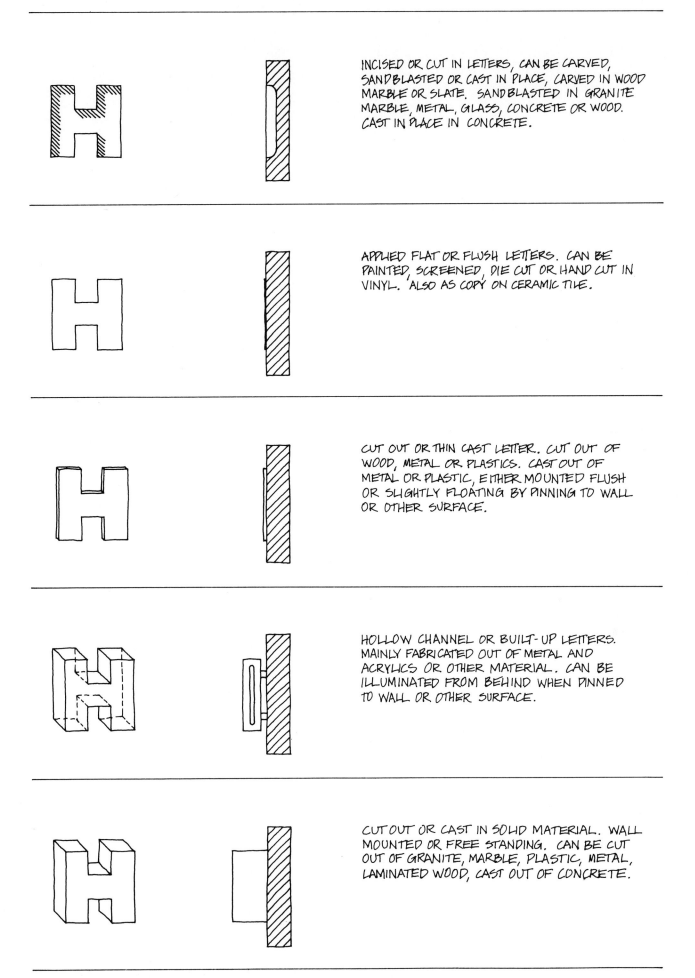

INCISED OR CUT IN LETTERS, CAN BE CARVED, SANDBLASTED OR CAST IN PLACE, CARVED IN WOOD MARBLE OR SLATE. SANDBLASTED IN GRANITE MARBLE, METAL, GLASS, CONCRETE OR WOOD. CAST IN PLACE IN CONCRETE.

APPLIED FLAT OR FLUSH LETTERS. CAN BE PAINTED, SCREENED, DIE CUT OR HAND CUT IN VINYL. ALSO AS COPY ON CERAMIC TILE.

CUT OUT OR THIN CAST LETTER. CUT OUT OF WOOD, METAL OR PLASTICS. CAST OUT OF METAL OR PLASTIC, EITHER MOUNTED FLUSH OR SLIGHTLY FLOATING BY PINNING TO WALL OR OTHER SURFACE.

HOLLOW CHANNEL OR BUILT-UP LETTERS. MAINLY FABRICATED OUT OF METAL AND ACRYLICS OR OTHER MATERIAL. CAN BE ILLUMINATED FROM BEHIND WHEN PINNED TO WALL OR OTHER SURFACE.

CUT OUT OR CAST IN SOLID MATERIAL. WALL MOUNTED OR FREE STANDING. CAN BE CUT OUT OF GRANITE, MARBLE, PLASTIC, METAL, LAMINATED WOOD, CAST OUT OF CONCRETE.

Figure 33. These schematic drawings indicate various ways of designing architectural letters, either cut into, flush with, or projecting from a wall surface.

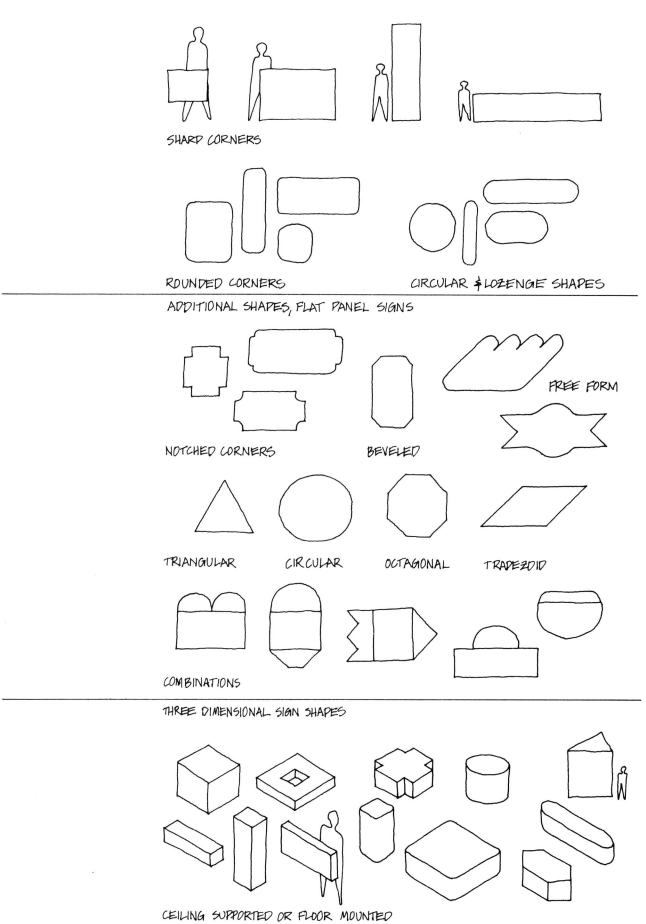

COMMONLY USED SHAPES, EXTERIOR OR INTERIOR FLAT PANEL SIGNS

SHARP CORNERS

ROUNDED CORNERS   CIRCULAR & LOZENGE SHAPES

ADDITIONAL SHAPES, FLAT PANEL SIGNS

NOTCHED CORNERS   BEVELED   FREE FORM

TRIANGULAR   CIRCULAR   OCTAGONAL   TRAPEZOID

COMBINATIONS

THREE DIMENSIONAL SIGN SHAPES

CEILING SUPPORTED OR FLOOR MOUNTED

Figure 34. This page shows various shapes which can be used in organizing signs into so-called family groups of both interior and exterior signs.

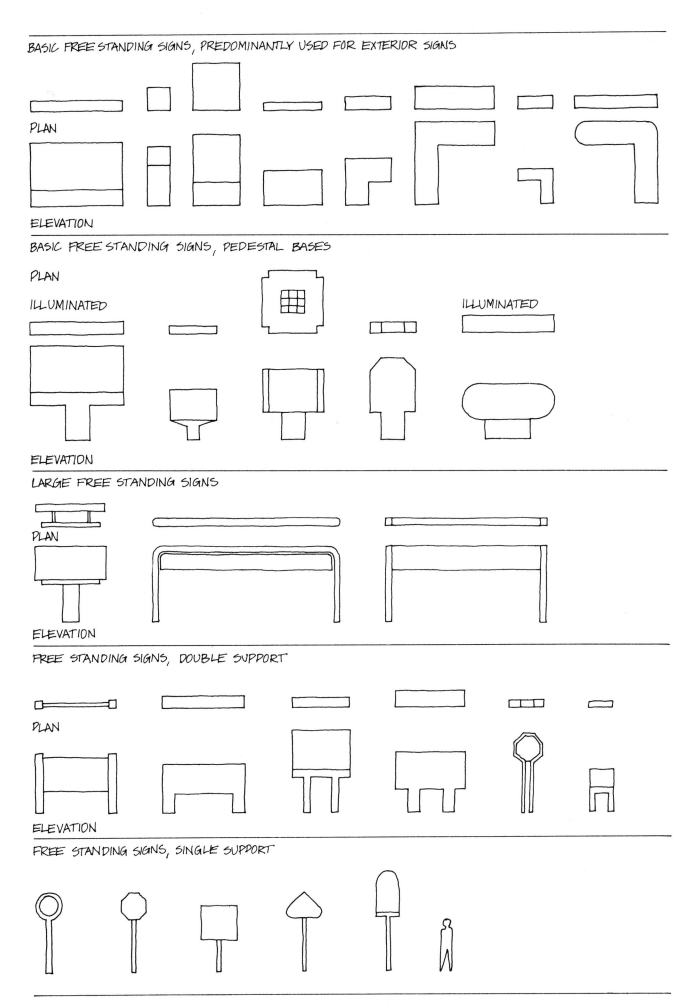

BASIC FREE STANDING SIGNS, PREDOMINANTLY USED FOR EXTERIOR SIGNS

PLAN

ELEVATION

BASIC FREE STANDING SIGNS, PEDESTAL BASES

PLAN

ILLUMINATED

ILLUMINATED

ELEVATION

LARGE FREE STANDING SIGNS

PLAN

ELEVATION

FREE STANDING SIGNS, DOUBLE SUPPORT

PLAN

ELEVATION

FREE STANDING SIGNS, SINGLE SUPPORT

Figure 35. Basic sign shapes for freestanding signs, predominantly used for exterior signs.

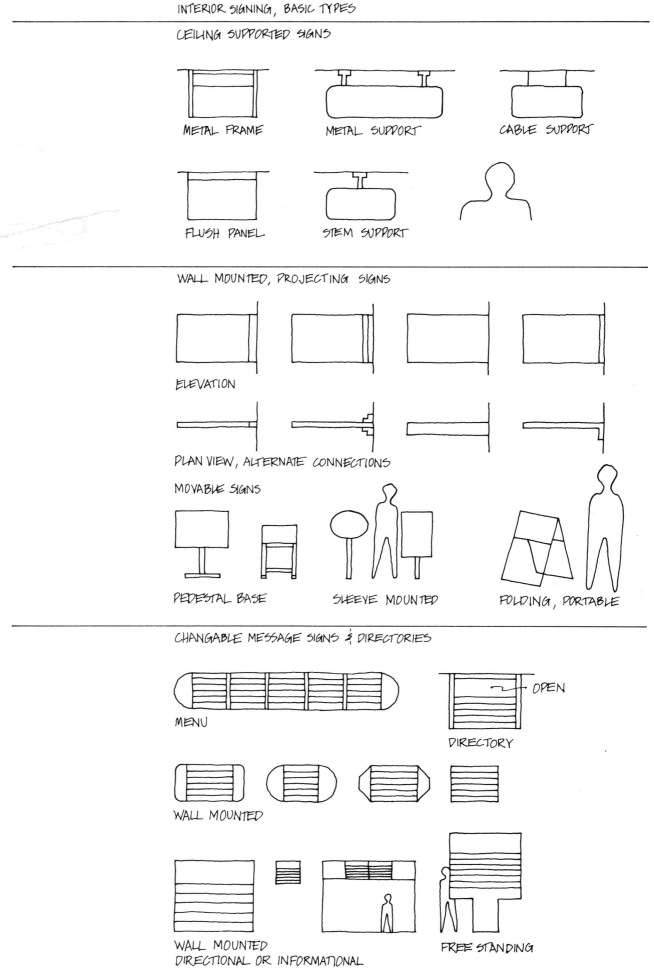

INTERIOR SIGNING, BASIC TYPES

CEILING SUPPORTED SIGNS

METAL FRAME   METAL SUPPORT   CABLE SUPPORT

FLUSH PANEL   STEM SUPPORT

WALL MOUNTED, PROJECTING SIGNS

ELEVATION

PLAN VIEW, ALTERNATE CONNECTIONS

MOVABLE SIGNS

PEDESTAL BASE   SLEEVE MOUNTED   FOLDING, PORTABLE

CHANGABLE MESSAGE SIGNS & DIRECTORIES

MENU   OPEN

DIRECTORY

WALL MOUNTED

WALL MOUNTED
DIRECTIONAL OR INFORMATIONAL   FREE STANDING

Figure 36. Basic types of signs frequently used for interior sign systems are shown here.

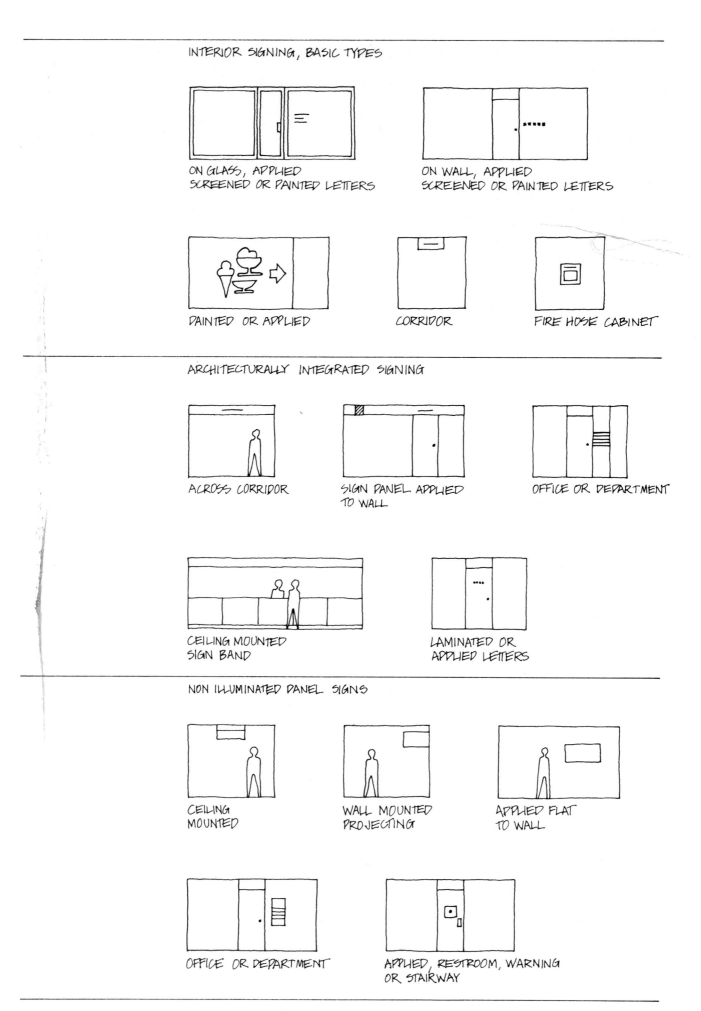

INTERIOR SIGNING, BASIC TYPES

ON GLASS, APPLIED
SCREENED OR PAINTED LETTERS

ON WALL, APPLIED
SCREENED OR PAINTED LETTERS

PAINTED OR APPLIED

CORRIDOR

FIRE HOSE CABINET

ARCHITECTURALLY INTEGRATED SIGNING

ACROSS CORRIDOR

SIGN PANEL APPLIED
TO WALL

OFFICE OR DEPARTMENT

CEILING MOUNTED
SIGN BAND

LAMINATED OR
APPLIED LETTERS

NON ILLUMINATED PANEL SIGNS

CEILING
MOUNTED

WALL MOUNTED
PROJECTING

APPLIED FLAT
TO WALL

OFFICE OR DEPARTMENT

APPLIED, RESTROOM, WARNING
OR STAIRWAY

Figure 37. These schematic drawings include basic interior signs and suggest possible ways of integrating signs with the architecture.

Figure 38. The word "Pull" is engraved into bronze door hardware, Security Pacific Plaza, Los Angeles.

Figure 39. Polished cast bronze sign identifies the auditorium, Security Pacific Plaza, Los Angeles.

Figure 40. To provide nighttime illumination for this Atlantic Richfield Plaza sign, a glass-covered troffer containing fluorescent light fixtures was built flush with the surrounding granite pavers.

occasionally if the situation justifies it. For example, if a lozenge shape is used for a group of directional signs, a nearby directory can be a rectangle with rounded corners. The rounded corners of the directory are a subtle relationship to the half rounded ends of the directional signs without slavishly repeating them.

Relating signs by shape is the most obvious way to create a family of signs, but there are many other design elements which can help to strengthen a basic family relationship. The use of one letterstyle or alphabet for all copy in a family group of signs is a normal way to create a strong visual link. Repetition of similar colors and materials creates another obvious relationship; less obvious are the repetition of construction details, sign supports, or fabrication methods.

Relating to Architectural Materials

A repetition of materials can help unify various signs into a system. In a similar way, some of the finish materials used to construct a building can often be used in fabricating its sign system. This repetition of materials such as polished bronze, dark anodized aluminum, and oak can help integrate signs with the architecture. These materials are adaptable to etching, engraving, and other normal sign fabrication techniques, and they result in signs which are very durable.

It is often possible to utilize existing building surfaces for certain sign items. The word "pull," for example, can be engraved into the bronze push plate of a door (Figure 38); floor indication numbers can be sand-blasted into the marble or granite wall of an elevator lobby. Signs can also be recessed into or "let-in" the building wall rather than sand-blasted into the wall surface. A shallow recess (sometimes called a "mortise") can be formed in the wall into which a bronze plaque or other sign is inserted (Figure 39). By creating a special place in the building wall for a sign, the designer gives it a sense of permanency and oneness with the building. This technique usually requires special planning and coordination with the architect while the building is being designed. In some cases, the architect must allow the proper back-up material for attaching the sign to the wall or ceiling.

Although not quite so permanent looking as letters sand-blasted or cast into a wall, those which are surface-mounted tight to a smooth wall can be very effective. Thick metal letters of aluminum, bronze, brass, or stainless steel, which are anchored to the wall with concealed metal pins set in epoxy, are permanent and solid looking. Letters with metal sides and Plexiglas face internally lighted with neon can avoid looking cheap and temporary if well fabricated of metal used in the building. For additional ways to build letters that are suitable for architectural signs, refer to Chapter 12, Fabrication.

Most signing programs will require many panel signs which cannot be built into the wall, but must be supported from the ceiling, project from the wall, or be freestanding. It is often not practical to make these of materials utilized in the building because of functional requirements, installation problems, or expense. Materials that are suitable for panel or freestanding signs are discussed in Figure 49 on page 50 in this chapter and in Chapter 12, Fabrication.

Sign Design and Color Usage

The sensitive designer is always aware of the esthetic relationship between the object he designs and the place where it is to be used; and this is particularly important in considering signing colors. As a design element, color is essential in making the sign system appropriate to its environment. Colors for sign panels and copy should not be selected arbitrarily or just because they go well together. Sign colors should relate to colors and materials of the building or space where the signs will be installed. Although "relate to" does imply "blend with," sign colors for some projects should contrast with building colors; other projects require a more monochromatic approach. Many large-scale, windowless work areas, often found in hospitals and schools, are very bland, and a decorative sign system can provide the needed scale and color.

However, if the building interior utilizes strong color extensively, the sign system can often be neutral in color. For example, a building of dark red brick suggests the use of sign panels slightly lighter or darker in value than the brick. If the designer wants to minimize the contrast between the brick walls and the sign system, he can choose a darker shade of the brick color for sign panels. However, it may be more appropriate to use black or dark gray sign panels, which would stand out nicely against the brick. In either case the copy message could be white or off-white for good legibility.

Signs of a neutral color may also be used effectively in airports, but for a different reason. These are restless, busy places which may have colorful concessionaire signs. A system of directional signs with black panels and white copy or the reverse may provide the kind of strong contrast needed to stand out against this colorful background of competing signs. By comparison, small polished bronze signs with engraved copy may provide ample contrast in elegant corporate offices involving a subtle blend of natural woods and fabrics.

Of course, there are purely functional color applications where the use of color is well established by convention or law. Boulevard stop signs, in most states, have red backgrounds. The Occupational Safety and Health Administration of the federal government has assigned specific meaning to certain colors to be used on safety equipment and signs or to define areas of a manufacturing plant. As noted in the chapter on Human Factors, people tend to have conditioned responses to some of these colors which can act as psychological reinforcement. This is why emergency signs at a hospital often involve the color red and why lighted traffic control signs also use red lights to indicate stop. Similarly, the color yellow is widely used on roadside signing or center divider stripping to indicate the need for caution.

ILLUMINATION AS A DESIGN ELEMENT
It is not the intent of this section to discuss architectural lighting at length but to present some basic information. This will help the reader understand the relationship between the architectural lighting of a particular project and lighting for signing and graphics in general.

Illumination is usually thought of as a functional element; it is a practical necessity which is largely taken for granted. But architects and designers also use light as a flexible design element. Light from various sources can help define forms and spaces and enhance details. Artificial light when used imaginatively can create psychological moods. Particularly when it is used in conjunction with colorful walls, light of the proper intensity and color can create excitement, dramatic emphasis, and emotional warmth.

Lighting Exterior Signs
Important architectural projects are often floodlighted at night. A headquarters office building is part of the corporation's public image, and proper exterior lighting enhances that image.

Nighttime illumination also helps identify shopping centers and other merchandising facilities where light is used to dramatize displayed goods. Incandescent light standards are installed in these centers to illuminate plazas and courtyards; incandescent fixtures are recessed into soffits over doorways to dramatize entries and welcome shoppers. Existing project lighting can sometimes be used to illuminate signing elements if signs are properly designed and located to take advantage of it.

There are several basic lighting techniques which relate to the illumination of exterior signing for architectural projects. These are flood- or spotlighting, ambient lighting, internal lighting, and external lighting.

Flood- or Spotlighting. In some situations exterior signs or letters which are cast into the building wall or set flush with it can be illuminated by spill light from existing or supplementary floodlights. This is often an appropriate and subtle way to identify dignified office buildings.

Great care should be taken when floodlighting raised, three-dimensional letters of any thickness because shadows cast from the letters can interfere with legibility. Of course, shadows cast by such letters is a common problem in signing, whether caused by floodlighting or the sun. However, the designer can sometimes overcome these difficult conditions by choosing the right material or finish. For example, aluminum or bronze letters mounted on a dark granite building will be quite legible under varying light conditions, if a bright satin finish is used. The designer must always keep in mind the specific environmental lighting when designing each sign, adjusting the design and lighting where possible to work together.

Major identification signs for a project are often quite large in size and located in such a way that floodlighting cannot be used. Special lighting must be devised, as in the following example: one of the main identification signs for the Atlantic Richfield Plaza project is a granite monolith with the project name sand-blasted into its surface. To light this sign, fluorescent lamps housed in a waterproof trough were used as a light source (Figure 40). The trough was designed flush with adjacent walkways and covered with a protective glass diffuser. This design provides an unobtrusive source of even illumination which extends the full length of the sign. Conventional spotlights would have created hot spots, glare, and uneven illumination.

Ambient Lighting. In the form of spill light from existing architectural lighting, ambient lighting may produce adequate illumination for many pedestrian-oriented signs. For example, the address numbers or identification signs at a building entrance can be illuminated by spill light from overhead entrance lighting if colors and materials of these signs contrast well with their backgrounds.

The intensity of ambient light frequently is a critical factor. In parking lots where existing light standards may produce only a few footcandles of illumination, parking entrance signs usually require internal illumination. Signs within the parking lot frequently utilize special vinyl letters which reflect the light of approaching vehicles.

Internal Lighting. Internal lighting of exterior signs is very often necessary to make them legible at night or to give them special emphasis. The following discussion describes several ways to design signs with internal lighting.

Signs with Illuminated Routed Copy and Opaque Backgrounds (Figure 41). This type of sign is widely used for a variety of

Figure 41. The copy of this sign is routed out of the aluminum face and backed up with internally lighted acrylic plastic. The T-shaped structure is steel tubing, McCarran International Airport, Las Vegas, Nevada.

Figure 43. This number is fabricated hollow of metal with concealed neon lighting that produces a halo effect.

Figure 42. Project identification sign, Belmont Savings, Belmont Shores, California.

projects from office buildings to airports. Compared with a similar design having an internally illuminated background, this technique can create a more refined, subtle effect. However, the surface brightness of the letters should be limited; otherwise, a halo or overglow at night may distort the letterforms.

Internally Lighted Signs with Translucent Panels and Opaque or Translucent Copy (Figure 42). Either the copy or sign background can be white or in colors. Because of the color potential, signs of this type are widely used in shopping centers and other merchandising facilities. Bright colors can help individual merchants fill their need to create a distinctive image and to attract attention.

Channel Letters with Internal Lighting (Often Called "Reverse Channel Letters"; Figure 43). These are normally made with metal face and sides and lighted with neon tubes concealed by the letters. These letters are pegged out from the wall, creating a rather soft halo of light, with the letters in silhouette. Similar letters can be fabricated with acrylic sides and face or metal sides and acrylic face, each creating a different effect.

External Lighting. This category includes any technique utilizing a light source outside the sign, whether attached to it or located elsewhere. Floodlighting, discussed above, is one such technique. Others include the use of exposed neon tubes, clear or frosted incandescent bulbs, very small so-called seed lights, high-intensity lamps, and various kinds of spotlights. Except for flood- and spotlighting, most of these techniques are more appropriate for merchandising sign applications.

Incandescent bulbs, when exposed, create a warm, romantic quality of light that is familiar in amusement parks or on theater marquees. Exposed lighting of this kind provided much of the nighttime charm of old Times Square in New York; it still provides the special ambience for Tivoli Gardens in Copenhagen and many other entertainment facilities. Incandescent bulbs can be programed to flash on and off in any sequence, providing sparkle or a dynamic sense of movement.

If used with good taste and imagination, exposed lamps can add a decorative quality to signs for shops and restaurants (Figure 44), which provide much of the color and warmth needed for evening operations of shopping center malls. Neon has an even greater decorative potential—when used as an external source of colored light. For signing, exposed neon tubes can be formed to the shape of most letters or linear designs. Many tubes used side by side can cover broad areas, but it is more economical to illuminate the well-defined areas of channel letters. When neon is combined with the broad color spectrum of plastics and colored glass, the design possibilities are limitless.

Lighting Interior Signs

For the interior spaces of most projects, the architect or interior designer establishes an overall design concept for lighting. If the project is already functioning, the sign designer can visit the site to observe how each area is lighted. If possible he should obtain footcandle readings of each area; they provide a more exact basis for determining where internally lighted signs are needed. From a design point of view, the visit will give him an idea of the *quality* of light in each space so that he won't provide lighted signs which contrast too harshly with existing lighting.

If the project is yet to be built, the sign designer can obtain projected footcandle ratings from the electrical engineer. He should also review lighting plans which show the placement and type of each light fixture. Becoming familiar with project lighting is very important because it is the source of ambient lighting.

Ambient Lighting. The most energy-efficient method for lighting interior signs is ambient lighting. Spill light often exists within project interior spaces in sufficient quantities to illuminate most signs wherever they are needed.

Compared with ambient light of exterior spaces, interior light seldom changes from day to night. However, the intensity of this ambient light may vary greatly from one area of a project to another. For example, workspaces in an office building are often very bright, perhaps 100 footcandles. But light levels in the building's public corridors may be as low as 25 footcandles. This variation may result from differences in both functional requirements and design intent. Bright workspaces stimulate activity while softly lighted corridors can produce a feeling of calm and elegance. Light fixtures in these corridors may be far apart, producing uneven lighting. This often means that there is no fixture near a planned sign location. The ability of the eye to adjust to different levels of illumination usually allows nonilluminated signs to function even under such difficult viewing conditions. When in doubt, the designer should test a mockup using actual sign colors and materials in the space where the final sign will be installed.

Adjusting the Design. If a mockup seems difficult to read in a specific area, several options should be tried before installing an internally lighted sign. Merely changing sign backgrounds from light to dark gray will often increase contrasts sufficiently if sign copy is white. This change should be consistent throughout a group of signs. If this change is not effective, then bulbs of higher wattage should be installed in the problem areas.

Figure 44. Small incandescent lamps in this sign are wired to blink on and off in a random sequence, Curtain Call Restaurant, Los Angeles.

Considering design continuity of signs within a group, if only one is internally lighted, it will appear out of place unless there is some very special reason for emphasizing it. The amount of ambient light falling on each may vary considerably, but so long as signs are legible, the eye will adjust to that variation.

While existing lighting is adequate for most hanging or wall-mounted signs, it is usually inadequate for lighting large graphic walls. Most recessed ceiling fixtures light walls unevenly, producing scallops of brighter light.

For lighting graphic wall designs, which may extend from floor to ceiling, it is often desirable to install "wall-washers." These incandescent fixtures are engineered to be installed flush with the ceiling and to light a wall evenly. Lighting manufacturers can provide technical information about such fixtures.

"Framing projectors" are special incandescent fixtures which are useful for illuminating a sign or graphic item very dramatically. For instance, if the designer wants to highlight a carved, gold-leaf sign in a dimly lighted restaurant, this fixture can be adjusted to light the exact area of the sign.

Spot- or Floodlighting. Floodlighting is a less precise way of lighting an interior sign or special graphic. Spotlights can be partially built into the ceiling, but this is difficult unless planned for as part of the building construction.

Internal Lighting. Internally lighted signs are infrequently used for projects such as office buildings, banks, hospitals, schools, and similar facilities. There are exceptions, such as directories or exit signs which are sometimes internally lighted. Building codes vary throughout the country, but some do require exit signs to be illuminated, especially for theaters which have stringent exit requirements.

By contrast, within shopping centers, signs identifying specialty shops, stores, restaurants, and the like are usually lighted from within. What has previously been said about various internal lighting techniques for exterior signs applies equally well here.

FUNCTIONAL FACTORS

Exterior Signs

Size and Shape. The size of exterior signs is often closely related to the size of copy they display. The basic size of the copy message depends upon two factors: how long the message is and how far away it must be legible. Legibility of all exterior signs is influenced by several factors, which are discussed in Chapter 2, Human Factors. Any exterior sign, such as one giving parking directions which requires the driver to stop, slow down, or change directions, must be legible from a greater-than-normal distance, allowing the driver time to respond to whatever directions are indicated.

After the letter height for a particular sign has been determined, rough layouts of the copy message can be made. If the basic shape of the sign panel has not been predetermined, these layouts can help in determining its final shape. For example, a freestanding sign may involve a six-word message. Assuming 12-inch (30.5-centimeter) high letters, it might not be practical to run the message in only one line. This would make the sign over 30 feet (9 meters) long. By trying rough copy layouts in two or three lines, the designer can determine an appropriate panel size. At the same time, the designers should explore various shapes, in his search for a shape that will meet all requirements. To become well integrated with other signs in the system, the shape of this particular sign must become part of a family group.

Location. It is assumed that general locations of all signs have been determined during the planning phase. These general locations are based upon a careful analysis of existing site and building plans, parking area layouts, and so forth. Before assigning specific locations, it is helpful to visit the existing site and make a photographic survey of all pertinent conditions. Such conditions might include corners of the site, major street intersections, building entrances, and other situations for which signs are planned. Photographs should be taken from the approach used by normal viewers; this will help the designer visualize trees or architectural obstructions which might not be shown on plans. Of course, if signs are for a new project, the designer must refer to landscape and lighting plans or work with consultants who can revise the location of trees or lighting if they conflict with important signs. For both new and existing projects, the ultimate size of trees must be considered to prevent future growth from blocking out signs. Other basic factors to consider are

1. The basic internal operations of the buildings or project. If the project is a parking structure, the designer should review plans that the architect or parking consultant has produced indicating traffic flow.
2. The movement of vehicular and pedestrian traffic within the site. Signs must be located for maximum efficiency of traffic flow.
3. Physical characteristics of the building such as columns, projecting canopies, overhangs—anything that may interfere with planned locations of the signs.
4. Temporary sight-line obstructions. Pedestrians or vehicles may temporarily obstruct sight-lines, unless signs are located above these obstructions.
5. The relationship between various signs, either existing or planned for. This must be considered to avoid interference with sight lines.
6. Number of directions from which the sign must be viewed. A directional sign at a street or road intersection may require information on two, three, or four sides.
7. The visual angle from which a sign is normally viewed. The angle as measured on plans between the line of sight and face of the sign should not be less than about 60° to avoid interfering with legibility.
8. All pertinent sign codes governing locations and height requirements. For any sign in or projecting over a public walkway, clearance dimensions [approximately 8 feet (2.4 meters)] are regulated by most local sign codes.
9. Location of signs requiring a vehicle to stop, slow down, or turn. Such signs must be placed far enough from the point of decision for the driver to make the change safely. This depends upon the speed of the vehicle. Refer to the case study of legibility in Chapter 2, Human Factors.

Enclosures and Supports. Many more exterior than interior signs are freestanding and illuminated. They are more often seen from several directions, which suggests that they may have copy on two to four sides. Multiple-sided signs can have a sculptural or structural character which is more architectural than the "lollipop" look of a single panel mounted on a thin post. Monolithic or columnlike forms with sign copy running vertically are often good solutions for constricted exterior spaces (Figure 45).

The sign enclosures of exterior illuminated signs usually need to be quite thick to house interior lighting equipment. These signs often look top heavy if mounted on a small steel post even though it may be adequate structurally. The visual mass of the base can be increased to balance the heavy top.

In other signs the steel or wooden supporting structural members can be expressed, rather than hidden inside the sign, to create an interesting support system for the sign panels or enclosures (Figure 46).

Most sign enclosures are rectangular because this shape is easy to make of sheet metal, but many other shapes can be fabricated. Because of the many techniques available, sign craftsmen are capable of making hollow metal letters or enclosures in very complex shapes: round, oval, lozenge, rectangular, or nearly any shape the designer can imagine. Refer to the schematic drawings on pages 37-41 of this chapter.

Materials. The range of basic materials used for exterior signs is somewhat limited because of the damaging effect of sun and weather and the practical considerations of fabrication costs.

The following materials are only the most basic and widely used for exterior signs. Other materials and various processes are described in Chapter 12, Fabrication.

Sheet Metal. Iron or steel is the dominant material traditionally used for exterior signs. In the hands of skilled craftsmen, very thin sheets can be formed into complex shapes and three-dimensional letters in heights from 1½ inches (3.8 centimeters) to 30 feet (9 meters). However, compound or warped surfaces (shapes like autobody parts) are usually beyond the capability of metal sign fabricators. Sheet metal can be welded, riveted, soldered, brazed, and fastened with a variety of mechanical fasteners. Sheet metal must be plated or painted to prevent rusting.

Steel Structural Shapes. Rods or tubes with square, rectangular, or round cross sections are commonly used to support small signs, but large tubes can be used for very large ones, such as billboards or freeway signs. Strong for their relatively light weight, these shapes can be welded or bolted to sign panels. Like all steel parts, they must be plated or painted to prevent rust.

Wood. Solid wood is one of the oldest materials still used for sign posts or other support members. Signs subject to damage or replacement every few years are frequently constructed of plywood panels fastened to fir posts. Redwood, cedar, or cypress are used for carved signs. These can be left natural, stained, or painted, and all have good weathering characteristics. A special grade of pine can be used for carving individual raised letters to be gold-leafed. Properly sealed and finished, such letters have lasted 30 years outdoors.

Exterior Grade Plywood. Made with waterproof glues, exterior grade plywood is widely used for inexpensive exterior signs. Duraply™ is plywood with a fiberboard face; it is warp resistant and has a smooth surface for painting, but edges should be well sealed against moisture.

Acrylic Plastic. Plexiglas is one of the best known tradenames, but there are many manufacturers of acrylic, which is the most widely used plastic for illuminated faces of exterior signs. The designer should be aware of a basic characteristic: it has a relatively high rate of expansion/contraction during temperature

Figure 45. Project identification sign, Atlantic Richfield Plaza, Los Angeles.

Figure 46. Directional sign in parking area, McCarran International Airport, Las Vegas, Nevada.

changes [approximately 1/16 inch (1.6 millimeter) per foot]. If not adequately considered, this characteristic can be a source of problems. For example, a sign enclosure constructed entirely of black acrylic with cemented joints can break in the sun's heat. However, it is an excellent material when properly used. To avoid problems, technical information should be obtained from the manufacturer.

Bronze and Aluminum. Both of these metals are suitable for cutout or cast letters and plaques. Some bronze alloys will verdigris (turn green) outdoors if not given a statuary (oxidized) finish or a protective clear coating. Many alloys of aluminum will oxidize or pit if not protected by anodizing, which is available as a clear coating or in colors. Aluminum is also excellent for sign panels and enclosures and is also suitable for painting.

Stone. Marble, granite, limestone, and other stones can be used to make monolithic signs, with carved letters either cut in or projecting. Some of these are easily stained or attacked by smog (especially limestone and marble). Hand carving of stone is a vanishing, very expensive art; letters can be sand-blasted into stone at lower cost, producing a round-bottomed cut.

Concrete. This is a strong, relatively inexpensive material for signs or sign bases. Small items can be precast in a shop or formed on the job site. Letterforms can be cast into concrete surfaces using wooden letter patterns which are removed when the concrete is set. With this technique it is possible to cast letterforms into the concrete wall of a building if planned well in advance of actual construction.

Fiberglass. This is made of polyester resins reinforced with glass fibers. It can be used to form one-of-a-kind shapes using hand lay-up methods or to produce a quantity of items using production molds. Lightweight, compound shapes made of fiber can be opaque or translucent. When properly lighted from inside, the entire shape can glow, making it suitable for illuminated map-type directories or sculptural sign items. However, it is difficult to achieve uniform light transmission with fiberglass.

Designing with Good Maintenance in Mind. Maintenance of exterior signs can be reduced by using durable, low maintenance materials and techniques, although initially these are more expensive. Natural materials like stone and certain weathering woods require little care, except for periodic cleaning. The finish of painted metal signs, similar to automotive finishes, should be cleaned and waxed periodically. Many sign companies offer maintenance programs on a contract basis.

Several methods of copy application minimize maintenance. For example, sign copy which is printed on the rear face of clear plastic is protected by the plastic. Copy which is routed through the metal face of a sign, then backed up with Plexiglas, is quite permanent. Most methods where the copy is an integral part of the sign (rather than mechanically attached) can reduce maintenance. Copy painted on sign panels may have to be repainted in a few years. However, a final coat of linear polyurethane painted over sign surfaces will improve the life of the painted finish. This clear coating is so tough that even spray can paint graffiti can be removed from its surface using lacquer thinners.

Designing Vandal-Resistant Signs. Much of what has been said about maintenance also applies to making signs vandal-resistant. Select the right materials for the job. In a vandal-prone area, a sign of stainless steel with sand-blasted copy is hard to damage. Porcelain enamel on aluminum, used for boulevard stop signs, is very wear- and chip-resistant. A painted concrete panel with cast-in letters can be repainted after it has been covered with spray paint graffiti.

Another kind of vandal is the collector who finds small, beautifully detailed items almost irresistible. Multicolored, gold-leafed, or three-dimensional symbols can be installed with theft-proof fasteners.

Interior Signs

Before designing any specific sign for a system, it is important to review plans and schematic designs made during the planning process. While these designs are usually no more detailed than thumbnail sketches, they show the basic character of a sign as well as its relative size and shape. During planning, signs were given preliminary locations and grouped into sign types. During final design, the location, shape, and size of all elements should be reviewed and adjusted.

Location. The following should be considered when determining the final location of interior signs:

Characteristics of the Architectural Space. For example, parking structures usually have very few walls, suggesting that signs be ceiling-hung or painted on low beams.

How the Space Functions. In busy institutional corridors, such as hospitals, for instance, signs usually work best when ceiling-mounted or mounted at right angles to the wall well above head height. In less busy office building corridors, signs mounted flat to the wall function well.

Obstructions. There are two basic types of visual obstructions to consider. The first type, architectural or built-in obstructions, are usually shown on architectural plans. These include walls, columns, pilasters, soffits, stairways, escalators, or any built-in equipment which may interfere with signs.

The second type are furnishings or movable equipment which seldom is shown on architectural plans. These include plants, furniture, special light fixtures, or other items not shown on the plans.

Viewing Angles. If the viewer observes the sign from an acute angle, it may not be readable. At times, the sign must be readable from both sides or from three or four sides at once.

Relationship to Other Signs. Place signs to avoid interference with the intent or message of other signs.

Supports. Deciding whether to emphasize sign support hardware is an esthetic judgment. This depends upon how closely related the sign system details are to the building details. Signs can be wall-mounted with supports fully concealed, which makes them appear to float off the wall, or they can be bracketed out from the wall. Ceiling signs can be tight to the ceiling or spaced down from it and supported in obvious or unobtrusive ways. Some of the practical methods include suspending signs for interior corridors from metal cables, rods, tubing, or wood members. It is usually advisable to use two supports per sign panel to discourage pranksters from rotating directional signs to point the wrong way (Figure 47). Whether to mount ceiling signs tight to the ceiling or spaced down will depend on ceiling heights and head clearance under the sign. Suspended signs usually look best when all are mounted a consistent height from the floor, but high enough to meet code requirements.

A general word of caution about all ceiling-mounted signs:

they should not be fastened directly to acoustic tile or acoustic plaster ceilings. Sign hardware should be attached to metal ceiling channels or to the structural slab above the suspended ceiling. To avoid public liability problems, insist on having any doubtful connection engineered. Sign fabricators can usually calculate the safety of any hardware the designer might devise. Various manufacturers of standard interior signing systems have developed hardware for ceiling- and wall-mounting conditions. It is often possible to adapt this standard hardware for use with custom installations.

For parking garage signing, the least expensive method of supporting a hanging sign panel is by chains. Besides being inexpensive, chains allow the sign to swing if hit, rather than the support to break. If exposed chains are offensive to some designers, straight vinyl tubing can be specified to cover them. For garages located in very windy areas, it may be necessary to provide rigid supports to prevent excessive wind movement of signs.

Sign panels designed to be mounted flat to the wall surface present the least problem. They can be attached directly to a smooth, durable surface or spaced out a little from the wall, giving a floating appearance. A combination of contact adhesive foam tape and silicone adhesive or a spacer frame of the right dimension can usually create the effect desired. However, panel signs mounted at right angles to the wall with little or no flange supports are much more difficult to support adequately. Too often, panel signs of this type are vulnerable to being accidentally struck by maintenance men carrying ladders. Any designer who has used a claw hammer to pull nails can understand the basic principle of leverage involved when this kind of wall sign is struck. If the end of an 18-inch (45.7-centimeter) long sign is struck with a 30-pound (14-kilogram) force, the resultant force acting to bend the sign or pull mounting fasteners out of the wall can be roughly 18 × 30, or 540 pounds (250 kilograms). If possible, a breakaway or hinged connection should be used to prevent damage to the sign or wall.

Freestanding and Portable Signs. Few interior sign systems require freestanding signs, except special portable ones (Figure 48). These can have weighted bases, fit into built-in sockets, or be made of folding materials to drape over chains at parking lot entrances. They are usually used to warn of wet, slippery floors, out-of-order elevators, and similar temporary conditions.

Considering the heavy use of most interior spaces, there are seldom floor areas where permanent, freestanding signs can be placed to function well. However, if neither wall nor ceiling locations seem adequate, floor mounting can be used. A pedestal-type mounting is usually strongest, with concealed connections at the floor. If the element is quite large, such as a map-type directory, a reinforcing plate should be installed in the slab before final floor materials are placed; such connections should be engineered to ensure adequate strength.

Materials. Interior signs which are installed out of public reach lead a very sheltered life. Particularly in air-conditioned spaces, many materials can be used for such signs and will last for many years—if they have the proper finish. Some of the materials widely used for interior signs are listed in Figure 49.

Considering Maintenance. Interior signs installed above head height in buildings seldom require any maintenance except cleaning, but those within public reach should be protected or designed of wear-resistant materials. Signs in waiting areas, such as elevator lobbies, are subject to a kind of unconscious

Figure 47. Directional signs with removable copy panels, supported from the ceiling by metal frames, Hollywood Presbyterian Hospital, Los Angeles.

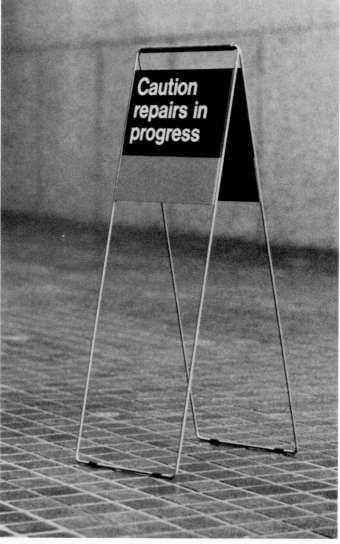

Figure 48. A portable sign which folds up when not in temporary use, Security Pacific Plaza, Los Angeles.

vandalism. When waiting in areas not under constant surveillance, some people tend to pick at signs. Vinyl letters are especially vulnerable to this kind of vandalism if not covered by a layer of clear vinyl, glass, or polycarbonate (Lexan).

As a general principle, all hard materials that are difficult to scratch are wear-resistant. Another general principle is to utilize fabrication and copy application techniques that are inherently maintenance-free. A few examples will illustrate this. Copy which is sand-blasted into a granite wall is both maintenance-free and vandal-resistant (Figure 50). (Hardly anything is vandal-proof!) A bronze plaque with cast-in letters presents fewer maintenance problems than individual pegged-out bronze letters, which can sometimes be pried off the wall. Painted interior signs with silk-screened copy can be protected with a clear coating of linear polyurethane or other durable clear, low-gloss finishes.

Flexibility and Changeability. For interior signing systems designed for facilities with many different internal departments or functions, it is often desirable to consider a modular approach to signing. Departments may grow or shrink and have to be relocated from one floor or area of a building to another. Clinics within a hospital may outgrow one building and be moved to another. To cope with these changes, directional signs can be composed of modular, changeable elements. Rather than discarding many signs when the department moves, only the affected elements need to be reworked.

One disadvantage to the flexible/modular system is that its initial cost is usually higher than a nonmodular one. The frequency of change is an important factor in determining whether or not to use such a system.

Another kind of changeability should be considered for desk name signs where there is a high rate of employee turnover, or for bank tellers' signs where tellers frequently change places with one another. It is far less expensive to design these items with inexpensive removable name strips, usually photo positives or negatives protected by thin vinyl, than to replace the entire sign when an employee leaves.

Yet another kind of changeable sign is one with many removable strips, each one with different copy (Figure 51). This kind of flexibility is often needed in hospital signing. Mounted near patient room entry doors, the sign can be changed daily to display special treatment or feeding instructions for a particular patient.

There are clients who need to replace signing elements each week, such as name strips for directories or desk signs. Such clients may request that the designer help them set up a method of in-house copy reproduction or sign fabrication. The following is a brief review of the available methods:

Engraver Routing. A routing or engraving machine is used to cut letters into plastic, which is laminated of two colors. For example, routing through a black top layer exposes the white layer. The cutting tool is round and produces letters with

MATERIALS FOR INTERIOR SIGNS

Material	Variety or Trade Name	Use
Wood	Pine, mahogany, redwood	Carved signs, painted or gold-leafed, with carved or cutout letters
Plywood	Birch, White pine	Painted sign panels or cutout letters
Fiberboard faced plywood	Duraply™	Painted sign panels
High-pressure laminate	Formica, Micarta, Textolite, etc.	Laminated to plywood
Metal	Bronze and brass	Cast, fabricated, or cutout letters, plaques
	Aluminum	Cast, fabricated, or cutout letters, plaques
	Stainless steel	Fabricated letters, panels, supports
	Steel	Fabricated letters, panels
Plastics	Acrylics (Plexiglas, Lucite)	Fabricated letters, sign panels, miscellaneous items
	Vinyls	Die-cut letters, extruded shapes, frames, or protective covers
	Fiber-reinforced polyesters (fiberglass)	Fabricated irregular- or complex-shaped items (white FRP can transmit light, but not so efficiently as acrylics.)
	Polycarbonate (Lexan)	Shatterproof, transparent sheet plastic, used as protective covering over graphics instead of glass, acrylic
Plastic laminate	Two-color laminated plastic (engraving stock)	Routing or machine engraving copy through the first layer, exposing the second
Glass	Various	Transparent signs with silk-screened copy; can be sand-blasted (except tempered) or acid-etched; can be ground, chipped, or mirrored

Figure 49. Materials for interior signs.

round-ended strokes. Letterforms are limited to a few alphabets. Spacing of letters, done by eye, is limited to the skill of the operator so it is often quite uneven.

Film Strip. The film strip process utilizes photo techniques to produce film positive or negative strips. The copy is either clear on a black background or black on clear if a film negative and black on white or the reverse if it is a paper positive. No color is available. The selection and sizes of type are very limited or expensive to change and make the method suitable for use on interior signs of only a fairly small size.

Silk Screening. Based on the use of photo-produced screens, silk screening is more complex than those described above and may not fit well with an office building environment. It requires specially trained personnel and may only be practical if there is a painting shop or large maintenance shop available. Screens can be obtained from specialists rather than produced in-house, but this creates a delay in time which may be self-defeating. Sign copy can be well spaced and printed in most any size or color.

BUDGETING FOR FABRICATION

One of the first questions most clients ask is, "How much are the signs going to cost?" This question may result partly from curiosity, but it also may reflect a normal concern about the budget. When asked this question before he has planned the sign system, the designer has little basis for even an intelligent guesstimate.

He might respond by asking the client to tell him what budget has been established. Having little experience with signing, some clients have no budget established and expect the designer to recommend one. Others have budgeted an arbitrary amount, hoping that it will be sufficient. A few want the job done properly, regardless of cost, and may not ask for a preliminary budget.

Whether or not a budget has been established by the client, the designer should defer any estimate of his own until he has assembled sufficient information to recommend a realistic one. He should avoid, if at all possible, offering even a rough guesstimate at the outset of the job; these are rarely close enough to be of value. A low guess may have repercussions (clients have long memories about such figures). A high figure may convince the client to seek professional help elsewhere.

When to Present a Fabrication Budget

After long experience, some designers may be able to estimate sign fabrication costs with reasonable accuracy. However, for cost information, most will have to rely on fabricators, who in turn base these costs on information about the signs received from the designer.

Timing is very important. If estimates are made too soon in the design process, not enough is known for the estimates to be accurate; if made too late, the designer may not have enough of the fee left to make cost-cutting design changes and also provide other necessary remaining services. Just when to make up a fabrication budget depends upon individual design office procedures. Some offices provide a preliminary cost estimate based on schematic or conceptual designs and a final one during design development.

In general a fabrication budget should be provided to the client at the time of the major design presentation. Several weeks in advance of that presentation, the designer should review design drawings with various fabricators, giving them

Figure 50. Elevator lobby sign, with numbers sandblasted into granite indicating floors served, Atlantic Richfield Plaza, Los Angeles.

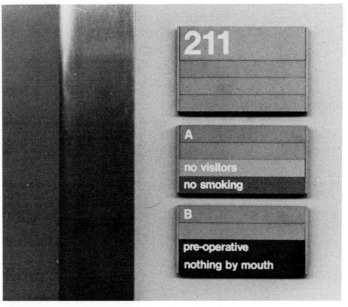

Figure 51. Located beside corridor door of multibed patient rooms, these signs display changeable messages, San Antonio Community Hospital, Upland, California.

Figure 52. This final design presentation of a site identification sign includes a schematic detail to show how internal lighting is handled.

Figure 53. This presentation drawing shows the plaza sign in relation to escalator. Photo cutouts of people are included to indicate a sense of scale.

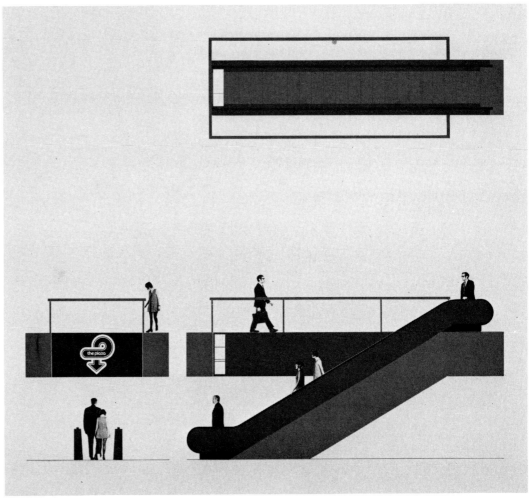

adequate time to assemble cost information. The following is a list of information they will need:

1. Quantities of each item
2. Shape and overall dimensions
3. Material and fabrication methods
4. Copy application methods
5. Lighting requirements

The more complete the information is, the more accurate the estimate can be. The more unusual or customized a sign system is, the more difficult it is to estimate, and the less accurate the estimate may be.

Assembling a Budget

Depending on the number of different fabrication techniques used in the sign system, the designer may have to obtain costs from several specialists. Several days should be allowed for assembling this information and calculating totals. It is usually wise to add a contingency factor of 10 percent or so to this total to cover unknowns. If there is a time delay of six to nine months before fabrication will be completed, another percentage should be added for inflation.

Presentation and Follow-up

Final designs can be presented to the client in many different forms—from scale models to perspective renderings—depending on the nature of the sign system, the time and fee budget available, and other requirements. For most situations, elevations of major sign items should be presented with copy wording applied in clearly readable form. Hard-line, to-scale drawings mounted on illustration board can have copy applied using transfer letters, similar to the examples in Figures 52–54.

If the client is very pleased with the design presentation, the budget may receive little attention, especially if the client feels that it is reasonable. However, there may be a serious gap between what the client had in mind and realistic budget requirements of the project. In such situations, the client may be willing to spend more or he may expect the designer to find ways to lower fabrication costs.

This can often be done without great changes to the designs—merely changes in detail. For example, on a recent project silk-screened copy was changed to a sand-blasted technique (a method of incising copy), resulting in a 50 percent reduction in costs. So, much depends upon the specific details of the system and how basic it is. If a low-cost system has been presented and even this costs more than the money available, there may be no viable custom design solution. The designer may have to suggest that the client use a mixture of standard manufactured signs and some custom designs. Or he may have to withdraw from the project.

Figure 54. This presentation drawing was produced using color-aid paper and transfer lettering.

6
Alphabets and Symbols

Many different terms are used by graphics specialists when referring to an English alphabet of 26 characters and 10 numbers. The printer or typographer may use the terms *font, face,* or *typestyle.* Sign painters and fabricators prefer the term *letterstyle.* Graphic designers may use any of the foregoing but seem to prefer the basic term *alphabet,* which is used in this book. The first part of this chapter is devoted to the selection, modification, and design of alphabets. These can be thought of as systems of abstract symbols (letters) which have no meaning until they are grouped to form words. The second part is concerned with symbols, nonverbal graphic forms, which have meaning when used independently of words.

ALPHABETS

Using Corporate Logotypes and Alphabets
The most important graphic element that the designer may have to incorporate within the signing program is an existing corporate logotype, which is used to identify corporate property and products. (Corporate, as used here, refers to a company, commercial organization, or noncommercial institution.)

National corporations often have distinctive logotypes which, when used in their advertising programs, project a strong public image. It is appropriate to treat such logotypes as unique designs to be used for identifying this corporation alone. The client's logotype may be used in major project signing to identify the site, the building, or a parking entrance.

If a client's logotype is based on a simple, legible alphabet, this same alphabet may also be suitable for all project signing. For example, both the Atlantic Richfield Company and Security Pacific Bank use Helvetica as a corporate alphabet. This alphabet was used on signing for their corporate headquarters in Los Angeles by mutual agreement between the client and designers. For both projects Helvetica was reproduced in a variety of materials, using many different fabrication methods (Figure 55). The excellent design and somewhat neutral character of Helvetica allowed it to be used for both elegant and utilitarian signs. Rather than using a secondary alphabet, a lighter or heavier version of Helvetica was used occasionally for special emphasis or proper scale.

However, if the logotype was custom designed and no alphabet for it exists or if the logotype has a strong, distinctive character, then a separate alphabet will have to be designed. The existing logotype will influence both the selection and the design of alphabets for project signing.

Modifying Existing Logotypes
The designer must be aware of some special problems in adapting an existing logotype for use in signing. For example, if a logotype based on a Bodoni-type style is to be translated into three-dimensional letters with internal lighting, the thin strokes may have to be increased to accommodate the neon tubing. Script letters with very thin strokes may be impossible to adapt for internal neon lighting, and they are often too fragile when cut out of metal or wood. Sometimes the overall weight of such logotypes can be increased to make them workable for internal illumination; this may be difficult to do without destroying the character of the logotype. To avoid this problem, it may be necessary to illuminate the logotype in some other way.

Designing New Logotypes for Signing
If the designer is asked to design a new logotype to be used in project signing, it should be based on a suitable alphabet which can be translated into three-dimensional letters or signs using a wide variety of materials and techniques.

Selecting Primary and Secondary Alphabets
The project alphabet that is used for the majority of signs within the system is referred to here as the *primary alphabet.* If the project image requires an alphabet that is particularly unique or distinctive, it may not be suitable for all the signs in a system. In such a situation, a *secondary alphabet* is often used for signs of less visual importance, for signs with very long copy, or for smaller signs of less functional importance.

For example, a secondary alphabet might be employed for a sign giving a quantity of detailed information, such as the statement of contract limitations in a parking facility. This kind of information is often required by code, but is seldom referred to by the sign viewer. When the information is very long, copy can be reproduced in relatively small letters for close-up reading. Many secondary signs are located in mechanical, storage, or parking areas where they are seldom noticed or even seen by the public.

Selecting primary and secondary alphabets which are compatible is a matter of design judgment. Because it is most important, the primary alphabet is usually selected first: it should be appropriate for the project, meeting both functional and esthetic requirements. In selecting secondary alphabets the most important consideration is their compatibility with the primary alphabet. An example of a suitable pair is shown in Figure 56.

ABCDEFGHIJKLMN
OPQRSTUVWXYZ&
abcdefghijklmn
opqrstuvwxyz
$1234567890

Figure 55. Helvetica Medium is the most frequently used typeface in signing. It is popular because of its extreme legibility and contemporary appearance.

Figure 56. This illustrates a suitable pair of alphabets for sign usage. The larger two-stroke alphabet is a modification of the Avant Garde alphabet shown below it.

ABCDEEFFGHIJKLM
NOOPQQRSTUVWXYZ
abcdefghijklmn
opqrstuvwxyz

Figure 57. This alphabet, modified by John Follis & Associates, is an example of a major change in the alphabet's design. It is based on the typeface Kismet.

Figure 58. By utilizing silvered light bulbs, this exterior sign identifies the John Street Building, New York. Designed by Rudolph de Harak.

Where Function Is Most Important

In some situations, such as parking structures, airport terminals, and other transportation facilities, it is most important that signs communicate information very clearly because the signs must be read rapidly. In parking structures, where signs must be read while driving an automobile down ramps, around columns, past pedestrians, an unclear sign may cause an accident. In airport terminals, where the viewer may be walking very fast or even running to catch a plane, certain alphabets may function better than others.

In these and similar settings where information is needed in a hurry, functional aspects of signing take precedence over esthetics. While typefaces such as Univers, Futura, or Grotesque would all do well in these situations, Helvetica is the most widely used for this and other signing applications because it reads most easily and quickly.

The Versatile Helvetica Alphabet. Helvetica has been widely—perhaps too widely—used for architectural signing from parking garages to mammoth prestige projects. First used with great distinction by Swiss graphic designers, it has now been adopted for projects throughout the world. Its popularity is based in part on its highly legible design and in part on its simple, timeless, classic quality. This makes it especially desirable for architectural signing because it will not detract from the architecture of any project and because it mixes well with other, more decorative or elegant alphabets.

Alphabets That Age Well. Most major architectural projects are designed and built to last at least fifty years, and many project signing elements are expected to last for the life of the building. In selecting alphabets for these projects, the designer should use those that are already well established so that the sign system's alphabet will not seem dated after only a few years. By contrast, in packaging and advertising the need for innovation creates frequent change. When an architectural graphics program does need to employ ephemeral designs, they can be executed in paint, so that they can be redesigned and repainted from time to time.

Changeable Letters and Copy Strips. For nearly every large project, some items will require standard changeable letters or copy strips. Items such as directories, menu boards, and desk plaques frequently utilize three-dimensional letters or photographically produced copy strips which are available as manufactured items. If the designer wants these standard items to match or be compatible with the project signing, he should check to see what is currently available. Usually Helvetica, Standard, and Grotesque alphabets are available from most manufacturers of such standard items.

Modifying Standard Alphabets

Existing alphabets may need major or minor changes to adapt them for signing use. The previous comments about modifying existing logotypes applies here except that many or all characters of an alphabet may have to be changed. Unless the designer has special training or experience in this area, he should only indicate design changes and leave the preparation of final artwork to a lettering specialist. Assuming they have a rapport, designer and specialist can work together, each adding his knowledge and expertise to the final result. Often the specialist will suggest alternates for some letters which may improve on the designer's modifications.

An example of a major change in alphabet design is shown in the Universal Studios signing project. The original alphabet, Kismet, lacked consistency for good signing and needed to be redesigned (Figure 57). In addition, Kismet was available only in uppercase; consequently a lowercase alphabet was adapted for use with it.

Even more specialized alphabets are found in unique architectural situations utilizing three-dimensional letterforms. The example shown was designed by Rudi De Harak for the John Street Building in New York (Figure 58).

These two examples are relatively unusual. Normal alphabet modification may range from changing basic ascender or descender dimensions to changing several characters of an alphabet. However, extensive changes may be easier to make than designing a new alphabet.

Custom Designing Alphabets

New alphabets are constantly being designed for typographic use in printed graphics. Some alphabet designers work in both printed graphics and architectural signing. Herb Lubalin, who has an excellent reputation for designing logotypes, alphabets, and other graphic items (Figures 59–61) says:

> There are at least 100 adequate typefaces available that, in my mind, meet the criteria for signage programs. Leading my list is Futura Light which has a warmth and appeal missing in Helvetica and yet retains an architectural quality. Architects also have a strong inclination towards sans serif faces rather than those with serifs. I myself have used Times Roman caps effectively for the signage for the Ford Foundation Building in New York. I believe all design solutions stem from the problem to be solved. Preconceived, narrow viewpoints hinder these solutions.

With so many existing alphabets to choose from, it seems only reasonable to avoid designing a new one. However, if a generous budget is available and the client insists on something quite distinctive, then it should be done—although not all designers are qualified to do alphabet design. It might be well to turn this work over to someone who excels in this area.

Checklist

When selecting or modifying alphabets for signing, the following questions should be kept in mind:

1. Does the alphabet have the appropriate character for the project?
2. Which weight (regular, light, medium, bold) should be used?
3. Will the alphabet be highly legible when viewed at the distance required? When illuminated at night?
4. If three-dimensional letters are planned for, will both upper- and lowercase versions be easily read when viewed from an angle? Some condensed alphabets may be hard to read in this situation, especially if letterspacing is tight.
5. Is the alphabet compatible with standard changeable letters, directory copy strips, or vinyl letters of other stock items need for the project?
6. Is the alphabet suitable for all the fabrication techniques planned? For example, if backlighted individual letters are to be fabricated, are the thin strokes wide enough to accomodate neon? In addition, a Roman-style alphabet with sharp serifs cannot be deeply sand-blasted into granite without losing much of its elegance, but it can be hand-carved into metal or slate.
7. Will fabrication of the alphabet be practical, considering the sizes required and the materials to be used? Script

ABCDEFGHIJKLMN
OPQRSTUVWXYZ

Figure 59. Avant Garde alphabet designed by Herb Lubalin for the International Typeface Corporation.

ABCDEFGHIJKLMNOPQRS
TUVWXYZ(&.,:;!?'""-$¢%/)
AACÆŒEAFAGGGHTKAIAIAM
MNTRRASSSTHUTVVW
abcdeefghijklmnopqrsttu
vvvwwwxyyyz1234567890

Figure 60. Lubalin Graph X-Light alphabet designed by Herb Lubalin for the International Typeface Corporation.

ABCDEEFGHIJKLLMNOPQR
STUVWXYZ (&.,:;!?"""-*$¢%)()
aabcdeeffghijkklmnopqrrsstt
uvwxyzz 1234567890

Figure 61. Serif Gothic Bold alphabet designed by Herb Lubalin for the International Typeface Corporation.

letters may have excessively thin strokes for cutout wood or even metal when fabricated in small sizes. However, script letters can be silk-screened or sand-blasted in small sizes on various materials.

SYMBOLS

The term *symbols* is used here to mean both symbols and pictograms. Although these two elements function similarly, they are quite different in origin. Symbols are abstract or geometric forms which are associated with an idea. For example, a certain kind of cross may stand for a hospital. Although most people in a culture may understand the meaning of a symbol, its meaning must be learned. Pictograms, by contrast, are based on recognizable objects closely associated with the idea they communicate; for example, a representation of a suitcase may identify a baggage claim area:

Arrows

Probably the most widely used and universally understood symbol is the arrow; consequently it can be used as an example of the problems in designing and choosing symbols. While the use of a pointing hand may have preceded the arrow, it has been used for centuries as a directional device. It is used universally today in directional signing for several reasons: it is understood despite language barriers; it is more flexible and requires less space than a verbal direction such as "to the left" which it might replace; it provides a consistent look to directional sign copy layouts.

Arrow Shape. While variations in arrow shape may be the result of designers' preferences for particular shapes, other variations can be traced to a functional basis. An interesting example is the evolution in arrow shapes used in British road signs over the last 50 years. Most of the changes indicated by the 10 variations shown in Figure 62 were made to improve legibility. But ironically, no one of these is outstanding in terms of legibility under all viewing conditions.

As the ratings indicate, some of the arrows in Figure 62 are more legible in sunlight, some in cloudy weather, and some at night. Factors such as the speed at which a viewer is traveling, color of the arrow and its background, and the viewing angle also affect legibility, with speed the factor that influences legibility the most.

While speed may also be a factor affecting legibility in some exterior signs for architectural projects, it is usually much less critical than for roadside signs. Within architectural projects, the vehicle-oriented signs are designed to be viewed at slow speeds under good lighting conditions, allowing the designer considerable latitude in the choice of arrow shape. For design consistency, most designers use one arrow shape for all directional signs within a project. Currently, subtle variations of the barbed arrow are widely used. Until a standard design for the arrow is accepted for international use, the one in Figure 63 seems appropriate for most architectural signing applications.

International Use of Symbols

Symbols and pictograms are seen with increasing frequency in facilities used by people all over the world. International trade shows, fairs, and airports are depending more and more on these graphic devices to help communicate information. Not too many years ago some of these facilities used signs in several languages. But today, partly because of the expansion of air travel to the Middle and Far East, multilingual signs are inadequate; too many languages are involved. International fa-

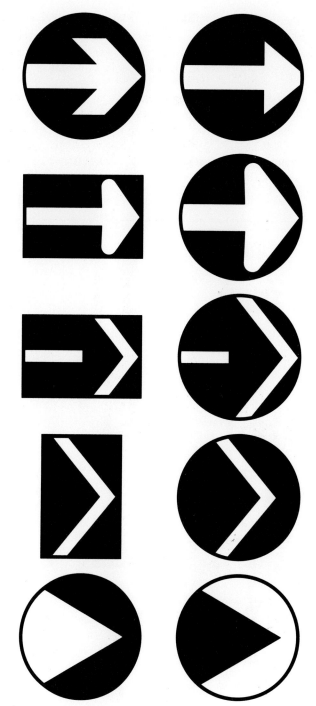

Figure 62. Arrows developed during the past 50 years for British road signs have the following legibility ratings under different conditions: sunlight: 9 (above 80% correct score); 3, 2, 1, 4 (above 60%); 8, 7, 5, 10, 6, (fall below 40%). Cloud: 4, 9, 1, 3, 2 (above 60%); 5, 6, (50–60%); 8, 7, 10 (all below 40%). Night: 5, 4, 6 (above 75%); 1, 9, 8, 3, 7, 2 (55–75%); 10 (below 20%).

Figure 63. Various versions of the barbed arrow are widely used today in signing systems.

cilities are using symbols as a kind of international language to communicate basic information. But they are not a panacea. A basic problem is that there are too many symbol systems, and no one system has been adopted for use in all countries.

Developing International Symbols. Programs are being tested at both national and international levels to reduce the number of existing symbols. Working through the American Institute of Graphic Arts (AIGA) in New York, Thomas Geismar directed the development of symbols for the U.S. Department of Transportation (DOT).

The DOT symbols are shown in Figure 64. DOT intends to standardize these symbols throughout the country in the way that certain roadside and traffic control symbols have been standardized. At present, the DOT symbols are going through a two-year period of testing and revision.

Evaluating Symbols. The AIGA committee assessed these symbols, using the following criteria:

Semantic. This refers to the relationship between the visual image and its meaning: does the symbol represent the message clearly to people of many cultures?

Syntactic. This refers to the relationship of one visual image to

Figure 64. These transportation-related symbols were developed for the U.S. Department of Transportation.

another: how well does a symbol fit into the entire system of symbols?

Pragmatic. This refers to the relationship between the symbol and its users: can it be seen clearly under varying conditions and when reproduced in various sizes?

These criteria should be used in evaluating any kind of symbol system.

International Standardization of Symbols. On the international level, designers such as Peter Kneebone are working through the International Council of Graphic Design Associa-
tion (ICOGRADA). This organization recommends the standardization of the image content of both symbols and pictograms, while leaving room for design variation. Just how much variation can be allowed without distorting the meaning of the symbols is yet to be decided.

However, a cursory review of the symbol systems designed for some recent international events will show that such standardization has not yet been accomplished. Different images have been used to communicate similar messages. A visitor to both Expo 67 in Montreal and the 1972 Olympics in Munich might have noted the two symbols for "telegram" shown in Figure 65.

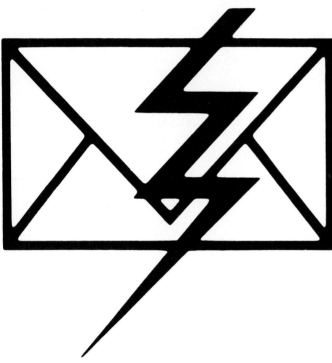

Figure 65. Both of these symbols represent the word "telegram." One was designed for Expo 67, Montreal, the other for the Olympic Games, 1972, held in Munich.

It should not be necessary to design a new system of symbols for each worldwide gathering. Considering today's worldwide traveler, the need for consistency in symbols used for international airport signing is obvious.

The telegram symbol example also demonstrates another problem of symbol design: technological change may render the symbol's image obsolete. Consequently, some revision of symbol systems will continue to be necessary even when an international system is widely adopted.

There are other problems in the use of international symbols. If, for example, a pictogram is going to represent an elevator, will it be understood by someone who has never seen an elevator before? Obviously not. Nor do existing symbols have the universality many people assume. Anthropologists such as Margaret Mead have reminded the designer that the skull and crossbones does not necessarily mean poison to the entire world nor is red a universal signal of danger.

Despite the obvious difficulties in developing internationally accepted symbols, progress has been made. Roadside and traffic control signs have been standardized through much of Europe and the United States. Many of these, being geometric in form and abstract in content, are more difficult to learn than pictograms, but they *are* being used successfully.

Symbols to Reinforce Sign Messages

Fortunately not all symbols must communicate to an international audience. There are many facilities—such as hospitals—for which symbols can help solve bilingual problems. It would be possible in such cases to display all sign messages in both languages without symbols. However, for the New York City Health & Hospital Corporation, designers E. Christopher Klumb Associates chose to use both symbols and verbal copy, creating signs which have strong visual appeal. The symbols are in color, and the meaning of the symbols is reinforced by verbal copy in two languages. Most of these symbols are pictograms, with obvious reference to a recognizable object: the eye stands for Eye Department and the tooth for Dental. The symbol for neurology is considerably less obvious, justifying the use of verbal reinforcement.

Klumb's solution seems to reach a happy balance between functional and esthetic requirements. The visually strong, simple pictograms can be recognized when viewed from a great distance. As the viewer comes closer to the sign, he is reassured by the copy that he is going in the right direction. This combining of pictograms and verbal messages (Figure 66) provides a more effective approach than bilingual messages alone.

The Future of Symbols

As international travel, commerce, and communications increase, the use in signing of graphic devices such as symbols will increase. It is difficult to predict whether the standards finally accepted will be abstract symbols, pictograms, or some combination of the two. It is probable that these symbol/pictograms will be developed by a group of international designers working together and revised or extended periodically to keep abreast of change. The AIGA–DOT program criteria indicate a possible direction for ICOGRADA to follow.

It is hoped that international symbols will be agreed upon in the near future. Until that is accomplished, all designers should utilize the DOT symbol program whenever possible rather than designing new symbols.

In addition, symbols applicable to hospital sign usage and other institutional signing should be adopted as an extension of the DOT program.

Symbol signs are something new for New York City hospitals. We hope to make a visit to a hospital easier by showing pictures of some of the hospital services for the visitor and patient. You will find these symbols useful in identifying those services which you may require.

El uso de símbolos es algo nuevo en los hospitales de la ciudad de Nueva York. A través del uso de figuras que representan varios de los servicios dados en el hospital esperamos que su visita se la haga más fácil. Estos signos le serán muy útiles para encontrar los servicios que usted requiera del hospital.

The New York City Health and Hospitals Corporation

1. Hospital or Medical Center	7. Pharmacy	11. Hydrotherapy	17. Female Care	22. X-Ray Department	25. Surgical Care
2. Playroom	8. Eye Care	12. Physical Therapy	18. Maternity	23. Ear, Nose & Throat	26. Medical Care
3. Wheelchair Access	9. Dental Care	13. Occupational Therapy	19. Child Care	24. Skin Care	27. No Entry
4. Information	10. Specialties	14. Speech & Hearing	20. Nursery		28. No Smoking
5. Appointments		15. Mental Health	21. Family Care Unit		29. Emergency
6. Registration		16. Orthopedics			

1. Hospital ó Centro Médico	7. Farmacia	11. Hidroterapia	17. Consulta Femenina	22. Departamento de Rayos "X"	25. Consulta de Cirujía
2. Sala de Recreo	8. Ojos	12. Terapia Física	18. Maternidad	23. Nariz, Garganta y Oído	26. Consulta de Medicina
3. Acceso Para Sillas de Rueda	9. Cuidado Dental	13. Terapia Ocupacional	19. Consulta Infantil	24. Piel	27. No Hay Entrada
4. Información	10. Especialidades	14. Habla y Oído	20. Recién Nacidos		28. No Se Fuma
5. Citas		15. Salud Mental	21. Servicio de Cuidados		29. Emergencia
6. Registro		16. Ortopedia	Atención Familiar		

N.Y.C. HEALTH SYMBOLS

Figure 66. When bilingual messages are combined with symbols, the information is communicated much more quickly. Designed by E. Christopher Klumb Associates, Inc. for the New York City Health and Hospital Corporation.

7
Typography

This chapter contains basic information about typography as it relates to signing. Most designers with a background in printed graphics are familiar with the problems of alphabet selection (called *letterstyle* in the context of specifying type for signs) and copy (message) layout. However, there are important differences between graphics for the printed page and for signing, particularly with regard to the functional aspects of signing such as legibility.

The last chapter on Alphabets and Symbols makes the point that only certain alphabets are suitable for signing because of these functional requirements. The relationships between let-terstyle, letterspacing, and legibility are reviewed in detail in this chapter.

Selecting the alphabet is a basic beginning, but how the message or copy layout is designed and located on the signface involves many more detailed problems, which are discussed here.

But first it is necessary to define terms: The term *signface* refers to the surface on which a message is placed. The term *message* refers to all items on the signface, that is, letters, arrows, symbols, lines. Message is also referred to as *copy, wording,* or *legend*.

LETTERSTYLES

The term *letterstyle* refers to the full range of characters of the alphabet of the same design. This means that each letter, numeral, symbol, and punctuation mark is designed to relate esthetically to all others. Each letterstyle as a whole is distinct from all other letterstyles. In printing the term "letterstyle" is referred to as *typeface*.

Elements of a Letterstyle

ABCDEFGHIJKLMNOPQRSTUVWXYZ

Uppercase letters (capitals or caps)

abcdefghijklmnopqrstuvwxyz

Lowercase letters

Numerals

1234567890

In most letterstyles the numeral "zero" is narrower than the letter "O" and is therefore considered a different character

$ ¢ % &

Symbols (ampersand represents "and")

. , : ; " " ( ) / ! ?

Punctuation marks

Incorrect

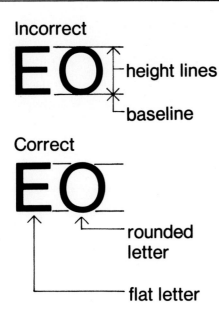

Correct

Visual Adjustment of Rounded Letters

In most letterstyle designs all letters with rounded forms are designed taller than the letters with flat bottoms and/or tops. This is necessary because so little surface of rounded letters actually touches the height lines that the rounded letters would look smaller if not visually adjusted.

The bottom height line is referred to as the *baseline* and is the imaginary line on which all letters align.

Flat letters: ABDEFHIKLMNPRTVWXYZ

Rounded letters: CGJOQSU

Note: One exception is the letterstyle Eurostile, where rounded letters are flat at the height lines.

Lowercase Letters

It is important to understand the terms used when discussing lowercase letters.

X-height. That part of lowercase letters that makes up the greatest portion of a letter is the x-height. It is also referred to as "the body of the letter." The actual dimension is taken from the flat letter. As with uppercase letters, lowercase letters with rounded forms are larger than flat letters.
Flat letter forms: fijklvwxz
Rounded letter forms: abcdeghmnopqrstuy

The letter "x" is used because in most letterstyles it is the one letter that is flat top and bottom.

For better legibility it is recommended that the letterstyle selected have an x-height that is approximately two-thirds the height of the uppercase letter.

Ascenders. The "up" stroke of a lowercase letter—bdfhkl—that extends from the top of the x-height to the top of the letter is known as the *ascender*.

Descenders. The "down" stroke of a lowercase letter—gjpqy—that extends from the baseline to the bottom of the letter is called the *descender*.

Overall Height. The area of the letter from the top of the ascenders to the bottom of the descenders is called the *overall height*.

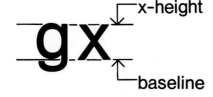

Normally the lowercase "g" is visually adjusted to the top of the x-height and does not sit on the baseline.

Melior
Times
Clarendon

Helvetica
Avant Garde
Eurostile

Optima

STOP
Kalligraphia
Futura Black

Helvetica Regular

Light **Medium** **Bold**
Condensed **Extended**
Italic Outline

Categories of Letterstyles
There are over 5,000 different letterstyles, and they fall into four general categories: serif, sans serif, transitional, and decorative.

Serif. Serif letterstyles are identified by short cross lines at the ends of the main parts of many letters. They have relatively good legibility, but not so good as that of sans serif letterstyles. Apparently, the serifs interfere with visual perception of spaces between letters. To overcome this, use serif letterstyles slightly larger than sans serif in comparable situations. Serif letterstyles can create a warm, classic look.

Sans Serif. Sans serif letterstyles have no cross lines. In signing they are the most legible because of their simplicity of form and close relationships to geometric shapes. They tend to create a clean, more modern look.

Transitional. Transitional letterstyles have the more classic look of serif letterstyles and are as legible as sans serif letterstyles.

Decorative or Display. Decorative letterstyles do not fit into the above categories. They are the least legible and are used when communicating information becomes secondary. They have to be greatly enlarged to be legible. Each design creates a unique look.

Many letterstyles have variations which differ from the basic letterstyle weight or proportions, as indicated by the following:

Basic letterstyle

Variations

DIRECTIONAL ARROWS
In signing an important part of the design is the directional arrow. The following are examples of some of the many different arrow designs:

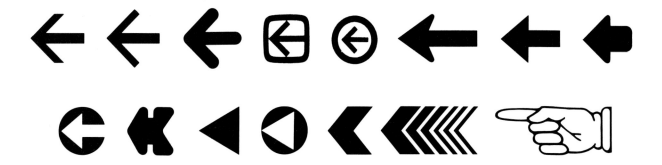

COPY (MESSAGE) LAYOUT

After the letterstyle has been selected and the message wording has been determined, the designer can begin laying out the copy on a scale drawing of the signface. The elements listed below all relate to the copy message. Each is an important step in the layout process; each is explained under a separate heading on the following pages:

Sizes of message letters and arrows
Capitalization of message wording
Letter- and wordspacing of the message
Line-to-line spacing of message wording
Arrow placement
Margin spacing of the message
Message space adjustments

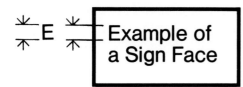

Sizes of Message Letters and Arrows
Uppercase or upper- and lowercase letters. The height of flat uppercase letters is used to state the size of letters.

Flat letters: ABDEFHIKLMNPRTVWXYZ

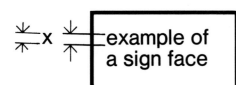

All lowercase; the x-height of flat lowercase letters

Flat letters: imnruvwxz

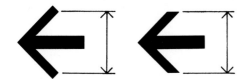

Dimensioning of arrows on copy layouts should follow the example shown here.

Capitalization of Message Wording
The following are five basic variations of capitalization style, along with a capitalization code as shown in parenthesis.

All Uppercase (uc). Uppercase letters tend to read individually and adversely affect the readability of the message. If it seems necessary to use all uppercase letters, it is recommended that they be restricted to short, three- or four-word messages.

All Lowercase (lc). Lowercase letters have greater readability because the ascenders and descenders help to visually define a word. Using all lowercase letters is not recommended because without capitals the message lacks the proper emphasis.

Initial Caps (inc). The most readable arrangement of letters for sign messages is upper- and lowercase letters. All words are capitalized except for articles, prepositions, and conjunctions.

Selective Initial Caps (inc as Typed). Selective capitalization can be used to place greater emphasis on a particular word within a phrase or sentence. This arrangement is recommended for signs with a large amount of copy.

Caps and Lowercase (clc). This arrangement is also very readable because words and phrases have good visual definition.

EXAMPLE OF
SIGN WORDING

example of
sign wording

Example of
Sign Wording

Example of
Sign wording

Example of
sign wording

Correct

Example of spac

Incorrect

Example of sp

Example of spac

Example of sp

Example of spaci

Example of spacin

Letter- and Wordspacing of the Message
The purpose of good spacing is to make all the intervals between letters and between words appear the same.

Words must be clearly recognized. Therefore, wordspacing should not be so tight that the words run together or so wide that the spaces interrupt the flow of reading.

It is important that the proper letter- and wordspacing be selected to meet the sign's functional and esthetic requirements. There are many possible variations but the following are the four basic types:

This spacing is recommended for most signing situations. It is visually balanced to the letterstyle and is very readable.

This spacing is used when signs have to be read from a great distance and tighter spacing would cause letters to visually run together and therefore cause letter and word distortion. It can also be used to create a desired look.

This spacing is often used when signs are to be viewed only at a close distance and a certain look is desired.

This spacing is used primarily for esthetic effect and not recommended for functional signing situations.

Letterspacing. The horizontal space between straight letters is the basic visual unit for letterspacing. The amount of this space depends upon whether normal, wide, tight, or touching spacing is desired.

All other letter combinations are visually adjusted to match this space by moving the letters closer together. This visual adjustment is referred to as the *color of the space.*

Normal Wordspacing. The space between words is one-half the height of uppercase letters.

This is true even when there are punctuation marks.

Normal Letter and Punctuation Spacing. The space between letters and punctuation marks is approximately one-sixth the height of uppercase letters.

Punctuation marks which relate to two letters should be spaced equally from both letters.

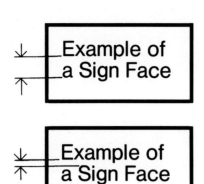

Line-to-Line Spacing of Message Wording

This dimension is necessary whenever the design of the sign face requires that the message be placed on more than one line.

These are two of the ways of indicating line-to-line spacing:

Baseline to Baseline. This dimension is given from the baseline of one line to the baseline of the next line.

Interline. This dimension is given from the baseline of one line to the top of the tallest flat letter of the next line.

It is imperative that the dimension be large enough so that the descenders of the top line do not touch either the uppercase letters or the ascenders of the next line.

Arrow Placement

Single Direction. The following are the three ways of placing a single arrow on one sign face:

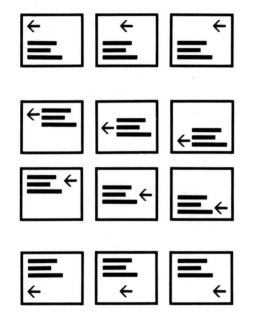

Arrow above wording

Arrow next to wording

Arrow below wording

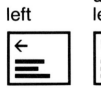

These are examples of arrow placement on a single sign face. The arrow and the wording are always flush left.

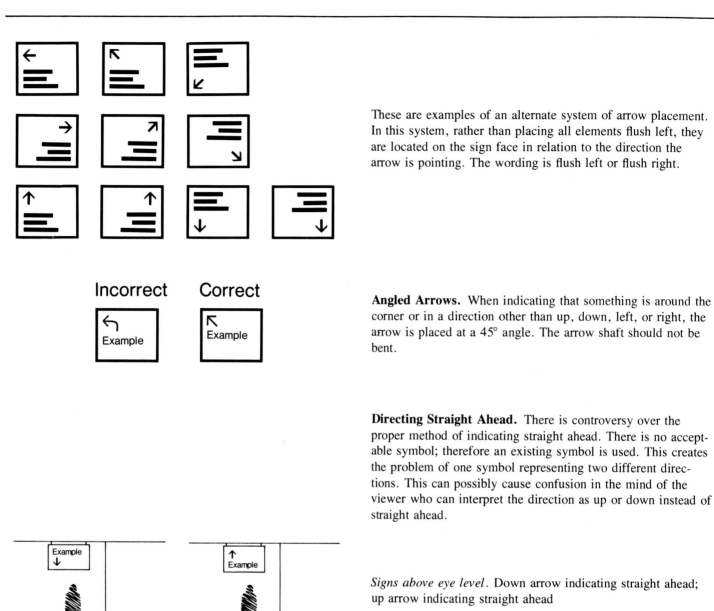

These are examples of an alternate system of arrow placement. In this system, rather than placing all elements flush left, they are located on the sign face in relation to the direction the arrow is pointing. The wording is flush left or flush right.

Angled Arrows. When indicating that something is around the corner or in a direction other than up, down, left, or right, the arrow is placed at a 45° angle. The arrow shaft should not be bent.

Directing Straight Ahead. There is controversy over the proper method of indicating straight ahead. There is no acceptable symbol; therefore an existing symbol is used. This creates the problem of one symbol representing two different directions. This can possibly cause confusion in the mind of the viewer who can interpret the direction as up or down instead of straight ahead.

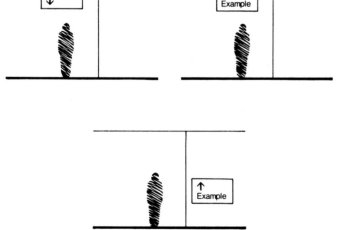

Signs above eye level. Down arrow indicating straight ahead; up arrow indicating straight ahead

Signs at or below eye level. Up arrow indicating straight ahead

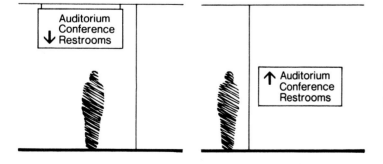

Two Ways to Indicate Order of Destinations. For signs that indicate more than one destination in a direction, the destinations should be alphabetized. They should be alphabetized top to bottom. This is true for signs above, at, or below eye level.

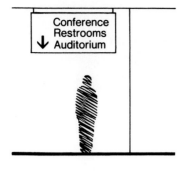

An alternate method of listing destinations for signs above eye level is to place the closer destination at the bottom and the next destination above that.

For signs at or below eye level the reverse order should be used.

Margin Spacing of the Message

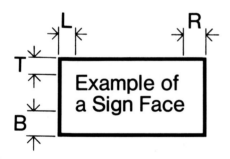

T (Top Margin). From the top edge to the top of the upper-case letter and/or the ascender.

B (Bottom Margin). From the bottom edge to the baseline of the last line.

L (Left Margin). From the left edge to the beginning of the message.

R (Right Margin). From the right edge to the end of the message.

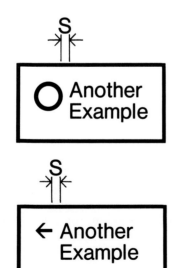

S (Symbol Margin). From the edge of the symbol to the edge of the message.

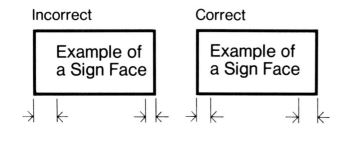

Flush Left and Flush Right Margins. For flush left layouts, the right margin should be equal to or larger than the left margin, and vice versa.

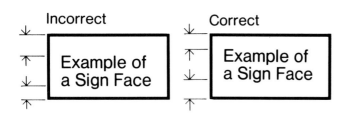

The bottom margin should be equal to or larger than the top margin. For visual balance it is generally recommended that the bottom margin be slightly larger than the top margin.

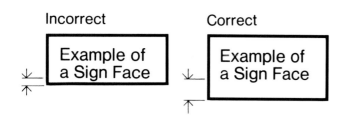

Descenders and the Bottom Margin. When determining the bottom margin, make certain that there is sufficient space for the descenders to fit within the signface.

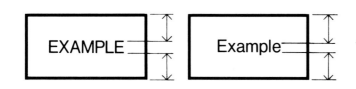

Top and Bottom Margins for Centered Copy. All uppercase: center. Upper- and lowercase: center on lowercase x-height.

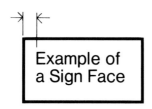

Flush Left and Flush Right Visual Adjustment. For flush left layouts the margin dimension is given to letters that have a vertical side.

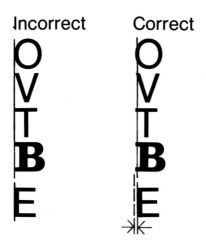

Letters that are rounded or angled, have thin horizontal elements on the left side or serifs should be visually adjusted a little closer to the edge of the sign face.

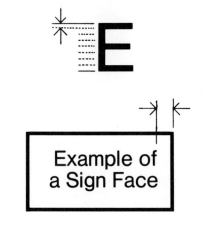

The visual adjustment should be approximately one-eighth the height of the uppercase letters.

Similar visual adjustments are required for flush right layouts.

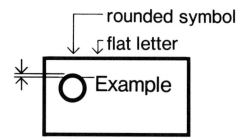

Visual Adjustment of Rounded or Angled Symbols.
Symbols which are rounded or angled should be visually adjusted a little closer to the edge of the signface.

Message Space Adjustments

Message Space Adjustments. If the longest line dimension is greater than the message space dimension, then the line will not fit on the signface and one of the following adjustments must be made.

Choosing the most appropriate adjustment is dependent upon a number of esthetic and functional considerations. In addition, if the sign in question is one of a system of signs, the adjustment chosen should be the one that least affects the other signs within the system.

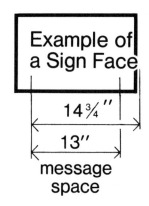

Reduce the Letter Height. Make certain that this will not adversely affect sign function. If the letterstyle is available in standard increments [for example, ½, ¾, 1 inches (12.7, 19.1, and 25.4 centimeters)] make certain the new letter height fits these standard heights.

Increase the Size of the Signface. If the signface fits within a frame, make certain it is not too big for the frame (increase the size of the frame, if possible). If there is no frame, make certain the signface is not too big for its environment.

Shorten the Longest Line. Make certain that this will not change the intent or meaning of the message.

8
Designers' Portfolio

Architectural signing and graphics is a young and rapidly growing area of design which is attracting designers with varied backgrounds. While some designers represented here practice interior or architectural design, most are skilled in all areas of graphic design. In selecting designs for this section we attempted to include a cross section of the best work produced during the last decade. Within the great variety of solutions, there appears one unifying principle: responsiveness to the unique requirements of each project rather than a reliance upon formula solutions.

Creative designs, when effective, satisfy both functional and esthetic aspects of a problem. Signing, even more than graphics, must involve methodology as well as intuition. But the search for what is appropriate in a given situation involves a subtle and often illusive balancing of often contradictory requirements. Final decisions rest on the experience and value judgments of the individual designer.

When asked for their design philosophy or statement of purpose, a few of the designers responded. Others preferred to let their work speak for them.

John R. Berry: Architectural signage and graphics provide the information which allows us to access and participate in the built environment. These elements which can be visually enhancing as well as informative should relate to the character of the space as well as exemplify the policies and attitudes of the responsible agencies. The role of the designer is to act as catalyst and collector of all related items and then to supply the services necessary to effectively and efficiently communicate.

Gerald Reis: Whether designing a complete and comprehensive signage system or a singular sign, our approach is to create a thing of beauty in and of itself. It should be comfortable in and compatible with its environment while fulfilling the purpose for which it is designed.

Larry Klein: Architectural signing and graphics projects are, to me, the most challenging and rewarding kind of design activity. The projects often have very large scope, require extensive analytical effort and synthesis, and can encompass very broad changes in scale, materials and kinds of expression. . . . The aspect that appeals most to me is that the completed work can be genuinely meaningful to people on many levels and it is *permanent*. You can't wrap the garbage in it.

Massimo Vignelli: "Discipline, appropriateness and ambiguity"—that's our motto. By "discipline," we mean that we are methodological; by "appropriate" we mean that we concentrate on the specific requirements of the project; and "ambiguity"

means many things—ambivalence, plurivalence, it is very hard to define. Basically, it has to do with "reading" things in many different ways. The Washington pylons, for example, are signs or signage or service conduits or milestones. . . . That is the ambiguity, a complexity of values.

William Noonan: We think good graphic design really works when all the elements are in harmony. What most people see is color, texture, and shape. What they don't see is the designer assessing the options he has in the use of materials, fasteners, cements, and paints. The depth of the beauty of the product is reflected in how wisely the materials are used. . . .

Sometimes one hears the metaphorical term "it's a zoo," which has the connotation of chaos and confusion. The San Diego Zoo has embarked on a design program that attempts to alleviate this image. It is keeping pace with other progressive institutions by recognizing the value and benefit of good signing and graphics.

Deborah Sussman: Dealing with regionalism—those traditions and forms particular to a geographic area or city—has been our major concern in design for the environment. Indigenous expressions of unknown designers have been an interest and influence on our work for many years. We attempt to bring to each solution a presence that grows from its place and history, along with trying to fulfill the needs of clients and users. In doing this one learns and sometimes uncovers fascinating ideas, occasionally buried or so obvious as to be easily overlooked. We are concerned that, along with the variety of foods, building types, languages, and plants that give regions their character, architectural graphic treatments contribute to such specificity. We try to build on, not erase, what is already there.

Bruce Hopper: One of the truisms I've learned is that the graphic designer can never be brought into a project early enough. Not only does ample design time help avoid having to "stick a sign" on the wall, but it enables us to more easily achieve integration of the signing with the architecture in terms of scale, material, color, and composition.

A problem that continually plagues a signing program is its position at the tail end of the budget line. If a project goes over in the construction phase (almost axiomatic), the cost-cutting inevitably seems to wind up with the signage allowance. The irony of this is that signs are among the most "looked-at" elements and therefore should be maximum in their quality and detailing. Fortunately, many architects and developers are becoming increasingly conscious of this discrepancy and the result is better looking and better functioning signing programs.

William Noonan

San Diego Zoo and
San Diego Wild Animal Park
San Diego, California

After training in Los Angeles, William Noonan became established as a highly respected graphic designer in the San Diego area. His practice included exhibits, printed graphics, packaging design, and illustration. Since 1974 he has been the director of the graphic design department at the San Diego Zoo and the San Diego Wild Animal Park, where he is responsible for the constantly changing graphic displays and signing. In the several hundred-acre area, there are many elaborate educational displays explaining and illustrating the main animal species. Noonan's responsibility includes concept and preparation of artwork for reproduction as well as supervision of fabrication of finished pieces, whether display, exhibit, or printed material.

1

2

3

4

5

6

7

1, 7
San Diego Wild Animal Park.

2-6
San Diego Zoo.

Design Planning Group Inc.
Chicago

The First National Bank of Chicago has recently put together a comprehensive signing and communications program that considers not only identification and directional signing, but how the bank's printed material is presented to the public. The result, achieved by the Chicago-based Design Planning Group, is a well-integrated architectural program. In addition to signing the office designs packaging, corporate identity programs, displays, and exhibits.

1

2

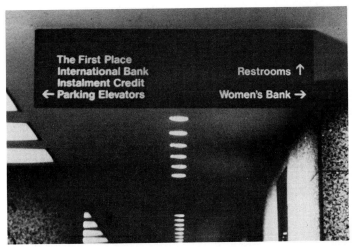

3

5

6

4

7

1
Logotype display panel,
Sears Bank and Trust Company,
Chicago.

2
Wall graphic,
Sears Bank and Trust Company,
Chicago.

3
Ceiling directional sign,
The First National Bank
of Chicago.

4
Primary identification plaque,
Water Tower Place,
Chicago.

5
Primary identification sign,
The Ritz-Carlton Hotel,
Chicago.

6
Interior pylon-mounted map,
The Carleton Centre,
Johannesburg, South Africa.

7
Special services banner,
The First National Bank
of Chicago.

Patrick Maddux

Patrick Maddux & Company
San Diego, California

Working in the San Diego area in graphics, architectural planning, space planning, and interior design, Patrick Maddux brings to architectural signing a flair for dramatic images. Pat is always willing to try something new; as a consequence his work can be playful and experimental. His practice includes a wide range of projects, while his most recent work has been with schools. This is unusual because school architects can seldom afford to hire a signing specialist.

1

2

3

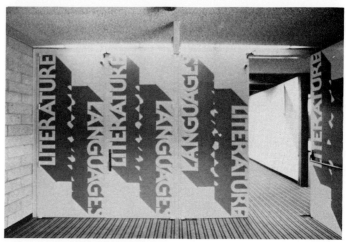

5

6

1
Exterior identification, gymnasium,
Torrey Pines High School, Del Mar,
California.

2
Main entrance identification,
Torrey Pines High School,
Del Mar, California.

3
Wall graphics, classroom divider,
Torrey Pines High School,
Del Mar, California.

4
Wall graphics, administration
building, Torrey Pines High
School, Del Mar, California.

5
Wall graphics, Torrey Pines
High School, Del Mar, California.

6
Wall graphics, language department,
Torrey Pines High School, Del Mar,
California.

Massimo Vignelli

Vignelli Associates/
Vignelli Designs Inc.
New York

It is unusual to be considered the best in two different design areas, but Massimo Vignelli of New York has achieved this distinction in graphic and interior design. He spent some years in Chicago as the principal designer with Unimark International where his work in roadside signing systems started a trend in the organization of conventional signing clutter onto vertical columns. Vignelli Associates, established in 1971 by Massimo and Lella Vignelli, is involved in the design of corporate identity and graphics programs; transportation and architectural graphics; books, magazines, and newspapers; exhibits and interiors; and furniture and a variety of products through Vignelli Designs. Examples of their graphic and product designs are in the permanent collection of the Museum of Modern Art in New York.

1

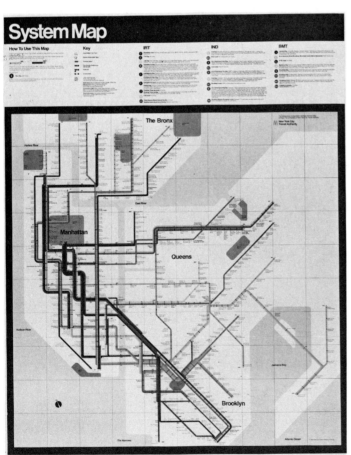

2

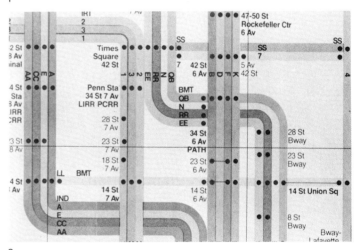

3

1
Exterior sign, Washington Metro,
Washington, D.C.

2
Subway signing and maps,
Metropolitan Transportation
Authority, New York.

3
Detail of subway map,
Metropolitan Transportation
Authority, New York.

4
Neon sign,
Greenwich Savings Bank,
New York.

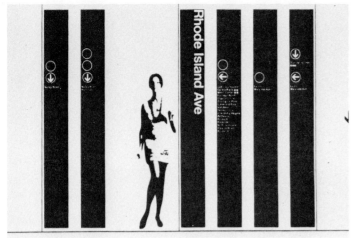

5

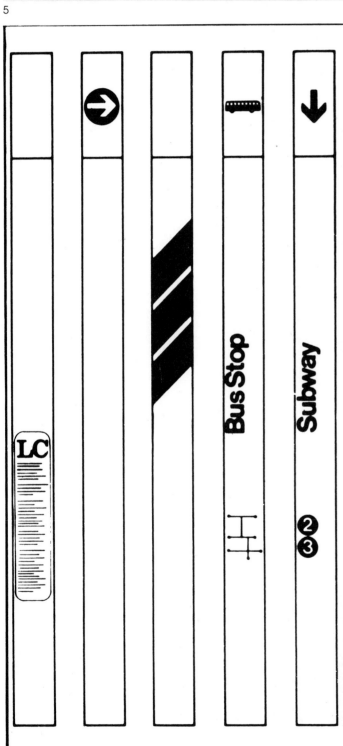

6

7

8

5
Direction, identification,
and information poles,
Washington Metro,
Washington, D.C.

6
Street and furniture signing,
53rd Street, New York.

7
Poster kiosks,
Museum of the Minneapolis
Society of Fine Arts,
Minneapolis, Minnesota.

8
Entrance,
Knoll Av Louvre,
Paris, France.

9
Plexiglas display cases,
Leigh Yawkey Woodson Art Museum,
Wausau, Wisconsin.

10
General directory,
Museum of the Minneapolis
Society of the Fine Arts,
Minneapolis, Minnesota.

11
Room identification,
Minneapolis Society of the Fine Arts,
Minneapolis, Minnesota.

12
Entrance sign,
Museum of the Minnesota
Society of Fine Arts,
Minneapolis, Minnesota.

9

10

11

12

James Hill
Skidmore, Owings & Merrill
San Francisco

Known for his playful use of colorful images, James Hill, now of Los Angeles, has slowly been expanding his graphic design vocabulary to include interiors. Before moving to Los Angeles, he was the director of graphic design for the offices of Skidmore, Owings, & Merrill in San Francisco and for Hellmuth, Obata, & Kassabaum, also in San Francisco. Many of his graphic designs work both to communicate information and to enhance interior spaces.

2

1

3

1-2
Reception, Weyerhaeuser Company,
Tacoma, Washington.

3
Carpet runners,
Weyerhaeuser Company,
Tacoma, Washington.

4-5
Directional signing,
parking structure, Irvine Center,
Newport Beach, California.

6
Schematic of kiosk,
Bay Area Rapid Transit (BART)
underground stations,
San Francisco.

7
Station interior,
kiosk and floor graphics,
Bay Area Rapid Transit (BART),
San Francisco.

8
Interior, Joseph Magnin Company,
Palm Springs, California.

4

5

6

7

8

9

9
Exterior building identification,
Joseph Magnin Company,
Fashion Square,
La Habra, California.

10
Entry, Joseph Magnin Company,
Fashion Square,
La Habra, California.

11
Interior, Joseph Magnin Company,
Fashion Square,
La Habra, California.

12
Elevator lobby,
Golden West Savings
& Loan Association,
Oakland, California.

13-14
Interior, Golden West Savings
& Loan Association,
Oakland, California.

10

11

12

13

14

Kenneth Resen
Page, Arbitrio & Resen, Ltd.
New York

The firm of Page, Arbitrio & Resen had its beginnings in the graphics department of I.M. Pei & Partners in New York. During the mid-1960s, they became a separate entity, providing a wide range of design services that include industrial design, corporate identification, and architectural signing and graphics. One of their most important graphic projects is the large-scale colorful designs for the Sears Building in Chicago. This is a good example of how architectural signing and graphics can relate to architectural design—by providing both a functional system and a unique design feature.

1

2

3

4

5

6

7

1-2
Interior directional sign,
John Hancock Building,
Boston, Massachusetts.

3
Storefront signing,
Place Ville Marie,
Montreal, Canada.

4
Exterior identification sign,
Chemical Bank, New York.

5
Exterior identification sign,
National Airlines Terminal,
John F. Kennedy Airport,
New York.

6
Ticket counter graphics,
National Airlines Terminal,
John F. Kennedy Airport,
New York.

7
Exterior directional signing,
National Airlines Terminal,
John F. Kennedy Airport,
New York.

Douglas Fast
Heckler Associates
Seattle, Washington

The only designer included in this portfolio who is also a fabricator, Doug Fast specializes in painting graphics on barns. His other design activities include the traditional sign painter's role of designing and painting signs for stores. As art director of Heckler Associates in Seattle, Doug is interested in combining traditional processes, techniques, and styles, such as gold-leafed Art Nouveau letters on glass. This approach produces designs which are decorative, intricate, and elegant.

1

2

3

4

5

1
Argus Press,
Seattle, Washington.

2
Heidelberg Beer,
Westport, Washington.

3
Heidelberg Beer,
Auburn, Washington.

4
Wine store,
Seattle, Washington.

5
Coldalls Boutique,
Seattle, Washington.

Glenn Monigle
Glenn Monigle & Associates
Denver, Colorado

Based in Denver, Colorado, Glenn Monigle & Associates specialize in meeting the design needs of petroleum and financial institutions. They offer a complete design service, which includes street furniture, printed graphics design, as well as architectural signing. An example of their overall approach can be seen here in their work for the Williams Center in Tulsa, Oklahoma, which covers several city blocks.

1

2

3

1
Bank lobby,
National Bank of Commerce,
Dallas, Texas.

2
Exterior identification,
National Bank of Commerce,
Dallas, Texas.

3
Tenant identification plaque,
Williams Center,
Tulsa, Oklahoma.

4

5

6

Williams Center Green

7

4
Transom sign,
Bank of Oklahoma,
Tulsa, Oklahoma.

5
Exterior identification,
Bank of Oklahoma,
Tulsa, Oklahoma.

6
Entrance monument,
Williams Center,
Tulsa, Oklahoma.

7
Freestanding sculpture,
Bank of Oklahoma,
Tulsa, Oklahoma.

8
Street furniture,
Williams Center,
Tulsa, Oklahoma.

9-10
Retail signing,
Williams Center,
Tulsa, Oklahoma.

8

9

10

Ivan Chermayeff and Thomas Geismar

Chermayeff & Geismar
Associates
New York

As creative and successful as any design firm in the United States, Chermayeff & Geismar have a broad variety of design projects and honors in their portfolio. Both Ivan Chermayeff and Thomas Geismar are sensitive and capable of executing art as well as design. Geismar headed up the design team from the AIGA that under a grant from the U.S. Department of Transportation developed the DOT symbol program (shown on pages 60-61); Chermayeff, who has written several architectural and children's books, paints for relaxation. Their firm continues to be a leader in the design fields of corporate identification, printed graphics, exhibits, and interior design.

1

2

3

4

5

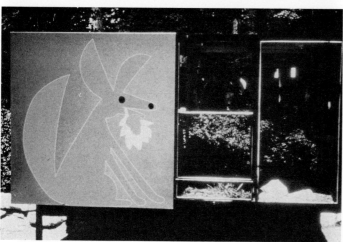

6

7

1
Identification monument,
Philip Morris, USA,
Richmond, Virginia.

2
Interior wall graphics,
Philip Morris, USA,
Richmond, Virginia.

3
Architectural graphics,
Philip Morris, USA,
Richmond, Virginia.

4-7
Sculptures, signing,
St. Louis Children's Zoo.

8
Identification sign,
Harper & Row Building,
New York.

9
Banners,
Museum of Modern Art,
New York.

8

9

10

11

12

13

14

10-11
Construction barricade,
Playboy Club, Chicago

12
Sculpture,
Solow Building Company,
New York.

13
Construction barricade,
Solow Building Company,
New York.

14
Showroom,
GF Business Equipment,
Merchandise Mart, Chicago.

15
Showroom,
GF Business Equipment,
Pan Am Building, New York.

15

Bruce Hopper
Bruce Hopper Design Inc.
Honolulu, Hawaii

Born and trained in Los Angeles, Bruce Hopper worked in New York and Paris before opening a design office in Honolulu in 1963. Although he is interested in many aspects of design, Bruce's strong interest in architectural signing and graphics is shown in his designs for the Honolulu International Airport. Bruce has also been responsible for selecting special color for use in architectural projects. Although the selection of wording in signing projects, particularly those of a proprietary nature, seldom falls on a designer's shoulders, this was not the case in Bruce's project for the Honolulu Bus System. More direct, appropriate titles than "The Bus Stop" and "The Bus" would be hard to imagine.

1

2

3

4

1
Room identification,
Bay Villas, Kapalua, Maui.

2
Auto directional sign,
Kapalua Bay Club, Maui.

3
Main entrance identification,
Kapalua Bay Club, Maui.

4
Auto directional sign,
Mauna Kea Resort, Hawaii.

5, 7, 9
Symbols for Honolulu
International Airport;
Wayne Creekmore, Bruce Hopper.

6
Identification sign,
Mililani Shopping Center.

8
Restaurant identification sign,
Dallas, Texas.

¥$£

Currency Exchange

5

6

U.S. Immigration

7

8

U.S. Dept. of Agriculture

9

10

10
Color scheme, shelter study
for city and county of Honolulu,
Honolulu Bus System.

11
Color scheme, logo
city and county of Honolulu,
Honolulu Bus System.

12
Exterior signing,
Honolulu International Airport.

11

12

Larry Klein
Redwood City, California

1

As one of the founders of Unimark International in Chicago and later the head of his own company, Larry Klein has contributed a wide range of projects to the field of graphic design, from illustration to elaborate sales offices for large real estate developments in the Midwest. After recently spending a couple of years as chairman of the exhibit department at the Field Museum in Chicago, Larry moved to Redwood City, California. The display for Harbor Point Sales Pavilion in Chicago is a good example of Klein's ability to handle a complex design problem. His solution cost $1,000,000 to fabricate. Few developers have been known to spend that much money for this type of facility.

2

3

4

5

1
Entrance,
Harbor Point Sales Pavilion,
Chicago.

2
Display,
Harbor Point Sales Pavilion,
Chicago.

3
Reception and waiting area,
Harbor Point Sales Pavilion,
Chicago.

4-5
Promotional signing
for an urban development area,
River Oaks, Illinois.

Irving Harper and Philip George

Harper & George, Inc.

New York

Well known for interior design with a flair for restaurants, Irving Harper and Philip George of New York often use flags and banners and striking, colorful configurations to enhance their projects. They have set a very high standard in airport interiors for Braniff Airlines, especially in their home base, the Dallas-Ft. Worth passenger facility. This work is rich in its handling of all aspects of design and even includes a place to hang a garment bag. This long-overlooked convenience typifies their concern for practical detail as well as good design.

1

2

3

4

6

7

1
Exterior paint scheme,
Braniff International airplanes.

2
Braniff logo for plane exterior.

3
Baggage claim carousel,
Braniff Terminal,
Dallas-Ft. Worth Airport.

4
Wall graphics,
Braniff Terminal,
Dallas-Ft. Worth Airport.

5-6
Exterior sign and logo,
Hall's Crown Center,
Kansas City, Missouri.

7
Signboard Bar,
Crown Center Hotel,
Kansas City, Missouri.

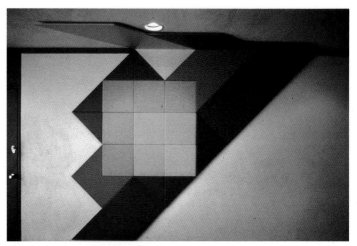

8

8
Braniff Terminal,
John F. Kennedy International Airport,
New York.

9
Ground Floor Cafe,
CBS Building, New York.

10
Braniff Terminal,
Kansas City International Airport.

9

10

Deborah Sussman
Deborah Sussman & Co.
Santa Monica, California

Deborah Sussman, a New Yorker who has lived in California long enough to consider herself a native, practices exhibit, packaging, interiors and graphics design, with Paul Prejza, her husband, who brings architecture and planning skills to the company. The firm is probably best known for incorporating color and sparkle into whatever it designs. A master of what Sussman calls the charrette, she and her office are used to working around the clock when necessary, such as when they designed and fabricated the Rolling Stones' concert environment in Los Angeles in less than a week. It may have been her years with the Charles and Ray Eames office that inspired her willingness and gave her strength to tackle such wild projects.

1

2

3

4

1
Main exterior identification sign,
Standard Shoes, Los Angeles.

2
Graphics and signing,
Standard Shoes, Los Angeles.

3, 5
Main exterior identification,
graphics and marquis,
Zody's, Los Angeles.

4
Wall plaque,
Chez Paul Restaurant,
Sun Valley, Idaho.

5

6

6
Architectural graphics,
office and apartment,
333 Bay Street
(in collaboration with Esherick,
Homsey, Dodge & Davis),
San Francisco.

7
Temporary signing,
California City, California.

7

Herb Lubalin
Herb Lubalin Associates, Inc.
New York

With an international reputation as an alphabet designer, Herb Lubalin is also active in print graphics and packaging as well as architectural signing. Of the many subsidiary design-related companies which he has formed is Good Book Publishing, a firm dedicated to book design, and ITC, the International Typeface Corporation, of which he is executive vice president. His latest contribution to the graphic arts has been the editing and design of *U&LC: Upper and Lower Case, The International Journal of Typographics.* Active in the international design community, Lubalin is a vice president of Alliance Graphique Internationale. Several of the typefaces that Lubalin has designed are shown in Chapter 6, Alphabets and Symbols. The draped sign for Jensen's is one of the most effective temporary signs ever designed.

1

2

3

4

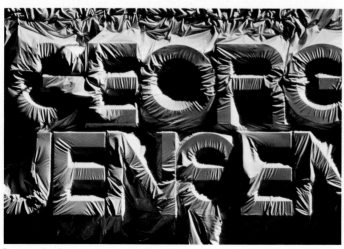

5

1
Logo for a hotel chain in Europe.

2
Logo for a hotel chain in Europe.

3
Logo for an office building
in Paris, France.

4
Detail of wall sculpture,
CBS Building, New York.

5
Barricade wrapping,
Georg Jensen Store, New York.

Marion Sampler

Gruen Associates
Los Angeles

1
Retail signing,
Joseph Magnin,
Century City, California.

2
Stained glass dome,
South Coast Plaza,
Costa Mesa, California.

3-4
Beef N' Counter,
St. Louis, Missouri.

5
Exterior identifications, Central City
Mental Health Facility, Los Angeles.

Besides his training in design, Marion Sampler brings an understanding and background in art to his practice of architectural signing and graphics. He heads up that department at Gruen Associates in Los Angeles, where he has been involved with graphics for urban complexes, shopping centers, hospitals, and restaurants. "It is difficult," says Sampler, "to make a unique statement about an activity as varied as architectural graphics, where all the rules, if there are any, have not been laid down." When sculpture, murals, and other works of art are needed to complete a Gruen project, Marion is the liaison with the artists engaged as outside consultants. Outside the office Marion continues his involvement with design in his home studio, where he makes drawings and collages that have been exhibited in Los Angeles art galleries.

1

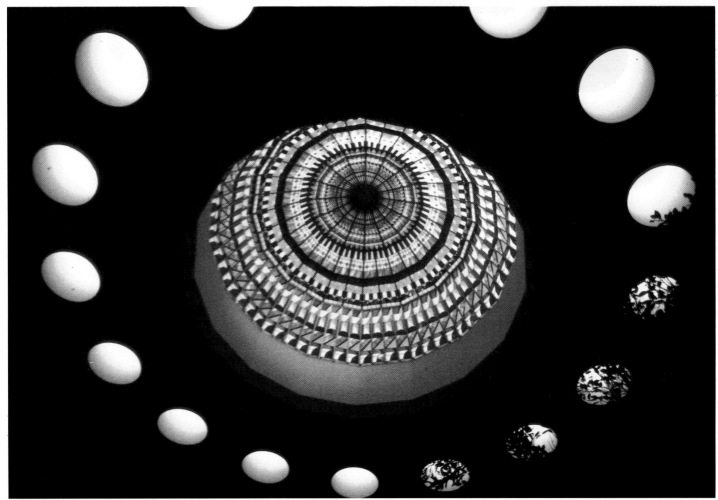

2

3

4

5

Milton Glaser
Milton Glaser, Inc.
New York

Well known for his work in printed graphics and illustration, Milton Glaser has recently become involved in architectural signing and graphics. A co-founder of Push Pins Studios and a member of the faculty at the School of Visual Arts and Cooper Union in New York, Glaser has had the distinction of one-man shows in Brussels, Paris, and New York. Rarely are graphic artists so honored. The designer of several magazines, Milton is now president and design director of *Esquire*.

1-2
Graphics and signing,
The Big Kitchen,
New York.

3
Federal Building,
Indianapolis, Indiana.

1

2

3

Rudolph de Harak
Rudolph de Harak, Inc.
New York

Established in New York for some 20 years, Rudolph de Harak has been involved in major exhibit design, extensive printed graphics, and corporate identification programs as well as totally unique signing programs, as illustrated here. Never one to shy away from total involvement in his many undertakings, Rudi is known for custom solutions to his many sizable projects. President of the U.S. Chapter of the Alliance Graphique Internationale, Rudi is Andrew Carnegie Professor of Design at the Cooper Union School of Art and Architecture.

1
Building identification,
127 John Street, New York.

2
Digital clock,
127 John Street, New York.

3
Entrance tunnel,
127 John Street, New York.

1

2

3

4

5

6

7
Entrance identification,
United Nations Plaza Hotel,
New York.

8
Directional signing,
United Nations Plaza Hotel,
New York.

7

8

Lance Wyman and
Bill Cannan
Wyman & Cannan Ltd.
New York

Symbol design, if not a specialty, can certainly be considered an unusual strength in Lance Wyman's design practice. His work has been seen at the Mexican Olympics in 1968, at the Washington Mall, and at the National Zoological Park, as well as in many other similar projects. Bill Cannan, his partner since 1971, brings interior, industrial, and package design expertise to round out their present partnership. The dramatic potential of form and color is fully utilized in their work.

1

2

1-5
Graphics program,
National Zoological Park,
Washington, D.C.

3

4

5

6

7

8

9

9-11
Graphics program,
XIX Olympiad, Mexico City, 1968
(Lance Wyman, Director
of Graphic Design).

10

11

12

13

12, 14
Temporary divider,
Edmonton Centre,
Alberta, Canada.

13
Directional signing,
Washington Mall, Washington, D.C.

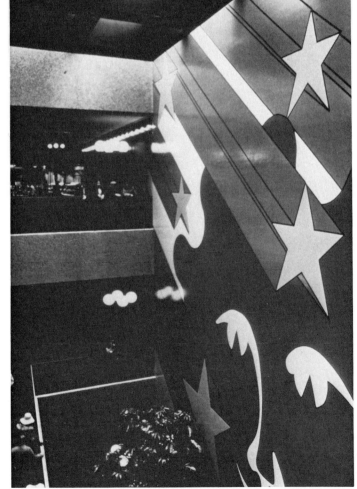

14

Gerald Reis and
Michael Manwaring
San Francisco

1
Graphics and banners,
The Wharf, Woodlands, Texas.

2
Identification sculpture
(Michael Manwaring),
India Basin Industrial Park,
San Francisco.

Although now working separately in the San Francisco area, Gerald Reis and Michael Manwaring were responsible during their partnership for some of the most poetic work done in the area of architectural signing and graphics. Their background in illustration and a shared interest in organic forms may have provided the necessary ingredients. Their use of well-scaled designs in full ranges of color has produced tremendously varied and dynamic design solutions. Like most of the designers in this book, they're very active in printed graphics, poster, and brochure design.

1

2

3

4

5

6

3
Exterior identification,
California Street Cooking School,
San Francisco.

4
Interior graphics,
California Street Cooking School,
San Francisco.

5
Showroom design,
Patrick Carpet Mills,
San Francisco

6
Interior graphics,
Museum Books Book Store,
Museum of Modern Art,
San Francisco.

7
Exhibit, Corning Glass Works,
New York.

7

8
Exterior identification sign,
Chinquapin, Lake Tahoe, Nevada.

9
Exterior signing,
Tanglewood Apartments,
Hayward, California.

8

9

John Follis
John Follis & Associates
Los Angeles

For the last 15 years, architectural signing and graphics has been a major design activity for the John Follis and Associates office in Los Angeles. Among the first to specialize in this field, the firm has designed signing systems for a wide variety of architectural projects, including multiuse office complexes, hositals, and theme parks. Enjoying diversity, the firm also designs printed graphics, interiors, and exhibitions. The firm draws on this wealth of broad experience to design signs and graphics programs which are well integrated with the project architecture; they function well and enhance the environment.

1-2
Interior sign,
San Antonio Community Hospital,
Upland, California.

3
Exterior signing,
Al's Garage,
Newport Beach, California.

1

2

3

4
Wall graphics,
Sea World, Orlando, Florida.

5
Parking area identification,
Sea World, Orlando, Florida.

6
Main entrance
identification and banners,
Sea World, Orlando, Florida.

7
Exterior identification sign,
San Diego Wild Animal Park.

8-9
Exterior information signing,
San Diego Wild Animal Park.

4

5

6

7

8

9

10
Main exterior identification,
Security Pacific Plaza,
Los Angeles.

11
Column and wall graphics,
Security Pacific Plaza, Los Angeles.

12
Directory, Security Pacific Plaza,
Los Angeles.

10

11

12

Barbara Stauffacher Solomon
San Francisco

Probably the most respected designer in the field of architectural graphics, Barbara Stauffacher Solomon first became known for her work at Sea Ranch, California. There her graphics combined with the architecture of Charles Moore showed clearly how graphics could enhance architecture in a very positive and strong manner. Her work has freed the art of environmental graphics from a single wall treatment to designs that may encompass the entire interior space—walls, ceiling, and floors. Currently a full-time student of architecture, she, more than any other designer, has made the use of large-scale graphics appropriate for architecture.

1
Exterior signing, Sea Ranch Store,
Sea Ranch, California.

2
Interior graphics,
Sea Ranch Swim & Tennis Club,
Sea Ranch, California.

3

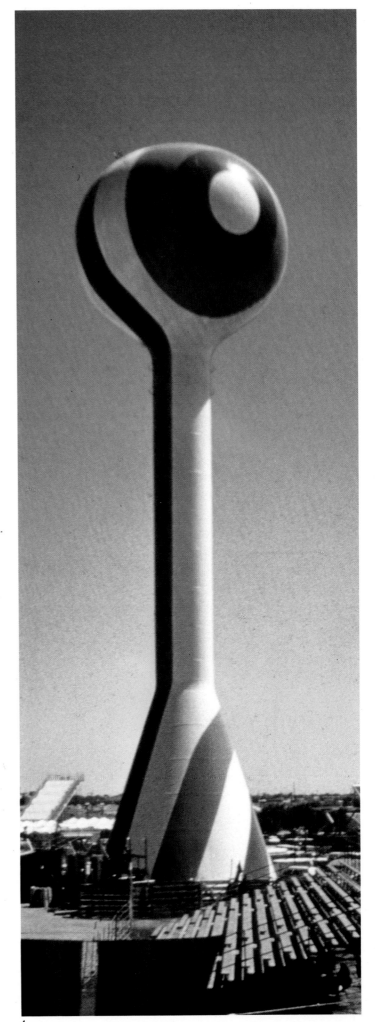

4

5

6

7

John Berry

Smith, Henchman & Grylls
Associates Inc.
Detroit, Michigan

As head of the graphics and signing design department in a
large architectural firm, which recently spun off on its own,
John Berry is as close to an architectural signing and graphics
specialist as anyone in this book. It is his main activity,
through which he has fine tuned the procedural process of designing communication systems for large corporate entities. In
addition John's work includes printed graphics for architectural
projects. Berry is a past president of the Society of Environmental Graphics Designers, a group headquartered in Chicago
whose primary interests are in signing and architectural graphics.

1

2

3

4

5

6

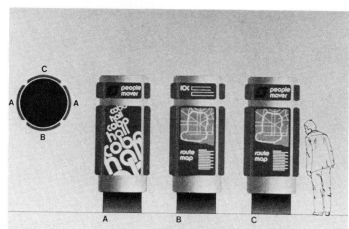

7

8

1
Wall graphics,
John Deere Engine Works,
Waterloo, Iowa.

2
Wall graphics,
Caterpiller Tractor Company,
Engine Plant,
Mossville, Illinois.

3
Interior identification banner,
Deere and Co.,
Waterloo, Iowa.

4
Changeable wall graphic,
Federal Office Building,
Detroit, Michigan.

5
Exterior identification,
S.S. Kresge Company Headquarters
(now called K Mart International),
Troy, Michigan.

6, 9
Wall and identification graphics,
State University of New York,
Stony Brook Campus, Long Island.

7
Kiosks, people mover system,
Detroit, Michigan.

8
Department identification,
Smith, Henchman & Grylls,
Detroit, Michigan.

9

Saul Bass
Saul Bass and Associates, Inc.
Los Angeles

Saul Bass, considered one of the founders of American graphic design, has gained considerable fame for his film work. Starting with designs for film titles, for which he has won many awards, Bass's practice today includes directing major film productions. Much of Saul's signing effort goes into producing large corporate programs for such clients as the Bell Telephone System, United Airlines, and Exxon. Some of his signing solutions, such as the vibrantly colorful configuration designed for the Fuller Paint Company, verge on sculpture.

1

2

3

4

5

6

7

1
Sculpture of Celanese symbol,
New York.

2-3
Color spectrum sculptures,
Fuller Paint Company,
Anaheim, California.

4
Identification sign,
Lawrys, California.

5
Lobby sign,
Warner Communications,
New York.

6
Building identification, AT&T.

7
Ticket counter graphics,
United Airlines.

8
Building identification,
Security Pacific Bank,
Los Angeles.

8

J. Malcolm Grear
Malcolm Grear Designers, Inc.
Providence, Rhode Island

Formerly the head of and still associated with the graphic design department at the Rhode Island School of Design, Malcolm Grear has headed up his own firm in Providence, Rhode Island, since 1960. Its wide range of graphic design activity includes work for organizations, companies, and communities, both nationally and internationally. Malcolm's range of architectural signage is also quite wide, starting with typical identification signing and extending to colorful and intricate environmental graphics. A good example of the latter is shown here in the Horace Mann/Andrew Jackson School in Brighton, Massachusetts.

1

2

3

4

1
Exterior sign,
Bonanza Bus Terminal
and *Providence Journal-Bulletin*,
Providence, Rhode Island.

2
Main entrance identification,
Bonanza Bus Terminal,
Providence, Rhode Island.

3
Exterior signing,
Interstate North Office Park,
Atlanta, Georgia.

4
Main entrance sign, Big Canoe,
Cousins Properties Development,
Atlanta, Georgia.

5, 8
Painted wall graphics,
Horace Mann/Andrew Jackson School,
Brighton, Massachusetts.

6-7
Painted wall and ceiling graphics,
South Block Nurse's Residence,
Boston City Hospital,
Boston, Massachusetts.

5

6

7

8

Charles P. Reay

Hellmuth, Obata & Kassabaum, Architects
St. Louis, Missouri

The head of a graphic design department within an architectural office, Charles P. Reay skillfully balances not only illustration and interior signing design solutions, but large, colorful, and sometimes complex graphics for Hellmuth, Obata & Kassabaum, Architects, of St. Louis. The graphic program for the Smithsonian's National Air & Space Museum in Washington, D.C., is typical of the many large projects which HOK routinely undertakes. These involve Reay in subsidiary design problems, such as developing color schemes, merchandising sign criteria, and other design decisions related as much to architectural design as to graphics.

2

1

3

4

5

6

1-3
Wall graphics and banners,
Community School,
St. Louis, Missouri.

4
Identification kiosk,
National Air & Space Museum,
Smithsonian Institution,
Washington, D.C.

5
Glass divider,
National Air & Space Museum,
Smithsonian Institution,
Washington, D.C.

6
Gallery identification signing,
National Air & Space Museum,
Smithsonian Institution,
Washington, D.C.

7

8

9

10

11

12

13

7
Directional sign,
Missouri Botanical Garden,
St. Louis, Missouri.

8
Building identification,
Missouri Botanical Garden,
St. Louis, Missouri.

9
Building plaque,
Missouri Botanical Garden,
St. Louis, Missouri.

10
Artwork,
Incarnate Word Hospital,
St. Louis, Missouri.

11
Gate banner and directional sign,
West Texas Regional Airport,
Lubbock, Texas.

12
Department signing,
Penroze Library,
Denver, Colorado.

13
Jet way gate identification,
West Texas Regional Airport,
Lubbock, Texas.

9
Graphics, Flags, and Banners

There are many design elements, basically decorative in nature, which can be used to enhance the architectural environment. This chapter is about some of them—namely, graphics, flags, and banners.

GRAPHICS

Graphics has come to mean so many different things in the field of design that no concise definition is adequate. This discussion is limited to graphics designed for commercial architectural environments. The primary function of architectural graphics is enhancement, not communication of information. For example, a supergraphics number which designates a floor level is not a good example of architectural graphics but should be thought of as part of a signing system.

By architectural graphics we mean nonfunctional, decorative designs which enhance architecture in various ways, such as providing an effective focal point; adding color, detail, or a sense of scale; reinforcing the architectural design; or supporting a thematic idea. A particular design may enhance the architecture in any of these ways; indeed, the most effective graphic designs function in all these ways.

Applications

Two interrelated questions should govern decisions about the applicability of architectural graphics:

1. What kinds of projects lend themselves to large-scaled graphic designs?
2. What subject matter seems appropriate to these projects?

On the most general level, large-scale graphics are most appropriate for large public or private areas. For example, baggage claim areas of airports are frequently crowded with people who are a captive audience. In these areas, graphic designs can enliven the wall surfaces, changing a boring waiting period into a visually interesting experience.

Many projects have large wall spaces to be decorated. Foyers of theaters; lobbies of sports arenas; government buildings; walls of libraries, restaurants, cafeterias, coffee shops, department stores, and auditoriums—all these—may provide opportunities for graphic designs.

The question of which walls are best for graphics is often decided by the project architect or interior designer, not the graphics consultant. Many interior walls are designed to receive architectural finish materials, and only a few may be available for graphics, but these designs need not be restricted to walls.

Floors and ceiling surfaces as well may be treated with graphic designs.

In the past, graphics were defined as flat, two-dimensional designs; but today architectural graphics may have three-dimensional characteristics. A good example of this is the wall designed for CBS by Lubalin, Smith, and Carnese, which is shown on page 107 in Chapter 8, Designers' Portfolio.

Subject Matter

When considering subject matter for a particular architectural graphic, the designer must rely on his own experience and design judgment in determining what is appropriate. However, the following questions, when related to a specific project, can often suggest a direction for an effective solution:

1. Should subject matter of the graphic design relate to how this project functions?
2. Can subject matter relate to the physical characteristics of the architecture?
3. Should the subject matter be abstract, providing a graphic design element which stands on its own?
4. Has a theme been established (as for an amusement park or restaurant) which the graphics can reinforce?

Fantasy. An attribute of architectural graphics which is suggested by several examples in this chapter is their potential to create a world of the imagination. What could be more appropriate for the lobby of a children's hospital than a design which may take a sick child from the real world of pain to one of fantasy? Adults also respond to the poetic in art, and like art, graphic design has the ability to stimulate the imagination through the use of fantasy (Figure 67).

Focal Point

The basic design principle involved in the concept of designing graphics as a focal point of the environment is an old one in art and architecture. Paintings regardless of style usually have a center of interest, a focal point. Architectural structures of all eras have entrances, canopies, and stairways which become focal points. Complex modern projects have numerous possibilities for points of interest. For the exteriors of these projects, architects use landscaping, sculpture, and graphics to create focal points wherever they are needed to complete the design concept. Interior spaces of commercial projects are often too crowded for sculpture. Wall graphics consume no precious floor space, and yet they can have dynamic impact as focal points. The graphics shown in Figure 68 illustrate this concept.

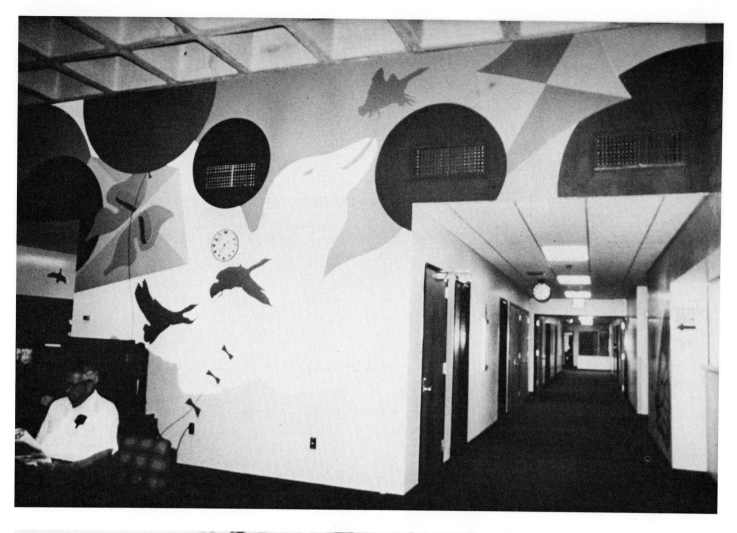

Figure 67. (above) Painted wall graphics utilizing poetic subject matter. Sidney Farber Cancer Institute. Malcolm Grear Design.

Figure 68. Canadian Theme Pavilion, "Man, His Planet, and Space," Expo 67, Montreal. At the entrance to the pavilion a symbolic picture of man was painted on a set of concentric aluminum rings which rotated at different speeds but came to rest in register. Designed by Rudolph de Harak, Inc.

Adding Color, Detail, or Scale

During the last few decades, the use of color for its own sake has been emphasized in certain architectural environments. Strong color combined with bold graphics creates design elements of such impact that they cannot be ignored. This application of graphics is widely used in projects ranging from fashionable shops to discotheques, creating a certain ambience which their clientele enjoys.

A wall in any of these projects may be so large that it needs some graphic detail to give it the proper relationship to people and to the space (Figure 69). This use of graphics is often referred to as *creating a scale relationship*.

Reinforcing the Architectural Design

When used properly, graphics can reinforce the architectural design by emphasizing building forms or strengthening a special feature. The water tank illustrated in Figure 70 is a dramatic example of how a very simple and direct graphic treatment can emphasize an architectural form. Without the graphic design, this tower would appear the same from different directions, but with the design applied, it presents a changing aspect when seen from every direction. The design reinforces the three-dimensional aspects (the roundness) of the tank and provides additional interest through the use of color.

Barbara Stauffacher Solomon was one of the first American designers to integrate abstract graphic forms and color with architecture. She designed graphics for this tower and also interior graphics for Sea Ranch, a housing development on the northern California coast. Charles Moore was the architect for this bold group of buildings, constructed predominantly of natural wood. The colorful interior graphic designs provide contrast and reinforcement for the geometric forms of these structures. Architecture and graphics are integrated, becoming a synthesis of space, decoration, and structure (Figure 71).

Another example of reinforcement is the hard-edge painted graphic designed by Harper & George for Braniff airlines (Figure 72). By applying bands of color and related geometric shapes to curved walls, the designers have emphasized the curvilinear quality of the space. On a subliminal level, the curves express the grace and freedom of air flight.

Supporting a Thematic Idea

In various parts of the country there are amusement parks or entertainment facilities based on a theme, which is usually expressed in the park's name. Sea World and Marineland, for example, are theme parks related to marine life. Sea World of Florida provides an example of the way large graphic designs used on exterior walls can help identify a thematic park (Figure 73). This facility, located near Orlando, Florida, is a series of sea-oriented exhibits and shows spread over a large site. The architect of this facility recognized the need for a program of architectural graphics to express the theme and help unify the buildings (Figure 74). In addition to signing, the program involved graphics in three ways: marine (cool) colors applied to painted building roofs; graphic designs of marine life applied to white building walls; banners with applied marine motifs. Because of budget constraints, the designers employed painting techniques for some of the designs while others were executed in durable materials, such as ceramic and glass mosaic.

Temporary vs. Permanent Graphics

The supergraphics of a construction fence may have only a few months of useful life, while a ceramic wall design may be enjoyed as long as the life of the building it enhances. But the

Figure 69. Graphic designs, when applied to architectural walls, can help provide a sense of scale, as indicated by this example. Designs by Gerald Reis and Michael Manwaring for Recreation Room, Tennis Club, Tanglewood Apartment, Hayward, California.

Figure 70. The form of this water tower, designed for California Expo in Sacramento, is enhanced and reinforced by a painted graphic treatment by Barbara Stauffacher Solomon.

Figure 71. Painted wall graphics on interior walls of the Sea Ranch project, Northern California. Graphics by Barbara Stauffacher Solomon.

Figure 72. The large B and painted bands of color reinforce the name "Braniff" and emphasize the curved walls of this air terminal design by Harper and George in the Dallas-Fort Worth Airport.

Figure 73. This whale is located near the entrance of Sea World of Florida in Orlando. The design is fabricated of glass mosaic tile for maximum fade resistance.

Figure 74. Inspired by a Japanese woodcut, this graphic design of stylized waves helps establish the ethnic theme of the Japanese Village built within Sea World and reinforces its marine theme. It is fabricated of custom-made glazed ceramic tile.

Figure 75. (below) A painted wall graphic design for McCarran International Airport is based on the numbers 7 and 11, appropriate to the gaming theme of Las Vegas.

useful life of many graphic designs may depend as much on their appeal as on time or durability (Figure 75). Graphics are designed for people, and if the same people see a design every day, they may become tired of it or come to ignore it. A painted graphic in a work area, for example, might be changed every few years just to improve employee morale. Painted graphics are appropriate also for projects where departmental changes require frequent remodeling of walls. The temporary nature of such designs should not affect their design quality, but in reality it often does. Because they are considered of less importance than permanent items, temporary graphics command lower fees and less design time.

A few permanent graphics for very important buildings and prominent locations may fall into a different category. It is understandable that the owners who establish budgets for prominently displayed items want to have them designed by well-qualified designers. Artists like Calder, Picasso, Moore, and Noguchi are commissioned to do sculptures for public spaces because they have a reputation for producing works of lasting value. Designers such as Herbert Bayer and Milton Glaser are asked to design architectural graphics for prominent locations for the same reason. Glaser recently designed a 600-foot (180-meter) mural for the New Federal Building in Indianapolis, Indiana (Figure 76 and page 110 in color). A work of this size and importance represents the kind of special challenge that a uniquely gifted designer or artist can meet.

Designers of signing and graphic systems may be involved with projects requiring a graphic of such importance. Realizing their own limitations, they may be able to recommend a designer of stature whom they respect for the commission. In this way they maintain a voice in the final outcome and a measure of control.

Durability. This is another aspect of permanency. There are many factors which can affect the durability of exterior architectural graphics, but the most important of these are the material used and the weather they are exposed to.

Materials. Most finish materials commonly used for the exteriors of buildings are suitable for graphics. The exterior signing materials, which are described in Chapter 12, Fabrication, are also suitable for graphics. However, the color stability of materials for exterior graphics is often of special importance where they are exposed to direct sun. Available in a broad range of colors, glass mosaic tile, glazed ceramic tile, and porcelain enamels are far more fade-resistant than paint colors or even baked enamel. The tiles, which are made in a broad range of modular sizes, are suitable for patterned, geometric, or free-form designs. Being glass, or glasslike, tiles have extremely dense, hard, nonporous surfaces. This makes them waterproof and weather-resistant.

Paints and Coatings. The durability or weather resistance of paints often depends on their lack of porosity or on surface density and hardness. Being hard and nonporous, high-gloss paints, porcelain, and baked enamels are generally more durable and easier to clean than low-gloss versions of the same material. This is also true of recently developed transparent coatings such as the polyurethanes. One of these, called linear polyurethane, is unique in its ability to protect painted surfaces and many materials. Most graphics when spray-coated with this material can have spray paint graffiti removed without being damaged. Additional paint and coatings information of a more technical nature is located in Chapter 12, Fabrication. For spe-

Figure 76. For the new Federal Building in Indianapolis, Indiana, Milton Glaser designed a 180-meter (600-foot) mural that completely surrounds the core of the building. Composed of bands of subtly modulated colors, varying in chroma and value, the design presents a different aspect from each point of view. (See the building in color on page 110.)

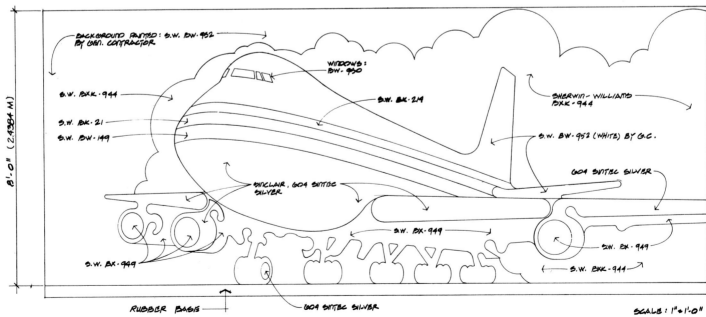

Figure 77. This drawing illustrates the kind of hard-line drawing usually required when hard-edge designs are to be painted directly on a wall. The accompanying photo shows the completed design. For Krueger furniture showroom, Pacific Design Center, Los Angeles.

cific problems, however, it is best to obtain information from a paint manufacturer.

Documenting a Graphic Design

The process of making final drawings for many kinds of hard-edge graphic designs is quite similar. The example illustrated in Figure 77 is for a typical hard-edge design to be painted directly on the wall. Documentation processes are outlined as follows:

1. Prepare a hard line drawing of the design to scale. A scale of about 1 or 1½ inches (25 or 38 millimeters) to the foot is usually adequate for simple designs.
2. Draw an outline of the edge of each area where there is a color change.
3. Note the color of each area using a code number from an accepted paint color system.
4. Attach a color chip of each color to a print when issuing the final drawing.

Documenting a soft-edge design normally involves a painting or a full-color rendering made to scale. A skillful craftsman-painter can enlarge this by eye or with the aid of an optical projector.

Execution

It is a common misconception that designers also execute what they design. This thinking may come from the time when artists conceived and painted murals because their ideas could not be interpreted properly by others. Today specialization has taken command; designers design, and craftsmen execute. Although problems of interpretation remain, they have become less critical. Certain graphic techniques have lessened the problems of translating creative ideas into graphics on building surfaces.

To help ensure that the final painted design will be durable, the designer should specify that painter's canvas be installed over the existing plaster or gypsum board wall to be painted. This will prevent minor surface cracks due to building settlement or wall movement. The craftsman who does final painting can also apply a proper prime coat to this wall. Using full-size patterns produced by optical projection, the craftsman will transfer the design to the wall; this is done by applying pounce (chalk dust) through perforated lines in the pattern. When the outlines are ready to be painted, the designer should inspect the design. He should also approve actual paint samples which the craftsman has mixed to match specified colors.

Depending on the size of the job, an inspection may be required during progress of the work and another upon its completion.

FLAGS AND BANNERS

Flags, banners, pennants, streamers, and similar items have been used for hundreds of years as colorful eye-catching devices. In the past, most were made of fabric so they could flutter or wave in the wind, but today they are also made of plastic, metal, paper, and the newer synthetic fabrics.

Flags are usually rectangular shapes, flown horizontally, while banners come in a variety of horizontal and vertical shapes. There are long banners that seem to float, slowly and gracefully, streamers that ripple or shimmer, and metal banners that hang vertically, adding color and reflections but no movement.

Applications

Traditionally, towns and cities have used flags and banners to announce historical events, celebrations, political gatherings, and holidays. Strung across Main Street, banners may announce the county fair, a 4th of July picnic, or the Christmas season. But when considered in relationship to architectural spaces, the use of these devices is extremely varied.

Modern shopping centers, which have large open or air-conditioned malls, have the space to use banners effectively to add color and movement or to announce important sales events (Figure 78). Museums use specially designed banners to announce current exhibits; these are often well-designed works of art in themselves. Much of the impact of these applications also depends upon proper timing; banners are only displayed when events are current.

Fairs, trade shows, and outdoor entertainment facilities of all kinds are traditionally major users of flags and banners. Theme parks, such as Disney World and Sea World of Florida, use flags and banners extensively to add color and excitement and to help establish the identity and theme of the park. For example, the sea life theme of Sea World is reinforced by banners, which utilize wave motifs and cool aquatic colors (Figure 79).

The national flag and state flags are traditionally displayed both outside and inside government buildings to help identify and indicate the special purpose of these facilities. Organizations ranging from schools to national governments display their own flags. Commercial projects could have their own flag, but rarely do. When displayed en masse, as in front of the United Nations Building in New York, flags of member nations add dignity and symbolize international cooperation.

Material Selection and Durability

Interior spaces provide great latitude in the selection of banner materials because weather factors need not be considered. Thin sheets of mylar, stainless steel, fabrics, and a variety of plastics are all suitable as banners. With these materials the designer is only limited by the kind of inks or paints used to apply any graphic design. Banner makers are usually knowledgeable about what is technically feasible, recommending durable reproduction techniques for specific materials.

Exterior spaces, where banners and flags are exposed to sun and weather, present an entirely different set of problems. We can only generalize here, because each project has its own microclimate affecting durability. Durability has two aspects: fade-resistance depends on the actual color, the dyes used, and the kind of fabric or basic material used; fray-resistance depends primarily on the kind of fabrics or material used.

Probably 95 percent of exterior flags and banners are made of fabric, and flag nylon seems to be the most practical fabric to use, considering all aspects of durability. The weight of the fabric depends somewhat on the size of the item, but heavier fabrics are not necessarily more durable. For sewing, synthetic thread, such as dacron or nylon, is more durable than cotton. Heavy folded seams at the end of a flag may reduce durability because this seam acts like a weight, making the flag snap in the wind and causing the edges to fray more quickly.

It is very difficult to project the life expectancy of any exterior fabric which is constantly exposed to the weather. While sunshine seems to have the fastest deteriorating effect, there are industrial pollutants which also cause rapid deterioration. Identical banners might last three months in one location and six in another, if flown continuously.

Support Devices

Flag and banner poles are manufactured in many standard sizes and designs and of various materials. Three of the most widely used pole designs are *straight, sectioned,* and *swagged* or *tapered.* Straight poles are made of one piece of steel pipe or tubing. Sectioned poles are fabricated of several pieces of straight pipe or tubing which slip together like parts of a telescope; these are normally made of steel but can also be made of aluminum. As the name implies, tapered poles are larger at the ground and smaller at the upper end. Normally made of special aluminum alloys, they are available with enameled paint finishes or with a variety of anodized finishes which have greater durability than paint.

The upper ends of poles can be designed with rotating attachment hardware, which can help prevent the wind from tangling flags or banners. Poles can be provided with various rope and pulley arrangements for raising and lowering flags; motorized hoisting devices can be installed where flags must be raised and lowered daily. For some installations where vandalism is a problem, motorized controls are often protected by locked boxes. All such flag-hoisting arrangements can become quite complex; designers should work with flag and banner manufacturers to solve problems of this kind.

Maintenance

Proper long-term maintenance of these decorative graphic devices, especially when used outdoors, is essential. An adequate maintenance allotment should be established for these items as part of the overall operating budget of the project. Otherwise, they will soon look shabby and ineffective.

A reputable manufacturer of flags and banners can provide technical information and help in recommending budgets. On installations where flags and banners must fly continuously, manufacturers may suggest an average replacement interval of from three to six months. To determine the exact interval required to keep them looking fresh will require an actual period of use. Once this has been determined, the manufacturer will normally recommend ordering a two-year supply of items which can be stored in vinyl bags. The manufacturer can also provide maintenance service, such as sewing frayed ends of flags or banners, which can greatly extend the useful life of these decorative items.

Figure 79. Design motifs inspired by ocean waves are silk-screened in aquatic colors on nylon fabric in these banners designed for Sea World of Florida.

Figure 78. (left) Stainless steel banners with silk-screened designs are displayed in the mall of The Plaza, Atlantic Richfield Plaza's underground shopping center. Designs by Jerzy Pujdak and Mark Bielski.

10
Design Development

Design development is a design activity which may begin during the design phase and extend into the documentation phase, as these phases are defined in this book. Most of this activity, however, occurs after presentation designs have been approved and before working drawings are started. It involves both technical and esthetic aspects of the designs which either were not or could not have been resolved in the presentation design drawings.

The presentation design drawings are two-dimensional in form and basic concept. While they are drawn to scale, they do not contain details and may not contain material notes or dimensions. Design development concentrates on the process of translating these two-dimensional concepts into practical design documents that contain all information needed by the fabricator, who will then convert these designs into the actual three-dimensional signing elements.

SCOPE OF THE PROCESS
Design development entails the following:

Developing all sign structures or supports, details, and connections

Resolving code-related problems

Gathering information about materials, methods of fabricating signs, and copy application techniques to be noted on the working drawings or in the specifications

Selecting or designing lighting, electrical, or mechanical equipment

In short, it is concerned with resolving *all* aspects of the designs so that design documentation can begin.

Various aspects of this process are outlined in the following discussion, which describes the development of a typical sign composed of a sign panel mounted on a supporting post. For the presentation drawings, the sizes, proportions, and relationships of post and panel are normally determined by their visual appearance—by what looks right. Determining the size of the post may also be based on what is called *intuitive engineering*; using past experience, the designer indicates what he judges to be a large enough post to function properly. During the design development, the size of the post is studied thoroughly, considering sizes of available post materials, their strengths, and other technical properties. The results of these studies may indicate a need for a change in the size of the post from what was originally shown. If the change is substantial, it may require restudy of the panel or other aspects of the sign.

Code Requirements
Signing designers of both exterior and interior signs should familiarize themselves with local sign codes obtained from building departments to be sure that all signs comply with applicable codes. This should be done as soon as designs are final or before designs are put into working drawing form. Basic code problems are usually identified early in the planning stages, but often not completely solved until the design development stage.

Fabricators are required by code to provide engineering of signs and to obtain permits from the appropriate government agencies before installing most signs on public or private property. These code requirements are written to protect the public safety, but being general guidelines, they are subject to interpretation. Permits for signs which do comply with the code are relatively easy to obtain, normally requiring only a few hours' time. However, if there is a code problem, the sign fabricator acting as agent for the client must file for a variance, which may or may not be granted, to install a sign which does not strictly comply with the code but is within limits of public safety. Depending upon the specific situation, this may require changes in the design and may take several hours or days to process.

Materials and Fabrication Methods
If the typical sign in our example has a painted metal sign panel and support post, the type of metal to be used and its thickness should be decided at this stage. Factors that may influence this decision are

Strength of the material

Availability of material in sizes to meet design requirements

Cost of the material

Ability of the material to be fabricated in the shape designed

Maintenance factors

Available finishes

Copy applications

Copy Applications. The method of copy application will often determine what material should be used for the sign background. Metal is often used as a background for lighted plastic letters. If these are to be routed through the face panel, aluminum should be used for the panel rather than steel; being softer, aluminum cuts more easily and can be finished more quickly than steel.

The method of copy application may also determine the kind

of detail that should be included in the working drawings. For instance, alternate methods of fabricating the letters can be considered (Figure 80): (1) recessed behind the metal face, (2) flush with the metal, and (3) projecting from the metal surface. A final detail should be developed for the method selected.

Lighting Applications

During this stage, the exact method of lighting the plastic letters for this sign should be determined. Studies might compare the feasibility of neon and fluorescent, for example. Fluorescent lighting usually requires a sign to be 8 to 10 inches (20.3 to 25.4 centimeters) thick, but neon is practical for much thinner signs. Either will require a removable panel for replacement of lamps or maintenance of electrical wiring or components. The location and attachment details of this panel should be studied to make it look as inconspicuous as possible.

Installation Techniques

The designer should be aware of correct installation methods for freestanding exterior signs so that he can specify them properly, as follows:

Sign Supports of Wood. Being relatively inexpensive, wood is the best material for sign posts on many projects (Figure 81), but it must be properly treated to prevent decay. Wrapping the part below ground with asphalt-coated cloth is one effective method. After coating, the post is surrounded with tamped earth fill and gravel for drainage at the bottom or set in concrete.

Sign Supports of Metal. Metal supports should be galvanized or coated with rust-proof paint near ground level and below to prevent rusting. Depending on engineering requirements, metal supports are usually set in concrete, referred to as a foundation or footing. This varies in size according to windloads, size of sign, and other structural requirements. Where signs are located in lawns or other planted areas, the exposed surface of the concrete can be square or round when viewed from above and sloped away from the post for proper water drainage. If located in paved areas of brick or tile, this paving should extend up to the post. Special conditions such as hillside installation should be detailed to show the desired result.

WHO DOES DESIGN DEVELOPMENT?

The design studies described here can become quite technical, exceeding the normal experience of graphic designers. To cope with these kinds of problems, offices that design signing should have someone on staff who is familiar with three-dimensional problems and who understands construction techniques. A background in architectural and industrial design is helpful for any signing designer and particularly to that designer responsible for design development work. Even some structural engineering knowledge is helpful, but usually intuitive engineering based on practical experience is adequate. Keep in mind that the contractor is responsible for structural engineering of all signs, including their internal construction. But exterior details which affect the appearance of the signs are design development responsibilities.

Sources of Information

It soon becomes obvious that construction and appearance are interrelated; to control the design fully, the designer must know the basics of construction. Designers can acquire a basic understanding of metal, plastic, and wood fabrication by visiting several sign manufacturers specializing in these techniques.

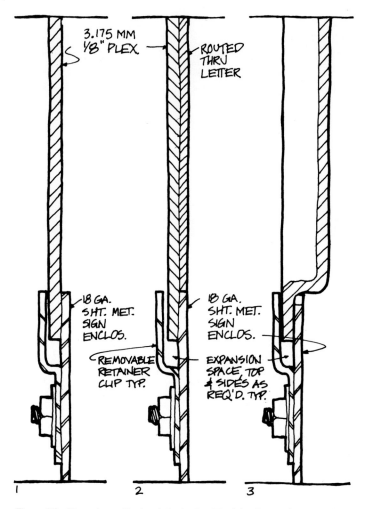

Figure 80. Alternate methods of designing Plexiglas letters for routed metal signs.

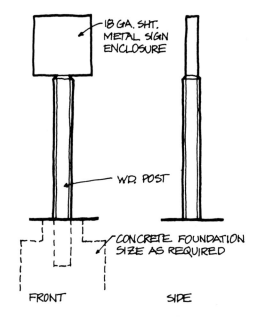

Figure 81. Study shows the relationship between a wood support post and a metal sign panel.

Here they can learn about the practical limitations of these materials and processes.

Basic information about the most common sign materials and fabrication processes is included in Chapter 12, Fabrication. Technical books about wood and metal fabrication (some of which are noted in the Selected Readings) are readily available at most libraries. More detailed information about various materials or equipment is usually available at little or no cost from manufacturers. Catalogs from steel or aluminum manufacturers list sizes and other pertinent facts about sheets, bars, and tube shapes supplied. Rohm and Haas provides a particularly helpful and well-written catalog about acrylic products for sign usage, but other plastics manufacturers also produce useful printed information. Lighting manufacturers such as General Electric, Sylvania, and Westinghouse will provide catalogs indicating pertinent data related to all incandescent, fluorescent, and floodlighting equipment they manufacture.

While plastic-forming and -molding processes are often very sophisticated, wood and metal technologies are fairly simple and well established. The designer needs only a general understanding of what can be done with these various materials, not a detailed knowledge of all the processes involved. He should know enough about the strength of materials, for example, to know when to specify metal tubing for a sign support post and when to specify wood. He should be familiar with the special properties of common sign materials such as glass and acrylic, so that he can intelligently decide which is best for a particular application.

Cost Information

A design development study may necessitate a cost comparison of two designs. If the designs differ only in materials, it is relatively easy to obtain cost comparisons from material suppliers, but if the two designs differ in both material and fabrication methods, cost estimates should be obtained from a sign fabricator. Frequently, such cost comparison can be made on the basis of very rough sketches if the designer only wants to know which design is the most expensive.

Information from Fabricators

During this part of the design process, the most valuable source of general information is an experienced sign fabricator, especially one who understands a variety of methods and materials. Most well-organized fabricators devote a portion of their time to advising designers and potential clients. The designers can utilize the fabricator's time most effectively by meeting with him to review a set of designs. These can be Xerox prints of presentation drawings the client has approved.

These drawings should include notes indicating the materials to be used, method of sign illumination, rough freehand sketches of edge details and connections—in short, any design information affecting the exterior appearance of the signs. The designer should prepare a checklist of technical questions about each sign type for reference as items are discussed. Preparing information and questions gives the designer an opportunity to think through the entire sign system; this will help him organize and simplify construction details which may be utilized on the many different items. The fabricator will also be looking for ways to simplify items to make them workable or less expensive to build. He may suggest alternate materials or fabrication methods which the designer has not considered; having a different and often more practical point of view is one of his valuable assets. Fabricators rarely suggest changes which will affect the basic appearance of a sign. Rather, they are interested in finding ways to turn design concepts into functional signs.

Most fabricators seem willing to provide a limited amount of technical advice without charge, but they may require a fee to provide extensive engineering studies or to help write technical specifications. They give some free advice during this phase, with the expectation of bidding on the designs once completed. Design review meetings allow the fabricator to become familiar with the designs and informed about projected fabrication schedules well in advance of the bid period.

Models, Mockups, and Prototypes. A majority of signs in a system tend to be basically two-dimensional or panellike, but most involve some three-dimensional aspects. Nearly every system contains some three-dimensional signs, such as a freestanding directory or large project identification sign, which is usually seen from many directions. A scale model of such items is often used in the design phase to visualize relationships with surrounding buildings. During design development, a full-size mockup of small items is often more helpful than scale models. Quickly made mockups of cardboard can show much about scale relationships and indicate where design details are needed.

Better than mockups are sign prototypes made from actual construction materials to exact dimensions and specifications. On large jobs, the sign fabricator can be required by the specifications to make prototypes for approval of certain sign types prior to making them in quantity. Although mockups are primarily for the designer's use, prototypes benefit both designer and fabricator in terms of working out design problems. However, there isn't always time or necessity for prototypes. One-of-a-kind signs or large signs are usually worked out on paper, often with the help of a knowledgeable signing fabricator. He can determine feasibility of a sign very quickly and will often suggest alternate ways to build the sign at lower cost. Sometimes cost savings can be dramatic. On one large project which was about $20,000 over the budget, the fabricator suggested leaving metal seams of all exterior signs unfilled. This changed the appearance of the joints but not the overall design appearance or durability. By reducing hand labor, this change held costs within the budget.

SELECTION OF INTERNAL ILLUMINATION AND SIGN STRUCTURE

The kind of internal illumination selected for a specific sign may affect the design of the exterior or its structure. For example, fluorescent lights must be far enough behind the plastic face of a sign to illuminate it evenly. This section describes the lighting and structural problems encountered during this phase of the work.

Internal Illumination

Although the designer concentrates his attention on sign exteriors, lighting is one aspect of interior construction that he can't ignore. A description of basic types of internal illumination for signs is included in Chapter 5, Design. During design development, one of these basic types should be studied in detail for each lighted sign or item. The following questions about lighting often arise as the designs are refined.

Backlighted Channel Letters. These are hollow, fabricated letters of metal or plastic, usually lighted by neon.

What diameter neon tubing should be used?

How many rows of tubing should be used side by side within the letter?

How big will the transformer be and where can it be located?

How far out from the wall should letters be located to get an adequate halo of lighting around them?

Hollow Letters with Translucent Acrylic Face and Metal Sides

How deep (front to back) should letters be made to accommodate neon tubing?

Can a neon tube be used in the narrowest part of every letter?

How thick should the acrylic face be?

What metal detail should be used with the acrylic face?

What thickness of metal should be used for sides?

Where will electric wiring come through the building wall?

Large Signs with Internally Lighted Translucent Face

If copy is on one side only, what front to back dimension should the sign housing (cabinet) be, assuming fluorescent lamps as a light source?

Should fluorescent lamps run vertically or horizontally?

How far apart should lamps be? What length lamps are required?

What access is required for replacing lamps?

How thick should the plastic face be?

How should opaque copy be applied to the sign face?

Translucent copy?

Where will internal supports be located?

Where will lamp ballasts be located?

Large Signs with Opaque Face and Routed-through Copy Internally Lighted

Should sheet metal or aluminum be used for signface? What thickness?

How should the plastic letters be held in place (if they are flush with metal signface)?

What dimension is required (front to back) for sign housing (cabinet)?

Will one row of fluorescent lamps behind each line of copy provide even illumination? [This is normal for copy approximately 4 to 6 inches (10.2 to 15.2 centimeters) high.]

What access is required for relamping?

These questions are not all-inclusive but serve as a guide to the kinds of questions that should be asked. Some of the answers may affect the basic design; for example, the design proportions of a sign housing may have to increase to provide space for adequate internal lighting. Some lamp manufacturers, such as General Electric, have technical salesmen who may be knowledgeable in this specialized field.

One of the main reasons for obtaining answers to the foregoing questions is to provide information to be included on working drawings and specifications. Only if this information is complete and accurate can comparable bids be obtained. The bidding process is explained in Chapter 11, Documentation and Bidding.

Sign Structures

Internal construction of signs, particularly of illuminated ones, is a specialized art. Internal structural members must be engineered to allow space for electrical equipment, accessibility for relamping, and so forth. Because of the complexity of these construction problems, sign fabricators are best qualified to solve them. However, the exterior structure of any sign is the concern of the designer. In most cases the fabricator can build the exterior structure exactly as shown on the final design documents. If the designer has doubts about the strength of any structure he has designed, he can ask a fabricator to evaluate it, using accepted structural engineering methods.

If the designer conceives of a very large or unusual sign structure, it may require extensive engineering studies, which are too much for the consultant fabricator to do on speculation. It is advisable in such cases to hire a licensed structural engineer on a consultant basis who can provide calculations and structural drawings that will be issued with the designer's working drawings. Such a consultant would also supervise fabrication and installation of the structural work he has engineered.

The exterior sign system for McCarran International Airport involved several large signs which required the services of a consultant structural engineer. This engineer worked closely with the designers, checking the strength of each design as the development work proceeded. Basic problems and solutions that came from this collaborative effort are outlined in the following case study.

CASE STUDIES

To demonstrate the process of design development with actual sign problems, the following examples of exterior and interior signs were chosen from the authors' own experience:

Exterior Signs: McCarran International Airport

In this example, existing conditions influenced the design studies and ultimately the final solution.

Givens

1. Strong desert winds of up to 80 mph often carry sand. Wind may blow signs over or blow out plastic signfaces. Sand may sand-blast the signs' finish.
2. Signs in parking area are vulnerable to damage by carelessly driven vehicles. Tipsy drivers abound.
3. Multilane circulation road requires signs to span up to 45 feet (13.5 meters).
4. Major identity sign at site corner should be tall and visually strong. Engineering problem indicated because of strong winds.

Development Studies

1. For sign panels consider alternate materials and methods to avoid plastic signfaces:
   a. Steel sign panel with vinyl copy.
   b. Alternate: aluminum panels with cutout aluminum copy.
2. For sign supports consider alternate methods and materials (Figure 82):

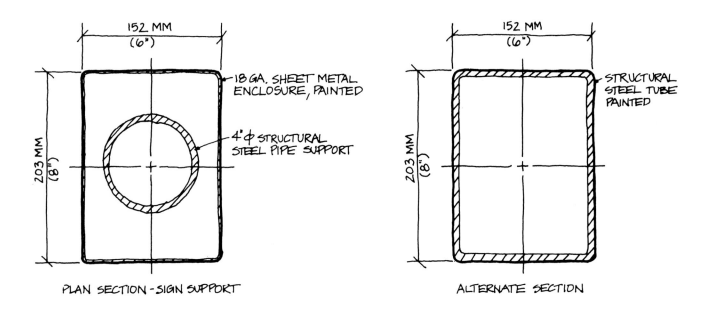

152 MM
(6")

203 MM
(8")

18 GA. SHEET METAL
ENCLOSURE, PAINTED

4"∅ STRUCTURAL
STEEL PIPE SUPPORT

PLAN SECTION - SIGN SUPPORT

152 MM
(6")

203 MM
(8")

STRUCTURAL
STEEL TUBE
PAINTED

ALTERNATE SECTION

Figure 82. These section drawings compare two methods of designing a sign support.

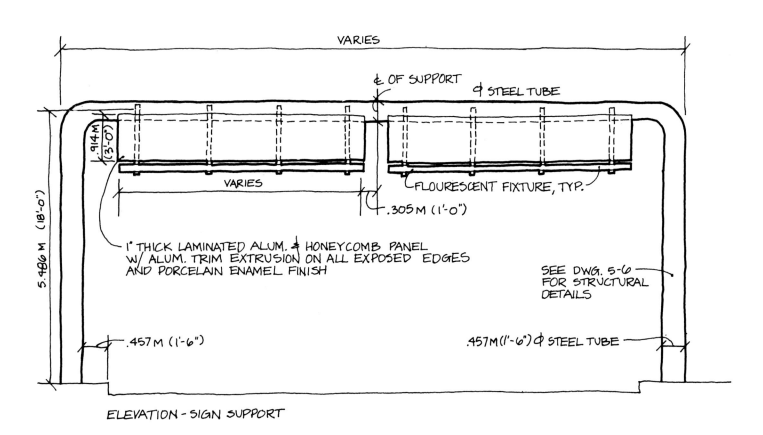

VARIES

₵ OF SUPPORT

∅ STEEL TUBE

.914 M
(3'-0")

VARIES

FLOURESCENT FIXTURE, TYP.

.305 M (1'-0")

1" THICK LAMINATED ALUM. ₵ HONEYCOMB PANEL
W/ ALUM. TRIM EXTRUSION ON ALL EXPOSED EDGES
AND PORCELAIN ENAMEL FINISH

SEE DWG. 5-6
FOR STRUCTURAL
DETAILS

5.486 M (18'-0")

.457 M (1'-6")

.457M (1'-6") ∅ STEEL TUBE

ELEVATION - SIGN SUPPORT

Figure 83. Study of steel tube structure for a sign which spans several lanes of roadway.

a. Thin metal enclosure over heavy steel pipe inner frame.

b. Alternate: heavy structural square, round, or rectangular tubing to serve as both inner and outer frame.

3. For multilane road signs investigate the following:

a. Freeway-type sign structure with truss spanning between vertical pipe supports.

b. Alternate: special support structure of heavy wall pipe with elbows connecting vertical supports to horizontal member (Figure 83).

4. For major identity sign study honeycomb core aluminum panels for signface with porcelain enamel finish, as used on freeway signing. Consider major identity sign to be 50-foot (15-meter) tall square tower (Figure 84):

a. Steel frame with attached porcelain steel sign panels and silk-screened copy.

b. Alternate: honeycomb panels as used on freeway signs over structural steel frame, with attached cutout copy.

Solutions

1. Nonilluminated signs along perimeter road

a. Sign panels: honeycomb core panels, aluminum face with porcelain finish and applied metal letters.

b. Support structure: heavy wall steel tube all-welded construction for maximum strength; epoxy enamel finish over hot-dipped galvanized coating for durability (Figure 85).

2. Internally illuminated signs

a. Sign panels: heavy aluminum plate signface with cut through copy backed up with acrylic plastic mechanically attached internally, so it can't blow out of frame (Figure 86).

b. Support structure: same as nonilluminated signs.

3. Multilane road signs

a. Sign panels: honeycomb core panels with aluminum face, porcelain finish, applied metal letters. This construction is light, strong, durable, and well-tested by existing freeway applications.

b. Support structure: special heavy wall round pipe, with elbow connections flush welded and ground smooth (Figure 87).

c. Illumination: fluorescent in trough supported by the panel.

Note: The typical freeway truss construction was just as expensive and visually more complex than this solution.

4. Major identity sign: Tower

a. Sign panels: typical honeycomb aluminum panels with cutout and applied metal letter (Figure 88). Porcelain steel panels rejected on basis of warpage problem in processing.

b. Support structure: prefabricated inner steel engineered to resist high wind load factor.

Interior Signs: St. Joseph Medical Center

The requirements for an interior sign system for this hospital included the following:

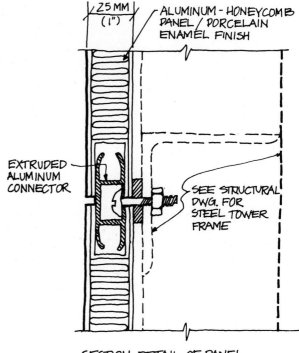

SECTION DETAIL OF PANEL

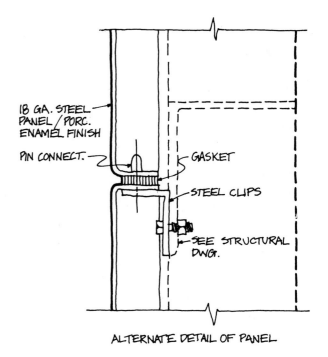

ALTERNATE DETAIL OF PANEL

Figure 84. Alternate methods of fabricating and attaching sign panels to the supporting structural frame.

Figure 86. Copy is routed out of the aluminum background and backed up with white plastic. Sign is illuminated internally. McCarran International Airport, Las Vegas, Nevada.

Figure 85. Heavy wall steel tubing was used for the structure of this parking area signing, making it practically indestructible. McCarran International Airport, Las Vegas, Nevada.

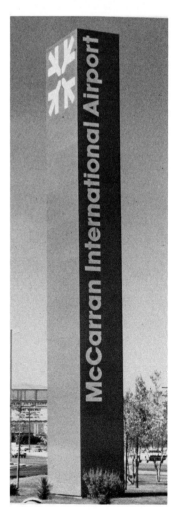

Figure 87. Spanning several lanes of roadway, this sign support is designed of structural steel pipe. Sign panels are of aluminum with honeycomb core and cut-out copy of porcelain-coated aluminum; face is illuminated by fluorescent troffers. McCarran International Airport, Las Vegas, Nevada.

Figure 88. This 50-foot (15-meter) high sign tower identifies the airport from a distance. It is fabricated of porcelain-coated aluminum honeycomb panels attached to an inner structure of steel which is designed to resist strong desert winds. Copy is cut out of aluminum with porcelain finish.

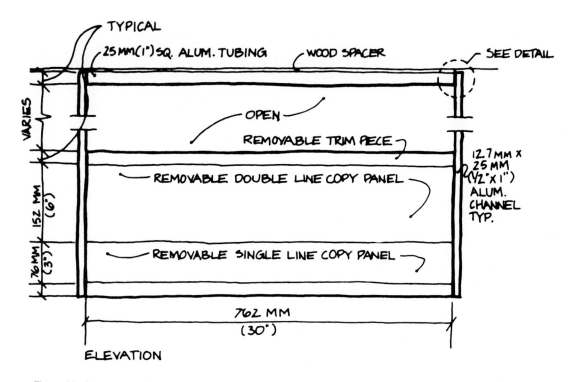

Figure 89. Design study for ceiling-mounted signs with metal support frame and removable copy panels.

Givens

1. Narrow corridors preclude use of projecting wall-mounted signs.
2. Certain directional signs should display message on both front and back.
3. Interior signs should have changeable message elements to allow for future relocating of departments, clinics, laboratories, and other functional areas.

Development Studies

1. Study various removable attachments of message elements to a sign panel:
   a. Magnetic fasteners; plastic interlock; Velcro.
   b. Alternate: methods of stacking message element panels one on top of another and held at the sides by a metal frame (Figure 89).
2. Consider use of signs supported from the ceiling which will accommodate messages on front and back of sign panels. Investigate ways to connect sign assembly to the ceiling. Consider vulnerability of sign: can it be struck by maintenance crews? Connection should be resilient or movable if sign is struck.
3. Study materials for message surface which will allow wording to be revised:
   a. Painted wood (can be repainted); formica (old copy can be removed and new copy applied); dark anodized aluminum.
   b. Alternate: silk screening, vinyl letters, surface printing.

Solution. A system of message elements was designed of formica over plywood with silk-screened copy (Figure 90). The elements are held in place by concealed snap fasteners and can be removed from the backup panel. The sign assembly is attached to the ceiling with a hook connection (Figure 91), which allows the entire sign to swing if struck by maintenance crews. Copy wording can be removed with lacquer thinner without damaging the formica.

Figure 90. These ceiling-mounted signs have metal frames which allow the copy panel to be removed if changes are needed. St. Joseph Medical Center, Burbank, California.

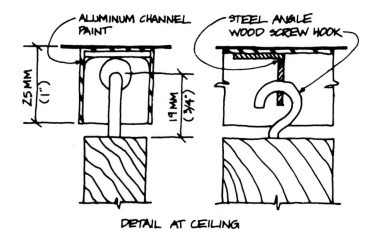

Figure 91. Studies for a hook attachment which allows sign panel to swing if accidently struck.

11
Documentation and Bidding

Experienced graphic designers are knowledgeable about so-called finished or final art used in the reproduction of printed items. While such art is adequate for the documentation of these two-dimensional items, signs require more complex working drawings and specification, primarily because signs are three-dimensional objects often made of a variety of materials.

This chapter describes various techniques for making the final working drawings for signs and outlines methods for writing specifications. It also covers bidding procedures for fabricators who will execute the designs from the drawings.

DOCUMENTATION
The term *documentation* covers all final drawings and written specifications which communicate information about the signing or graphic designs to the client, sign fabricator, and installer.

How Detailed Should the Drawings Be?
Before discussing the preparation of these documents, there are basic considerations affecting the amount of detail to be shown on the drawings:

The type of sign or graphic item to be documented

Construction methods and materials involved

The fabricator's qualifications

Fabricator's contract arrangements

The Sign Type. The type of sign or graphic item is the most important factor in determining the form and complexity of the final drawing needed. Items to be documented may vary from a simple, temporary sign painted on plywood to a very complex

BLACK COPY .836 M | WHITE PANEL
(2'-9")

.254 M (10")

No Smoking
Violators subject to fine L.A.M.C. 4151

TEMPORARY SIGNS - 10 REQ'D.

• PROVIDE PLY. PANEL & PAINTED COPY
• PROVIDE FULL SIZE SAMPLE FOR APPROVAL

Figure 92. This illustrates how to document the simplest kind of temporary sign that requires a minimum of information.

freestanding sign internally illuminated. The temporary sign can be documented by making an elevation drawing of the panel including a layout of the copy to scale (Figure 92). As a guide for the sign painter, copy can be set in phototype and a proof sent with the drawing. If paint colors and materials are noted directly on the original drawing, no separate specifications are necessary.

A complex sign made of several materials and with internal illumination requires a more complete drawing, details, and specifications. After basic front and side elevations are drawn to scale, it is often advisable to call in an experienced sign fabricator to talk over construction methods, materials, lighting, and any special structural problems which may exist. He can give advice about the amount of detail necessary to complete drawings and specifications. He can supply technical information about neon or fluorescent lighting, transformers, ballasts, and other electrical sign equipment.

The following examples further illustrate how the type of item may affect documentation:

1. A wall-mounted plaque or sign panel. This is basically two-dimensional in form and can be drawn simply as indicated in Figure 93 with pertinent dimensions shown. Specifications of materials, color, finish, and mounting hardware can be noted on the drawing or in specifications.

2. A freestanding, three-dimensional sign to be read from different directions. Note in Figure 94 that internal lighting is shown schematically. Details of how various materials connect should be shown at a larger scale. How the sign post is to be anchored to the concrete footing is shown only in outline form.

Construction Methods and Materials. If the sign is designed to be built of only one material, it is often relatively easy to draw up. For a simple plywood panel with copy silk-screened on the surface, the material, thickness, finish, and other specification information can be noted directly on the drawing. Only an elevation is needed to show the size of the panel and copy layout.

Another example of a relatively simple drafting problem is an all-metal sign, monolithic in appearance, with no interior illumination (Figure 95). Again, only exterior appearance details need be shown because interior construction will be indicated on the shop drawings. Include only the front and side elevations, detail of the corner, and the copy layout.

It is far more complicated to draft a sign designed of several materials, especially if it is also internally illuminated. In addi-

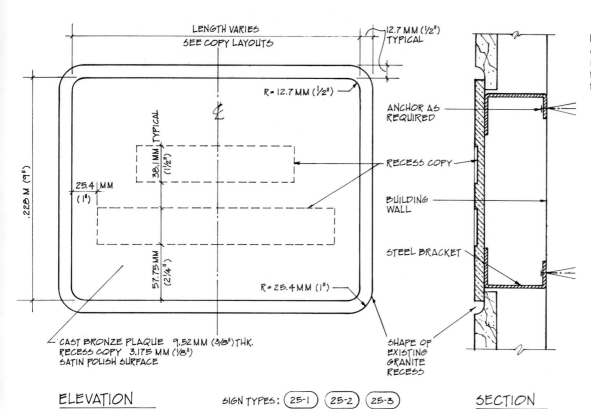

LENGTH VARIES
SEE COPY LAYOUTS

12.7 MM (½")
TYPICAL

R = 12.7 MM (½")

.228 M (9")

38.1 MM TYPICAL (1½")

25.4 MM (1")

57.75 MM (2¼")

R = 25.4 MM (1")

CAST BRONZE PLAQUE 9.52 MM (3/8") THK.
RECESS COPY 3.175 MM (1/8")
SATIN POLISH SURFACE

ANCHOR AS REQUIRED

RECESS COPY

BUILDING WALL

STEEL BRACKET

SHAPE OF EXISTING GRANITE RECESS

ELEVATION   SIGN TYPES: (25-1) (25-2) (25-3)   SECTION

Figure 93. Wall-mounted plaques, depending on their design, may require an elevation and a section to indicate how they are to be attached to the wall.

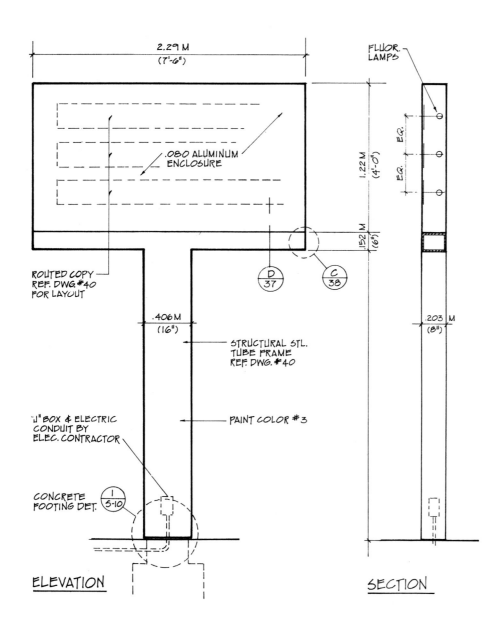

2.29 M (7'-6")

FLUOR. LAMPS

.080 ALUMINUM ENCLOSURE

1.22 M (4'-0")

E.Q. E.Q.

E.Q. E.Q.

.152 M (6")

D 37   C 38

.203 M (8")

ROUTED COPY
REF. DWG. #40
FOR LAYOUT

.406 M (16")

STRUCTURAL STL.
TUBE FRAME
REF. DWG. #40

"J" BOX & ELECTRIC
CONDUIT BY
ELEC. CONTRACTOR

PAINT COLOR #3

CONCRETE
FOOTING DET. 1 / 5-10

ELEVATION   SECTION

Figure 94. A freestanding sign fabricated of several materials and lighted internally, as shown here, may require details to be shown at a larger scale on additional drawings.

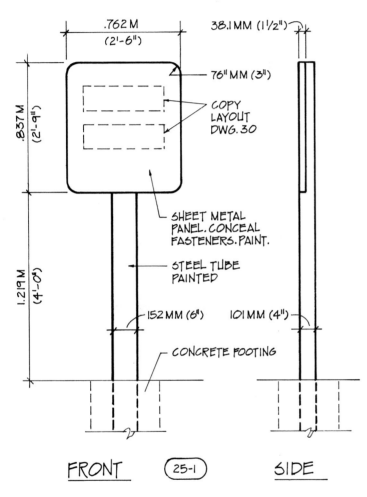

.762 M
(2'-6")

38.1 MM (1½")

76" MM (3")

COPY
LAYOUT
DWG. 30

.837 M
(2'-9")

SHEET METAL
PANEL. CONCEAL
FASTENERS. PAINT.

STEEL TUBE
PAINTED

1.219 M
(4'-0")

152 MM (6")   101 MM (4")

CONCRETE FOOTING

FRONT   (25-1)   SIDE

Figure 95. An example of the kind of drawing needed for a painted sign constructed of metal without interior illumination.

tion to the normal elevation, a section drawing is needed to show lighting, the thickness of the sign, and the relationship of various internal parts (Figure 96). Details should be added to indicate how metal and plastic connect and how the sign is anchored to a footing or attached to a building.

The Fabricator's Qualifications. It is possible to prepare drawings without considering the fabricator's qualifications. However, sign fabrication is a craft, not a science; it is largely custom work, dependent on the skills of individual craftsmen.

Although reputable fabricators can all be trusted to build signs which are strong and durable, there are often noticeable differences in the detailing and finishing of signs made by different fabricators. Some of the factors which cause these variations are

1. Shop practices—the typical details and techniques used in sign construction—vary from one shop to another.
2. One shop may have better craftsmen than another.
3. One shop may spend more time on hand-detailing and finishing than another.

The designer can control the first factor by carefully detailing the exterior appearance of signs on his working drawings. Otherwise, the fabricator will use his own standard shop details.

The second and third factors can be controlled to some extent by establishing standards of workmanship in the specifications and by proper supervision.

With this in mind, the designer must provide the fabricator with *all* information which in any way affects the design appearance. Design information has to be either on the drawings or in the specifications. Verbal instructions should be avoided except when there is insufficient time to produce adequate documents or when working on a unique item which has special problems, requiring verbal explanation.

Information can sometimes be shown schematically on the drawings, if fabrication is to be done by an unique and very skilled fabricator whose work is known by the designer. This fabricator can be depended upon to make signs which conform to his own standards of quality.

Fabricator's Contract Arrangements. Contracts between client and fabricator may be the result of competitive bidding or of a negotiated fee. Competitive bidding, especially for elaborate government projects, requires the designer to prepare completely detailed drawings and specifications for all sign items so that many different bidders will know exactly what is required of them. The bidding period is usually short (approximately two weeks), and there is no time for the designer to have discussions with each bidder to clarify design intent or discuss fabrication techniques.

By contrast, if a time and materials contract or negotiated fee is acceptable between fabricator and client, the designer can work out some details with the fabricator's help and then show them schematically on working drawings. This presumes that the fabricator is a trusted and skilled craftsman who will deliver a quality product within a predetermined budget. This method can save design time and reduce fees for the client and avoid the delays involved with bidding.

Even though time could be saved by eliminating shop drawings, they should always be provided by the fabricator regardless of the contract arrangement. These show exact construction details, which the designer can review and approve for all items. Shop drawings are the final word on fabrication and, once approved, supersede the designer's drawings.

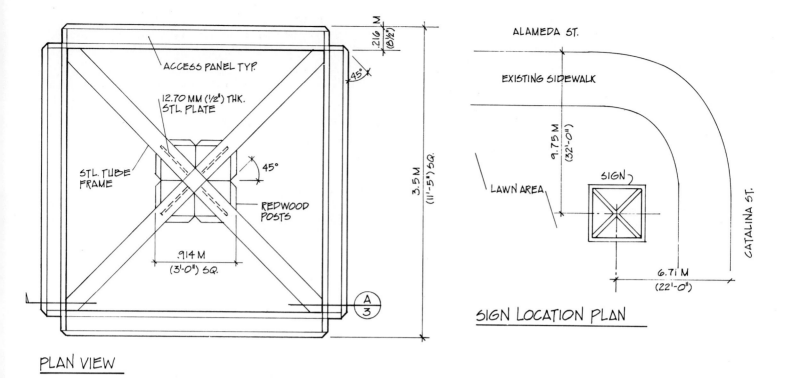

PLAN VIEW

ACCESS PANEL TYP.

12.70 MM (½") THK. STL. PLATE

STL. TUBE FRAME

REDWOOD POSTS

45°

45°

.914 M (3'-0") SQ.

.216 M (8½")

3.5 M (11'-5") SQ.

A/3

SIGN LOCATION PLAN

ALAMEDA ST.

EXISTING SIDEWALK

9.75 M (32'-0")

LAWN AREA

SIGN

6.71 M (22'-0")

CATALINA ST.

ELEVATION

ROUTED COPY. REF. DWG. 6

EQ.

EQ.

EQ.

D/10

1.37 M (4'-6")

EQ.

EQ.

EQ.

63.5 MM (2½")

SQ. POSTS LAMINATE OF REDWOOD

2.134 M (7'-0")

FOOTING DETAILS

B/11

SECTION

A/3

WELD TO .23M (8") SQ. STL. TUBE

12.70 MM (½") THK. STEEL PLATE

FLUORESCENT LAMPS. REF. SPECIFICATIONS

.080 ALUM. TYP. PAINTED

Figure 96. A drawing similar to this is usually required for a complex freestanding sign made of several materials, especially if it is internally illuminated. Copy layouts, footing details, and typical design details are often shown at larger scale on other drawings.

Of the two basic methods for selecting a fabricator, competitive bidding is by far the most used. This method, commonly used in architectural practice, is accepted by clients as the best way to control costs. Bidding procedures will be reviewed in greater detail later in this chapter.

Preparing Final Working Drawings

Sign systems for different projects vary greatly in size and complexity, and the final working drawings detailing those systems reflect that variety. However, there are basic elements which all well-prepared sets of sign drawings should contain. These are outlined as follows:

1. Sign plans. Based on architectural plans, these show the location of each sign.

2. An index of drawings on which each item is shown. The graphic schedule form as shown on page 34 in Chapter 4, Planning, can be adapted for this.

3. A complete, accurate listing of all copy wording to appear on the signs. This is also included on the graphic schedule.

4. A reproduction of the alphabet(s) and all symbols to be used in the sign system.

5. Elevations, sections, and details (similar to those shown in Figures 92 through 96) required to describe fully the design of each item.

6. Specifications which outline the fabricator's responsibilities and describe materials and processes to be used in the fabrication of signs. Typed specifications can be included on drawing sheets and bound with the set for a small project. They can be bound separately if very extensive.

Before discussing some of the above in greater detail, technical information about drawing materials is provided.

Format and Materials for Drawings. Drawing papers are available in many different sizes and qualities suitable for working drawings. Dietzgen 1000H is of excellent quality, but others are also satisfactory. Selecting the correct sheet size to fit the project is most important. In general, plan drawings require large sheets; elevations, sections, and details fit well on small sheets.

Imprinting Title Block Information. Borders and title block information can be preprinted on drawing sheets of most any size. Obviously the designer or firm name and address can be imprinted with little extra cost, along with the following basic information:

Date:	Drawn By:
Drawing No.	Checked By:
Project No.	Revisions:

Often designers include a paragraph prohibiting the use of any designs shown on the drawings without permission (Figure 97). It is difficult to know how much protection this affords, but it makes the designer feel better.

On large projects it is common practice to imprint the client or project name in the title block. For smaller jobs, various preprinted stick-on labels or rubber stamps can be used to identify the project.

Preparing Signing Plans from Architectural Plans. For most signing projects, existing architectural plans can be adapted for the designer's use. For exterior signing, he should use plans which show how the buildings are arranged on the site (Figure 98); for interior signing, floor plans must show the detailed arrangement of areas or rooms within buildings, including stairways, doors, elevators, fire hose cabinets, and so forth.

On older projects which have been extensively remodeled, it may be necessary to draw plans of the existing conditions because as-built plans are not available. The designer should hire a drafting service to do this time-consuming and dull drafting or ask the client to have this work done.

Available architectural plans are sometimes too large to work with. At other times it is necessary to piece together parts of several plans, making one large plan of the entire project area. If this composite plan is too large to fit on one sheet, reduced prints can be made using an 1860 Xerox machine or equivalent. This machine will reduce a drawing by the following percentages in one step without the use of a negative film: 95, 75, 62, 50, and 46 percent. The 50 percent reduction is recommended because it will result in reproductions of a usable scale: ¼-inch down to ⅛-inch (.6- to .3-millimeter) scale or ⅛-inch down to 1/16-inch (.3- to .2-millimeter) scale. This machine produces a translucent vellum Xerox which can be used for making blue-line prints or mounted on opaque board.

The Convenience of Small Drawings. Paper sizes for all working drawings except plans should be kept small. One sign item, or perhaps two, will fit neatly on 14 × 17-inch (35.6 × 43.2-millimeter) paper. A drawing set of this size combined with large plans is a practical convenience when bound separately from the plans. This eliminates constant flipping from plans to details by anyone who has to use the set.

Another advantage is that small sheets can be reduced to 8½ × 11-inch (26.3 × 27.9-millimeter) Xerox prints for filing or easy reference. Notes and dimensions on reduced sets are large enough to be read easily. Yet another advantage to small sheets is that the size of the set and drafting time needed to produce it can be more easily estimated, allowing for one or two sign items per sheet.

Locating Signs on Plans. Each design office will develop its own method of designating a sign item on the plan. For example, in this book each sign has an item number enclosed in a

All ideas, designs, arrangements, and plans indicated or represented by this drawing are owned by and the property of the designer, and were created, evolved, and developed for use on and in connection with the specified project. None of such ideas, designs, arrangements, or plans shall be used by or disclosed to any person, firm, or corporation for any purpose whatsoever without the written permission of the designer. Written dimensions on these drawings shall have precedence over scaled dimensions: contractors shall verify and be responsible for all dimensions and conditions on the job, and this office must be notified of any variations from the dimensions and conditions shown by these drawings. Shop details must be submitted to this office for approval before proceeding with fabrication.

Figure 97. A statement such as this can be reproduced in the title block of all design drawings to help protect the designer's work and limit his responsibilities.

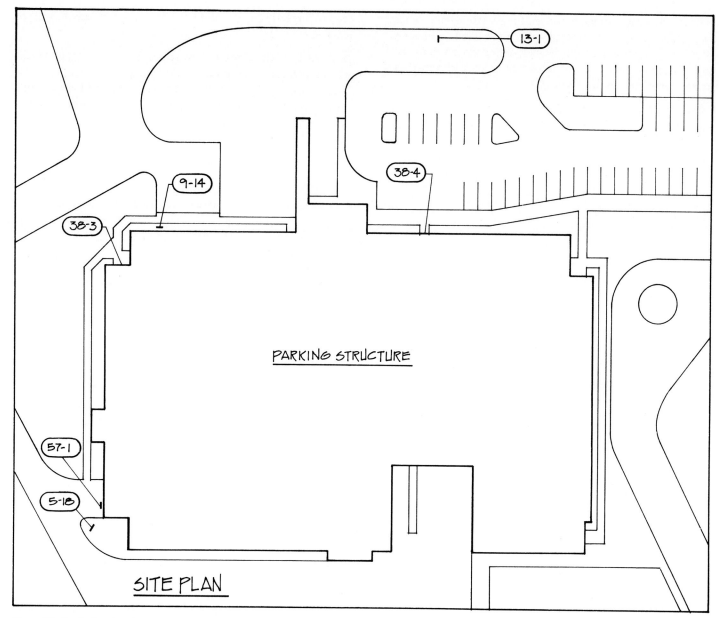

Figure 98. For indicating the general location of exterior signs, an architectural site plan showing buildings, walks, roads, and parking is normally utilized. Sign type item numbers are indicated here in lozenge shapes to make them easily identifiable.

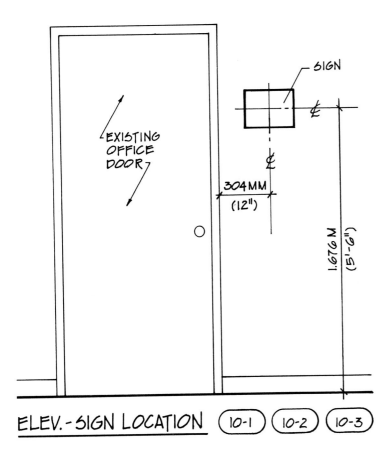

EXISTING
OFFICE
DOOR

SIGN

304MM
(12")

1.676 M
(5'-6")

ELEV.-SIGN LOCATION   10-1   10-2   10-3

Figure 99. Elevation drawings, such as this, can be used to indicate the specific location of interior signs.

lozenge shape, which is distinct from other drafting symbols. This shape is indicated on plan in the general area of the sign. Because of the scale of these plans, it is usually impractical to show the exact, dimensioned location of each sign. This is best accomplished by locating signs on elevations which scale 1/4 inch to 1 foot (Figure 99), where the dimensions from floor to ceiling and the horizontal dimension from some obvious architectural feature can be shown.

Even when dimensions have been shown, it is often necessary for the designer to coordinate this work with the installer, spotting exact locations on the job. Close coordination is particularly necessary where many signs are to be located in one small area.

Cross References Save Drafting Time. Given the problem of drafting a sign system, the inexperienced person tends to show an elevation of each sign separately on a sheet with the necessary notes and details grouped around it. He will soon discover that many of the signs within a system have similar edge details, supports, connections to the wall, and so forth. In other words, there are some details which are common to many different signs. These details, often called "typical," can be separated from elevation drawings and grouped together on a few sheets toward the rear of the set. Each should be given a separate cross reference number: for example, 1/101, where 1 is the detail number and 101 the sheet number. Cross referencing is done by indicating the reference number at the location on any sign elevation or section to which it applies and repeating it on the pertinent detail.

Cross referencing is also used on plans to designate the sign item or type number placed inside of a drafting symbol. The sign items are listed in a graphics schedule in front of the set, which contains the sheet numbers on which the sign item is drawn.

Indicating Copy Layouts. A sign of one design, which in this book is called a sign type, may require ten different copy messages. For example, a rectangular wall-mounted sign can be used for displaying the variety of directional and informational messages. The physical characteristics of the sign panel can be shown on one drawing. The ten copy layouts require only one other schematic drawing to show layout criteria (Figure 100). Since dimensions are given showing line placement, upper- and lowercase heights, there is no need to laboriously draw or trace individual words and letters. Drastically reducing the total amount of drafting, this technique presumes that one alphabet is used for most signs in the project. The project alphabet should be clearly reproduced and bound with the set of drawings. For detailed information about copy layouts, see Chapter 7, Typography.

Drawing Structural Items. Most freestanding signs require a support (post, standard, or base) and footings. The designer will determine the size and shape of these items to satisfy both esthetic and practical requirements during design development work. The draftsman shows exterior conformation of the support in sufficient detail and with dimensions to control design only; no internal construction is necessary. Just how much detail to show is often difficult to decide. Obviously if the designer wants to make a feature of fasteners or hardware connecting a sign panel to a post, these must be drawn or noted. If a joint or quirk between two elements or materials is a feature of the design, it must be detailed and dimensioned or at least noted.

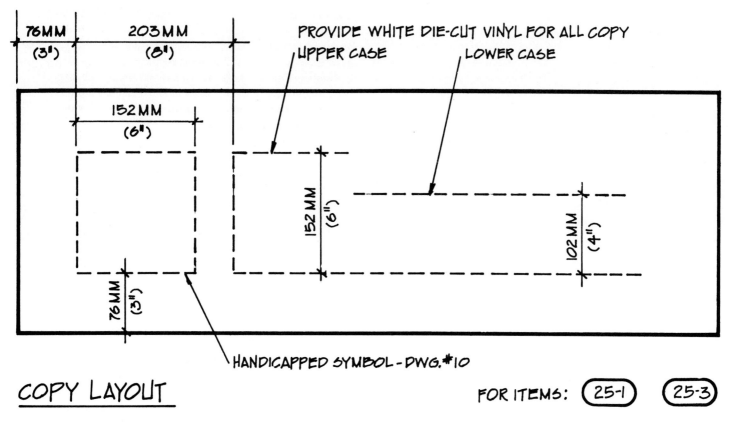

COPY LAYOUT

FOR ITEMS: (25-1) (25-3)

Figure 100. Copy layout drawings, such as this one, can be used to show criteria for size and placement of copy for many sign items.

Indicating Footings and Foundations. A footing and foundation is a mass of concrete, usually below ground level, which supports the signpost (see Figure 94). The extent of a concrete footing should be shown schematically, leaving the fabricator to show the final details on his shop drawings.

Notes on the Drawings

No drawing is complete without the specification of materials. The most basic method of specifying materials for a sign is by hand-lettering this information directly on the drawings. Hand-lettering is very time consuming, and because the same notes are often repeated on many sheets, they should be kept as short as possible. Use general terms and abbreviations whenever possible because the written specifications will cover the information in much greater detail. Examples of notes and related specifications are shown in Figure 101.

Types of Specifications

While architects are very well informed about specifications, few graphic designers know anything about this discipline.

Note on Drawing	Related Specification
18 ga steel	All 18 gauge steel shall be stretcher-leveled cold-rolled steel with factory-applied prime coat
Natural hardwood	All natural hardwood shall be American white oak, plain sawn, with a clear Rez finish
Plywood	Plywood shall be exterior grade ¾-inch (1.9-millimeter) thick fir plywood. Fill edges flush with waterproof filler and sand smooth

Figure 101.

Specifications are the formal way of providing verbal information which cannot be conveniently noted on the drawings.

In the field of signing, specifications can be thought of as all the written information and instruction which supplement and clarify the drawings. The specific content of specifications, their length, and complexity will depend on several factors: the nature of the design; how much information has been noted on the drawings; how many materials are involved in the designs; the number of sign types in the system being documented.

Outline Specifications. For the smallest jobs, involving a few sign types, concise specifications can be typed or hand-lettered on the drawings. Basically, outline specifications consist of a typed list of general notes supplemented by specific information noted on the drawings:

General Notes. The contractor shall be responsible for the quality of all materials and workmanship required for the execution of this contract including the materials and workmanship of any firms or individuals who act as his subcontractors. Contractor shall be responsible for providing subcontractors with complete and up-to-date drawings, specifications, graphic schedule, and other information issued by the designer.

Written dimensions on the drawings shall have precedence over scaled dimensions. Contractors shall verify and be responsible for all dimensions and conditions shown by these drawings. Shop details must be submitted to this office for approval before proceeding with fabrication.

Details shown on the drawings shall be followed for exterior appearance. Contractor may change interior construction shown on these details to conform with his shop practices.

Designer shall be notified of any discrepancies in the drawings or graphic schedule, in field dimensions or conditions, and/or changes required in construction details.

Copy, quantities, and references shown on the graphics schedule shall have precedence over drawings.

Location of signs: the locations shown on the plan drawings are for general information only. The fabricator is to arrange a meeting with designer at the site for final location of sign elements. All signs are to be located in one day with the use of numbered stakes tagged with correct item numbers.

Designer retains full rights to all designs shown or specified herein (refer to the statement of ownership in the title block on each drawing).

Designer hereby grants the contractor the limited right to fabricate designs herein for the sole purpose of completing his current contract. He may not manufacture, reproduce, or exhibit these designs or modify them for any other purpose without the written approval of designer.

Notes on the drawing should include:

1. A technical description of materials from which the item is to be made
2. A description of special fabricating techniques, if any, to be used
3. A description of the materials and processes for applying sign copy and paint or other finish
4. Notes covering installation of the sign

Complete Specifications. While the specifications for each signing project should be written specifically for that project, all specifications for large projects have similar sections which are outlined as follows:

1. General requirements. This section explains the responsibilities of the fabricator in general terms, covering such areas as:
    a. Scope: a description and listing of signs to be built and services to be provided
    b. Applicable documents: a listing of all drawings and pertinent documents
    c. Submittals: a listing of shop drawings, paint, and other samples
    d. Permits: code requirement permits obtained by the fabricator
    e. Engineering: engineer responsibility is assigned to the fabricator
    f. Guarantee: terms of guarantee to be provided by the fabricator
2. Materials and products
    a. General requirements: quality of materials
    b. Materials and products: alphabetical listing of all materials and manufactured products
    c. Listing of all hardware items
    d. Paint and finish materials
3. Execution
    a. Conditions (for example, skill of labor)
    b. Fabrication of metal items
    c. Fabrication of wood items
    d. Special items (for instance, plastic or glass)
    e. Painting, finishing, and plating application
    f. Methods for applying copy
4. Installation

Architectural and Sign Specifications Combined. At times the graphic designer acts as a consultant to an architectural firm on a large project. In this case sign specifications can often be included as a section of existing architectural specification for the project. The designer can usually get help from the architect's specifications writer, particularly with the content of general requirements as outlined above, for issuance with the architectural specifications.

Specifications for Governmental Jobs. Sign projects designed for local, state, or federal agencies usually require the most comprehensive specifications of all. While the general content of the sign specifications will include information similar to that outlined above, each agency may require different forms or format. It is best to get advice from appropriate technical people within the agency before proceeding.

Production of Final Art

It is seldom necessary for the designer to produce final or finished art for sign systems. Instead, he provides criteria in the form of copy layouts as part of the working drawings which also include a reproduction of the project alphabet.

Using this criteria as a guide, the fabricator produces full-size photo negatives or other material necessary to reproduce the copy.

If the designer has specified copy to be photo silk-screened, for example, photo screens will be prepared for the designer's inspection. If the copy is to be die cut vinyl letters, then these letters will be cut and applied to spacing tapes before they are actually applied to the sign panels. Each different method of copy application can be inspected by the designer prior to fabrication.

There are, of course, special items like directory maps which the designer develops for the project. If the fabricator does not have the facilities to make final art from design layouts or sketches, the designer should provide camera-ready art at about half (1/2) size. Maps of this kind may involve three or four flat colors and are often silk-screened; art should be prepared to facilitate making separate photo screens for each color.

BIDDING PROCEDURES

Client Review

After all working drawings and specifications have been completed and checked, they should be thoroughly reviewed with the client. This should not be a rubber stamp affair, but rather a working meeting to make last minute changes and to be certain that the client understands all aspects of the system.

Competitive versus Negotiated Bidding

Invariably, there will be questions about competitive versus negotiated bids. Large governmental and most private clients will insist on competitive bidding; in many cases this is required by law.

The process of competitive sign bidding involves from 2 to 10 qualified fabricators. All fabricators are given a fixed time period (usually 10 to 14 days) to figure their costs to fabricate and install all signs included in a specific set of drawings and specifications. All submit written quotations to the designer, who compares costs and recommends one to do the work.

Negotiated bidding usually involves one or two fabricators who submit estimates of their costs to do the work on a time-and-materials basis.

Selecting Competent Bidders

If the designer is experienced, he will have developed several lists of bidders to recommend for certain kinds of jobs. The client may also have had experience with fabricators and may be able to make suggestions. If any of the bidders are unknown to the designer, he should see both the fabricator's work and his shop facilities.

It is usually unnecessary to have more than three bidders, providing all produce work of equal quality. Fabricators who do work of low quality often submit low bids because they skimp on time-consuming finish work. Or they may not have the knowledge or skilled people required to produce quality work.

Invitation to Bid. If the sign system has to be built quickly, it is wise to ask all potential bidders if they have shop time available. Shop workloads can vary greatly. At one time a fabricator may be too busy to figure a job, while at another he may bid low because his shop needs work.

Issuing Bid Documents. Bid documents should go to all bidders along with a covering letter. The letter should include the following:

1. The bid period or the time when the fabricator's bid proposal is to be received. Usually 10 days to 2 weeks are allowed for bidding.
2. The project name and job site address.
3. Names and addresses of client and designer representatives. Duplicate copies of the bid proposal should go to each.
4. Date when the installation of the sign system must be completed.
5. Time schedules, if the system is to be installed in phases.
6. Special payment schedules, if any.
7. List of all item prices by sign type.
8. Applicable taxes and delivery charges.

Changes during Bidding. Errors or inconsistencies may be discovered in the documents during bidding. A written notice or addendum should be issued by the designer to all bidders before the end of the bid period so that all can adjust their bids accordingly.

Reviewing Bids with Client

After the designer has analyzed the bids for errors or discrepancies, he should review them with the client and make his recommendations. The low bidder should not always be awarded the contract, although for government work this may be required. If the low bid is very much lower than others, it may indicate that the bidder has overlooked items or figured too low. However, he may have cut his profit because he wants the work, or his overhead may be lower than his competitors. Frequently, small quality shops can bid lower than large shops because they are more efficient. All these factors must be considered in making a final recommendation.

Negotiated Bidding to Reduce Costs

At times, all bids exceed the client's budget. Unless the designer can suggest cost-saving changes, he may have to go back to the drawing board and redesign. If overages are small, one bidder may be willing to negotiate, with changes being made in materials or techniques. These can lower costs without substantially affecting the design intent. If the overage is more than 5 to 10 percent, then some items may have to be eliminated or drastically redesigned.

Client-Fabricator Contracts

Most clients have a contract or purchasing department which can help in awarding the contract. The bid proposal, when signed by both parties, will become part of the agreement, along with the working drawings and specifications. Public liability insurance, bonding requirements, and payment schedules are usually arranged without the designer's involvement.

12
Fabrication

This chapter contains detailed information about the most commonly used sign materials and techniques, many of which are illustrated. But because of the primary importance of the fabricator, the chapter begins with a general explanation of his role in the process.

THE FABRICATOR'S ROLE

While some large sign fabricators have design capabilities, few graphic designers are also fabricators. There are the rare designer-craftsmen who work in carved wood or with other specialized materials or techniques. But for the most part designers of signing systems must depend upon sign fabricators or contractors to build and install these systems.

Most custom signs are fabricated in job shops rather than in large production-oriented plants. Consequently, the individual craftsmen are key elements in the overall process. The skill and knowledge of fabricator/contractors is based on years of diverse shop and field experience. Many have grown up in a business which may have been in the family for several generations.

The designer should become familiar with the various sign fabricator/contractors in his area. The Society of Environmental Graphic Designers (SEGD) in Chicago has published a list of recommended fabricators located throughout the United States. This information should be especially helpful to designers interested in architecturally integrated signing. A sign system based on this approach may involve many different types of materials and methods, and it may require as many different fabricators to build it.

Kinds of Fabricators

It is difficult to classify sign fabricators into neat groups because there are so many crafts related to signing and so many methods of building signs. However, it is useful to discuss the various types of fabricators, even though there is not always a convenient label to distinguish one from the other:

1. General Sign Contractor (GSC). Whether small or large, the general sign contractor is usually quite rare. Having a broad knowledge of many techniques, this firm can handle a job of any size or complexity. It builds in-house what it can do most efficiently and jobs out the rest to well-qualified subcontractors whose work it supervises. The special value of general sign contractors lies in their flexibility, broad experience, and ability as coordinators. They are responsible for scheduling and supervising the work of subcontractors so that the entire sign system is built well and installed on time.

2. Custom Sign Fabricator. The custom sign fabricator can usually make signs of wood, metal, or plastic using a variety of techniques. It often concentrates on nonilluminated signs.

3. Electric Sign Manufacturer. An electric sign manufacturer may be a member of the National Electric Sign Exchange and often specializes in the fabrication of illuminated signs. It builds custom signs or limited production runs of signs for chain store outlets, banks, markets, and the like. This kind of firm can act as GSC in some cases.

4. Standard Sign Manufacturer. The standard sign manufacturer produces signs, letters, directories, or other cataloged items in quantity. It usually concentrates on small interior items and can produce custom variations of cataloged items if quantities are involved.

5. Technical Specialists. The technical specialists' category includes subcontractors who are very skilled in one material or technique, such as:

metal casting	silk screening
engraving	plastic forming
stone carving	concrete casting

They are not limited to producing sign items.

6. Artisan/Craftsman. The artisan/craftsman includes, among other specialists, wood carvers who specialize in making signs; stone carvers who specialize in incised letter work; or craftsmen who fabricate stained glass signs.

7. Sign Painter. Sign painters vary greatly both in the kinds of signs they paint and in their skill. Some paint small signs on store windows, while others specialize in executing huge signs on the sides of buildings. This group is important to the designer as a source of temporary and hand-painted signs.

8. Wall Graphics Painter. A relatively small group of craftsmen, wall graphics painters, specialize in painting hard-edged supergraphics, involving flat areas of color. They do not design, but enlarge the designer's original layout. Their reputation is spread by word of mouth, but the GSC should be able to recommend one or two.

Few sign fabricators can bid effectively on a complex sign system utilizing many materials unless they are GSC. There is no such listing in the telephone directory; the designer must find such a contractor himself or through SEGD.

A list of qualified fabricators is especially important during the bidding process, explained in Chapter 11, Documentation and Bidding. At least three fabricators are needed to bid in most situations. The ideal situation would be to find three fabricators of equal quality, all of whom could make all the signs within their own plant, but this is rarely possible. Several types of fabricators listed above may be capable of coordinating the system if it is limited in variety of materials and techniques.

Qualifications of a Fabricator

The firm to be given the responsibility of overall coordination should have prior experience related to the sign system to be fabricated. If, for example, many of the items are exterior signs requiring illumination, then type 1 and type 3 fabricators should be asked to bid. However, if most items are small interior signs, which could easily be adapted to the fabricator's existing techniques, then the list of bidders could be composed of type 2 or 4 fabricators. In general the designer's task of coordination is simplified during fabrication if he can work with only one fabricator rather than several.

In addition to having the prior experience outlined above, any fabricator who coordinates the entire job should meet the following qualifications:

1. Can read working drawings.
2. Can understand and follow specifications.
3. Understands designer's needs in terms of: ordering and enlarging typography and artwork; preparation of lettering guides or patterns to show exact size, spacing, and placement of copy; color matching samples; prototype samples and material submittals.
4. Can produce detailed shop drawings and understands submittal and approval processes.
5. Works well with designers and is good at translating his designs into practical signs, which are durable.
6. Works with a group of well-qualified subcontractors.
7. Stands behind his work and that of his subcontractors and makes corrections when required.
8. Can deliver signs on time if the time available is reasonable.
9. Can offer a consulting service to designers when needed.
10. Has adequate financial backing and follows good business practice.

Fabricator Responsibilities

During the fabrication phase of a project the fabricator provides certain services as he interacts with the designer. The following is an outline of basic steps that he follows in the fabrication process:

1. The fabricator reviews the designer's drawings and specifications to become thoroughly familiar with the sign system.
2. He submits a bid—an itemized list showing the costs to provide and install all items. Made out to the client, this bid is usually submitted to the designer for his review.
3. When awarded the contract, the fabricator prepares shop drawings (full size details and scale drawings) for designer's approval, which are based on designer's working drawings and specifications.
4. He surveys conditions of the project, if existing, to determine any problem of interference with the installation and operation of the signs.

5. He coordinates electrical, structural, or installation requirements with the general building contractor and informs the designer of any problems needing his attention.
6. If requested in bid documents, he produces prototype samples of certain items.
7. After receiving approved shop drawings from the designer, he proceeds with fabrication of the approved items.
8. The fabricator provides all labor and material to make and completely finish all signs.
9. During fabrication, he informs the designer when items are ready for inspection prior to being installed.
10. After obtaining the designer's approval of fabricated items, he arranges for their installation.
11. During installation he calls the designer for periodic inspection of the installed signs.
12. The fabricator makes any final corrections or adjustments based on a checklist submitted by the designer's supervisor.
13. If additional items are needed to improve functioning of the system, the fabricator provides these at reasonable additional cost.

MATERIALS AND TECHNIQUES

Graphic designers entering the field of signing design will soon realize that there are many ways to fabricate even the simplest of signs. By becoming thoroughly familiar with the basic materials and techniques, they will be able to select and specify ones best suited to a particular sign system. Only good design judgment is needed to select materials which are suitable esthetically; but to select those which function well in terms of durability, workability, and cost requires both knowledge and experience. Knowledge can be acquired by reading technical books, magazines, and manuals, such as those in the Selected Readings. Experience is probably a more useful source of knowledge; but direct personal experience is acquired slowly, often based on years of exposure to materials. The young designer has to rely on the experience of fabricators, materials salesmen, and technical specialists for much of the technical information he needs. However, he should retain a certain intelligent skepticism about word-of-mouth information. By talking to several technical salesmen about a new plastic, for example, he can soon determine if there is basic agreement concerning its performance characteristics.

Techniques are the processes or methods utilized in fabricating an object. It is important to realize that most custom-made signs involve methods requiring hand labor; the machines involved, however complex, are merely tools that assist the skilled craftsman. Because good craftsmen are paid a high wage, the more quickly a sign can be fabricated, the less expensive, in general, it will be. When designing low-budget jobs, the designer must utilize techniques which are relatively labor efficient and therefore low in cost.

The following discussion of materials and techniques has been excerpted from the *Environmental Graphics Sourcebook*, Part One, published by the Society of Environmental Graphics Designers.

Adhesive Film

Adhesive films are herein defined as extremely thin vinyl or plastic films with adhesive backings that can provide either permanent or removable messages. Both types are normally pressure sensitive, although other forms of adhesives are available.

A third type of adhesive film is reflectorized vinyl sheeting. Its adhesive is generally of the permanent type, and it will also withstand severe weather and handling conditions. Bonded in the plastic sheet are millions of microscopic glass beads, each one of which is an optically perfect reflex reflector that bounces incoming light directly back to its source with glareless brilliance. It provides effective reflection at severe angles and performs well under the heaviest rain conditions. Normally used for traffic control devices, there is a limited variety of other applications for signs that will be seen by motorists. This expensive material is not recommended unless it will be seen by motorists, as its effectiveness is limited to situations where strong light sources are beamed directly at it. It is used either for a background—with dead, nonreflective letters—or for letters only—with a dead, nonreflective background. Do not use for both letters and background. Once applied this material cannot be removed except by sanding or grinding.

Prespaced Messages. Die-cut messages are available as individual letters or as complete prespaced and prealigned legends. Individual letters cost about half of prespaced letters. Some companies furnish individual letters on a spacing and alignment carrier which gives in effect prespaced messages for the cost of unspaced, though handwork is still required.

Prespaced messages are furnished with tight, normal, or wide letterspacing per customer specification.

Transfers. Transfer letters are letters printed in vinyl inks on the back of a carrier sheet. The individual letters are then optically spaced and rubbed onto the sign surface by burnishing. Recommended use is for interior signs with protection from vandalism. Such protection can be a plastic frame, cover, or overcoating recommended by the manufacturer. Such coatings, however, are lacquer based and therefore susceptible to yellowing. Also, application of the coating can cause overspray in unwanted areas and cannot be masked over the individual letters. The background between letters and within negative spaces of the letters will appear darker.

Transfer letters can be purchased as stock items through any art supply company, and custom alphabets can be obtained from several sources with delivery times ranging from a few days to several months (from overseas manufacturers).

Decals. *Decals*, or self-adhesive markings, are a common method of applying printing to various surfaces which would otherwise not be receptive to a printing process. They are simple, one-step applications and avoid extraneous operations such as painting, riveting, or stenciling. They may, of course, be used in conjunction with these processes.

Decals are used for many sign requirements ranging from small-scale signs to identification of fleets, oil trucks, or airplanes. The two major categories of decals are pressure-sensitive and water-activated markings.

Photographic Film

Photographic film technology has only recently been used in signage. In its negative film forms, the technology requires special frames or carriers to hold the finished product. This also holds true in its positive paper forms, although this finished product may be adhered directly to any surface. Negative forms are clear or white images on a black film or paper background. Positive forms are black images on clear film or white paper.

Positive Processes. Processing equipment is, of course, necessary to produce the negative form, and a darkroom is necessary to produce finished positive forms from those negatives. In addition, products are available that produce messages on a paper strip in a one-step process. Alphabets are available on disks or filmstrips and are exposed onto paper or film, character by character. The strips can be used right off the machine or can be pasted up for a negative to be made from the copy camera.

Illumination. Illumination of negative form messages in a carrier is accomplished by fluorescent lamps located in a housing behind the negative sandwich. This sandwich consists, from front to back, of a clear or tinted protective face (glass or plastic), the negative film, and a translucent white backup sheet to tightly compress the negative. The distance between lamps, which should run the length of the sign, must equal the distance from the lamp to the white backup sheet.

Plastics

Types. Plastics have chemical names, generic names, and brand names. For example, acrylics—chemically speaking—are made of methylmethacrylate polymers. "Acrylic" is a generic term, and "Plexiglas" is a brand name. This section is not concerned with chemical names. Plastics, particularly acrylics and laminated plastics, are the most widely used materials for sign production.

Plastics, however, are sensitive to temperature change. Expansion and contraction allowance in the ratio of 3/16 inch (.5 millimeters) for every 4 feet (1.4 meters) is permitted by catching the sheet edge in a metal frame, allowing the face to breathe without restraint. Bolting or other inflexible fastening which does not provide for this expansion, may result in sign breakage. Large, flat, horizontally installed sheets will become deformed under continuous pressure from snow, ice, water, or their own weight. Because of different expansion coefficients, plastics bonded to other materials—such as metals—will pop off in extreme temperatures.

There are 9 types of plastic suitable for use in signage: *acrylics, acrylic-polyvinyl chlorides, polyvinyl chlorides (PVC), polycarbonates, butyrates, styrenes, polypropylenes, fiber-reinforced polyester (FRP)*, and *FRP-Nylon*. All other plastics are suitable only for packaging furniture, and other consumer purposes. Four types will be discussed here:

Acrylics. Acrylic plastics can be colorless, combining the transparency of glass with lighter weight and greater resistance to breakage, or colored to be opaque or semiopaque. Opaques maintain the most intense and even color quality and are used particularly in lighted signs to hide the light source. Acrylics have good resistance to weather and little fading from exposure to sunlight. They can be heated to conform to almost any shape and can be sawed, drilled, and machined like a soft metal. Acrylics have a generally low-impact strength, shattering easily, and a fragile surface that is easily defaced. It also tends to build up static electricity that accumulates dust and dirt particles to its surface. Some manufacturers of acrylic sheeting provide special hardcoatings that eliminate this static electricity. The appropriate paints, when properly applied, fuse with the surface and become integral with it. Surfaces can be ordered in gloss or matte.

There is a higher-impact acrylic called DR, which is modified to produce a tempered hardness that falls between acrylics and polycarbonates.

Acrylic sheeting is the most commonly used material for internally illuminated signs. Although sign fabricators have—over the years—developed an almost limitless repertoire of ingenious applications and uses, the normal method is to fuse letters cut with a band saw from opaque or translucent acrylic sheet 1/8 inch (.3 millimeters) thick to another translucent sheet. Alternately, the background may be opaque and the letters translucent. Care must be taken to ensure evenness of illumination of acrylic signfaces.

Polycarbonates. Generally speaking, polycarbonates have the properties of acrylic together with the enormous advantage of being virtually shatterproof. Even a bullet will pass through leaving only a burnt hole, with no shattering. In thicker sheets, a bullet cannot pass.

It comes in clear and a limited range of colors. Being shatterproof, it is useful for illuminated signs in locations where there has been a high evidence of vandalism.

Butyrates. Butyrate plastic is optically clear, impact resistant, and very easily formable. It is available in a limited range of translucent and transparent colors. Its deep-draw and durability properties make it especially adaptable for vacuum forming. Thicknesses range from .060 to .250 inches (.2 to .6 millimeters) for standard sheet and roll sizes.

Fiber-Reinforced Polyesters (FRP). The popular name for FRP is fiberglass. It is made from polyester resins impregnated with chopped glass fibers. It has visible texture and grain which, especially with a paint coating, can give it a somewhat wavy appearance. It is a high-impact material with light-diffusing ability. A light source held relatively close to the surface will not show a hot spot on the other side, for example, although its ability to transmit light is inferior to acrylic.

Vacuum Forming of Plastics. Vacuum forming is a process based upon air pressure differentials. Heated plastic is clamped directly to the edges of a female form and sucked into a mold by air pressure. It can be stretched to various sizes, depending on the thickness of the sheet and the amount of heat applied. Vacuum forming is used especially for large signs, as it tends to give greater strength and durability to the form. It also can be used for individual letter forms. Vacuum-formed letters have fairly round edges.

Molding. The process of molding is very similar to vacuum forming and is sometimes used in conjunction with it for more precise definition. A heated sheet of plastic is placed between male and female dies and pressed into a form. This method, though expensive, allows for good detail because two dies are used.

Engraving. Two-color laminated plastic (ES or "engraving sandwich") is generally used for engraving. The image is cut through the first color exposing the second and allowing the first to become the background. This process is more permanent than painting an engraved area. Engraving is most frequently used for small identification signs, and the corners of the letters are only as sharp as the engraving master and the size of the router will permit.

Sand-Blasting. For large signs, an image is sand-blasted through a rubber stencil laid on top of the plastic.

Casting. Casting is a cheap, fast process used to produce small letters in mass quantities. A silicone rubber mold is filled with polyester and allowed to cure. These letters are used primarily for bulletin boards, and range in size from 1/4 to 18 inches (.6 to 457 millimeters).

Embedding. Plastics, usually fiberglass, with embedded messages is a relatively new development. Messages can be on a substrate—usually silk-screened paper or vinyl letters—flooded with polyester resin. They can also be integral, requiring subsurface printing using a polyester resin ink system and a .015-inch (.4 millimeter) minimum thickness polyester gel coat as the background color. Ultraviolet inhibitors are incorporated into the sign materials to produce maximum color stability, and the sign is reinforced with chopped glass fiber strands. The resulting panels are often sandwiched over a core material of honeycomb cardboard, plywood, or high-density polyurethane foam. Cardboard must be completely enclosed or it will deteriorate and the FRP signface will warp.

Framing and Mounting of Individual Letters. A vacuum-formed letter cut with a lip can be inserted in a metal or plastic frame or can be mounted on canvas, metal, or plastic backgrounds. Large sawed letters can be glued (though not totally weather-proofed) or fused with ethylene dichloride to another plastic. This fusing process is only applicable between acrylic plastics or mylar.

Stick-on Letters. Either vacuum-formed or sawed letters can have pressure sensitive adhesive on the back. They adhere best to smooth, hard, nonporous surfaces and are not intended for use where a permanent bond is necessary, such as outdoors.

Magnetized Letters. Made of magnetic plastic, magnetized letters will adhere to any ferrous metal surface. They must be custom-painted.

Clip-on Letters. Clips are attached to the back of molded plastic letters. They can be made and used in a number of different ways: with tacked-on runners, placed directly on a corrugated plastic background, or pressed into the grooved backing of a bulletin board (cast letterforms are generally used for bulletin or menu boards).

Colors and Finishes. Multicolored plastic signs can be made using spray paint, silk-screen, or pigmented plastic. In hand painting, the paint (acrylic lacquer) is always applied to the back of the sign to ensure greater protection from weathering or normal abuse.

Spray Painting (Cut and Spray). A clear sheet of plastic is sprayed with a thin water-soluble rubber film or paper-masking material, which is then cut away (similar to a stencil) exposing the area to be painted. After the image is completed and all masking is removed, a fine coat of white paint is sprayed over the back of the entire sign to intensify the colors.

Silk-Screening. An image is silk-screened to a clear sheet of plastic, then sprayed from the back with another color to supply the background as well as to protect the first color. Painting can be done before or after the forming process. If paint is applied before forming, it becomes partially fused to the plastic and produces a permanent coloration.

A matte finish applied to plastic will reduce problems of glare and reflection; clear plastic remains transparent after application. These finishes will, however, cause copy to be fuzzed and not sharp on the reverse side of plastics of 1/8-inch (.3-millimeter) thickness or more.

Plastic Laminates. Used for interior signs, plastic laminates are generally bonded to such core materials as plywood, particle board, flake board, or metal. They are manufactured in different grades for both horizontal and vertical surfaces. They are manufactured by pressing melamine resin-impregnated overlay paper and a melamine-impregnated pattern paper over layers of phenolic-impregnated kraft paper at pressures approximating 1,000 lbs per square inch (70 kilograms per square centimeter) at temperatures in excess of 275°F (135°C). The back is sanded to maintain a uniform thickness and to facilitate bonding. A great variety of colors is available, as well as gloss, semigloss, matte, sculptured, and embossed finishes. Use for interior signs only.

Wood

Wood is one of the oldest and most common sign materials. Its lasting qualities vary according to location: woods in humid areas require special preservation treatment. Wood must, in any case, be specially treated or coated to begin to approach the effective outdoor life of other materials. These treatments, coupled with higher timber costs, make wooden signs competitive with other materials, and even higher in some cases.

Generally, the best woods for use in sign construction are those that are typically used in exterior architectural construction which have higher decay resistance. Because of the price, more exotic woods with pronounced grain patterns are best for interior use as decorative wall panels.

Types

Cypress. A closed-grained wood with a slightly red to yellowish-brown natural color, cypress is not generally available as plywood, and the maximum practical size limitations of lumber are 1 3/4-inch (4.4-centimeter) thicknesses, 9 1/2-inch (24.2-centimeter) widths and 16-foot (4.9-meter) lengths. Cypress has medium hardness and medium to high dimensional stability. It receives finishes well. Because of its long-lasting characteristics, it is very popular in the construction industry, and is therefore in short supply.

Douglas Fir. A closed-grain wood with a reddish tan color, fir is available in two grains: flat and vertical. The vertical grain is more expensive, but has better stability than the flat grain which tends to splinter and raise. Consequently, vertical grain is a little harder to find. Matching plywood is available in both grains. The maximum practical size limitations of fir lumber are 2 3/4-inch (7-centimeter) thicknesses, 11-inch (27.9-centimeter) widths, and 16-foot (5-meter) lengths. It is a soft wood with fair to good finishing characteristics and dimensional stability.

Mahogany. Only a few types of mahogany are suitable for exterior use. Lauan or light Philippine softwood mahogany is light to reddish brown in color, open-grained, more expensive than pine, cypress, or fir, and has fair finishing characteristics and stability. Maximum practical size limitations are 1 3/4-inch thickness, 11-inch widths, and 16-foot lengths. Matching plywood is generally available.

Oak. White oak, plain-sawn, is a grayish-tan open-grained hardwood available in a wide range of grain patterns and colors. Comparable in cost to African mahogany, it has excellent finishing characteristics for transparent rather than opaque coatings and is generally available in matching plywood. Practical size limitations are 1 5/8-inch (4.1-centimeter) thicknesses, 7 1/2-inch (19.1-centimeter) widths, and 12-foot (3.6-meter) lengths. It has poor dimensional stability, requiring expansion joints.

Pine. All pines are closed-grain soft woods that, like Douglas fir, are inexpensive and readily available. Pine plywood is generally not available, except for Ponderosa, the most widely used pine. All pines share the same practical size limitations: 2 3/4-inch thicknesses, 11-inch widths, and 16-foot lengths. They also share good to excellent finishing characteristics and medium dimensional stability.

Red Cedar. Also known as western cedar, red cedar is a soft, closed-grain wood of light to dark red color. It is economical, comparing in price to pine, and has high natural decay resistance. It has good finishing and dimensional stability characteristics. Practical size limitations are 1 5/8-inch thicknesses, 11-inch widths, and 16-foot lengths. Cedar plywood is difficult to find, and the lumber has limited availability. Cedar is one of the top three woods suitable for signs.

Redwood. Redwood is available under two grades: All-Heartwood which is highly resistant to termites and decay, and sapwood-containing. All redwood is closed-grain, deep red in color, moderate in price, and available readily in practical size limitations of 2 3/4 × 11 inches × 20 feet. It is a superior wood for exterior signage construction. Its tendency to weather check is inconspicuous, it has minimal tendency to cup and pull nails loose, it has high-dimensional stability, and it accepts paints and coatings of the widest range while giving good service.

Without benefit of special coatings, the two best woods are redwood and tidewater red cypress. They are the only two woods in the United States that are available in commercial quantities that are high in decay resistance and termite resistance. Red cedar is also an excellent wood.

Handcarving/Routing. Messages on wooden signs may be directly chiseled by hand or cut by routing machines which may either be controlled by hand or by a stencil. Stencil-cut letters are made with a pantograph machine, by which a stylus is made to conform to the outline of the small letters of the stencil. The pantograph mechanically transfers these small motions into larger identical motions which guide a router that cuts the wood. There are size limitations on these machines of approximately 3-inch (7.6-centimeter) maximum letter sizes on approximately 24-inch (61-centimeter) wide wooden surfaces.

Sand-Blasting. Messages may be sand-blasted into wooden signs by covering the surface with a rubber masking material, cutting out the characters, and blasting with a fine sand. The depth of the letters is determined by the softness of the wood and the length of time the sand can be sprayed before it eats through the rubber and destroys the surface. Sand-blasting is only recommended for woods that have a very even grain, like redwood, or else the surface will splinter and edges will be uneven. Size is not a limitation with sand-blasting.

Laminating. The most common laminated wood product for signage is plywood.

Standard Plywood. Made from any of the woods described above, standard plywood is most commonly made from exterior fir. Care must be taken to prepare plywood for use as a sign-face by filling and sealing all flaws and edges before applying the finish coats. Exposed edges, especially upper edges, should be weather-protected to prevent the wood from warping and delaminating.

Medium Density Overlay (MDO) Plywood. MDO plywood differs from standard plywood in that a layer of phenolic resin-impregnated fiber sheet is bonded to both its sides. This covering eliminates the grain of the wood and effectively seals both major surfaces of the panel. Edges are still unprotected and must be filled and sealed. The principal use for MDO is for highway signs where its durability has been amply proven. There is also a High Density Overlay (HDO) that may still be available, but is extremely difficult to find.

Metal-Clad Plywood. Although metal-clad plywood can be obtained on a more-or-less custom basis, some forms are stock items with lumber companies. This product is made by laminating aluminum, steel, or whatever material is specified to the two major surfaces of the sign. In stock forms, smooth or pebble-surfaced aluminums are most common. The sheets can be cut to the desired size, but the edges are always exposed and must be filled and sealed. Cladding is available on one or both sides.

Metals

Types. Metal is an extremely versatile material for sign fabrication. It is very durable and may be fabricated in a wide diversity of methods.

Steel. Steel is a very satisfactory material for signfaces that do not need internal illumination—despite the very real problems of rusting. These can be overcome, however, with adequate care in specifying undercoats and paints. One of the great advantages of steel is the fact that any small metal-working shop can fabricate signs with it, it welds easily (unlike aluminum), and it is relatively cheap. Messages are applied by silk-screening or by the application of die-cut vinyl letters.

Galvanizing is the process of applying a zinc coating to a steel sheet or core. There are basically two types of galvanizing: hot-dip and electro. Galvanizing is measured in ounces of zinc per square foot, total, both sides. A 1 1/2-ounce (44 milliliter) class coating will have a life of 7 to 14 years to first rusting. A 2 1/2-ounce (52-milliliter) class coating has a 14- to 20-year life to first rusting. Galvanized steel may also be painted with proper preparation.

Aluminum. Because of its nonrusting characteristics, aluminum is used extensively in the fabrication of signfaces. Sheet and plate are defined in the same way as for steel. Aluminum is generally hard-anodized, painted, or clad in adhesive films. Prepainted sheet with the same qualities and in the same thicknesses as steel is also available.

Aluminum is especially suitable for signfaces using cutout letters. In one technique the letters are cut out of the aluminum face, the cut edges painted or anodized to match the face, and the message backed up by a diffusing sheet of acrylic plastic. The negative letter spaces, such as the inside of an "o" or "d," are either glued onto the acrylic sheet in temperate climates or screened in severe climates to avoid expansion problems. They can also be cut from acrylic, painted to match the aluminum background, and fused to the acrylic backup sheet.

In a second technique—commonly called "cut-and-fill"—the letters are cut out of the aluminum face and used as patterns to cut acrylic letters of slightly smaller dimensions, the acrylic letters are then fused to a backup acrylic sheet, and the backup sheet is then attached to the back of the aluminum face so that the letters fill the cutout spaces.

Anodizing is a process which thickens the aluminum oxide film common to all natural aluminum. Color can be added by dying the clear anodic coating.

Bronze/Brass. Bronze and brass are primarily alloys of copper and zinc, plus traces of other metals, in varying proportions. They can be cast from ingots, sawn from sheet material or extruded. Smaller sign fabricators are generally limited in the size of sections that can be poured. Their bright finishes can be preoxidized by chemical attack or can be left to oxidize naturally in the weather. If oxidization is not desirable, manganese can be added to the alloy and the finish can be preserved through such coatings as lacquers or liquid plastics.

Red brass is an alloy of 84-86 percent copper and 14 percent zinc.

Yellow brass is an alloy of 70 percent copper and 30 percent zinc. Brass accepts chrome plating better than bronze, and is therefore favored for that purpose.

Casting. Cast metal signs are solid, one piece signs or individual letterforms of a relatively heavy gauge. They are often used when durability or prestige identification is required.

Mounting. Metal signs are mounted with metal-rod wall fasteners, various adhesives, or by welding, brazing, or soldering onto a metal surface.

Sawing, Cutting

Fabrication Process. A paper pattern is made and attached to a metal plate. Following the pattern, the sign is cut out with a band saw. Any metal is usable that can be sawed. Stainless steel, for example, can be used up to a thickness of about 1/8 inch (.3 millimeters) or aluminum up to 1/2 inch (1.3 millimeters). Finishing requires only the removal of any rough edges by belt sanding and filing. Further treatment may involve enameling, plating, or anodizing. Wall attachment techniques are basically the same as those for cast metal signs.

Fabricating Sheet Metal. Fabricated sheet metal signs are hollow, thin-walled three-dimensional signs. They are constructed by hand from many separate pieces. Sides and face of the signs are flat and usually broad in area. Various sheet metals such as stainless steel, copper, or aluminum may be used.

Fabrication Process. A paper pattern of the signface is attached to the metal and the forms are cut out. These forms are given depth with the addition of sides. Sides and face are seamed by either soldering for steel, heliarc welding for aluminum, or brazing for copper. Size limitations for this kind of sign are very flexible and can go up to 10 feet (3 meters) in length. The surface of the sign can be finished by polishing, plating, anodizing, or enameling.

Engraving. Engraved metal signs are cut as shallow negative relief, often filled with enamel to make the letters stand out. They are generally used as small identification signs or dedication plaques, having much the same quality as cast metal.

Fabrication Process. A pattern is usually cut into plastic or metal and can either be prefabricated or custom-made. To get good definition, the pattern should be slightly larger than the original. The pattern and a fresh plate are first locked into separate positions on the engraving machine. The position of the two plates determines the percentage of reduction. Engraving is done over a tracing device or pantograph. On one end of the device a needle or stylus follows the groove of the pattern; on the other end, a rotating needle routs out a groove on the fresh plate, reduced but exactly following the pattern. The width of the engraved line can be extended, but beyond a certain limit the quality of the engraving tends to decrease.

Enameling

Baked Enamel. Baked enamel provides a most satisfactory painted surface. If vinyl letters are to be applied to the baked enamel, however, ensure that there is no trace of free silicon in the paint used or the letters will not adhere. This process uses paints that are cured by heat.

Porcelain Enameling. Another common treatment for steel is porcelain enameling. Baked porcelain is permanent when properly fabricated and, if left alone, will withstand weathering over an indefinite period. But, if struck by a rock, bullet, or other projectile, it will chip, flake, and expose the steel base which will rust, starting a process that will continue until the sign invariably disintegrates. This process uses powders that are cured by heat and are available in any color. Integral porcelain messages are not sharp in the stencil process and will not stand close inspection. Silk-screened messages, however, will be as sharp as the screen.

Etching. Photoetched metal signs are thin plates that frequently have a large body of small or intricate design elements in extremely shallow, negative reliefs. Letterforms are often colored or filled with enamel to make them more visible.

Neon

Neon is an inert, colorless, gaseous element. When contained in a glass vacuum tube, through which an electrical current is passed, it produces a reddish-orange glow. *Neon* is the term generally used to describe lighted tubing of all colors. This misconception exists because at one time it was the most commonly used gas. Other gases are used, combined with liquid mercury and various fluorescent coatings to produce light tubing of various colors. Gas tubing can be bent to follow practically any pattern, enabling it to function simultaneously as light source and communication medium. In contrast to other lighted signs, neon signs are easy to maintain and have, under normal conditions, a very long life. With the increasing use of plastic and diminishing number of skilled neon craftsmen, neon is gradually being displaced as a sign medium.

Gas Color Equivalents. The various gases used are colorless and only take on individual color characteristics after an electrical current is introduced. The color equivalents of gases are

Neon	Red-orange
Argon	Ultraviolet, but in combination with a small amount of mercury it yields a blue light
Helium	White-gold
Xenon	Blue-white with a white cast
Krypton	Purple, in combination with a small amount of Argon

Other colors—yellows, greens, rose, copper, gold—are obtained by coating the tube with a fluorescent powder. Neon, for example, yields a rose color in combination with a blue fluorescent coating. Argon is green, in combination with a yellow coating. Deep rich colors such as ruby or very dark blue are obtained by using colored glass tubing.

Fabrication

Tube Bending. The first step is preparation of a pattern which reads in reverse on an asbestos sheet, so that all bends and electrodes are behind the readable portion of the tubing. A section of tubing to be bent is first heated over a low-intensity flame. As the glass begins to soften, the bend is carefully made

to conform to the pattern. When tubing is bent, it tends to flatten out, so it is reheated and air is blown into it until the diameter of the bend is uniform with the rest of the tube.

Channel Letters. Channel letters are three dimensional, usually fabricated from sheet metal with an open front. An open-backed letter is a "reverse" channel.

Open Front. Neon tube is mounted to the front of a metal letter, closely following its shape. The metal channel letter becomes the sign during the daytime and is practically invisible at night when it functions only to confine the light to the shape of the letter.

Open Back. Neon tube is attached to the back of a letter with a solid metal front. The letters are pin-mounted away from the wall. At night, the lighted tubing creates a silhouette of the sign. To disperse the light evenly, the background should be made of a nonreflective material.

Stone/Masonry

For signage purposes, the most common techniques used on stone are carving, sand-blasting, and using the stone surface as a background for stud-mounted metal or plastic letters. Hand-carving is expensive and difficult to obtain, although there are a few stonecarvers left in this country. Sand-blasting is more common, but it is becoming increasingly difficult to find good craftsmen. The best source is through a cemetery monument company. Stone can be blasted with various grades of sand, carborundum grit (best for granite), or metal spheres which can be reused.

Sand-blasting is accomplished through the use of a paper pattern which transfers the design to a rubber masking material [approximately 1/32 inch (.07 millimeters) thick] which is then cut to expose the stone beneath. Letters are generally blasted with the gun held at an angle to give a v-groove stroke. If the gun is perpendicular to the stone surface, a rounded stroke will result.

Magnetic Signs

Interior signs that require frequent name or insert changes often utilize 1/32-inch magnetic tape on the back of an insert. The insert then is applied to a frame which has a thin sheet of metal film applied over the basic plastic, aluminum, epoxy, or wooden frame material. The resulting magnetic bond has good holding strength and allows easy interchangeability. The technique is readily available throughout the sign manufacturing industry.

Imprint

Hot Stamping. Hot stamping is just that: metal type is locked up in position, electrically heated and stamped onto the surface to receive the message with a sheet of foil or film that transfers its coated color under heat. A wide range of colors, including metallics, is available. The finished product is a hard, permanent message fused under pressure to .003-inch (.01-millimeter) depth. It is highly vandal-resistant, under exterior or interior conditions, and can be further protected by laminating with clear film. Messages can also be applied to papers, vinyl notebook covers, etc.

Screen Process. Screen processing, or silk-screening, is a versatile method for imprinting messages on a wide variety of materials, from paper to steel. Messages can be imprinted either in the shop or in the field. A screened message is only as good as the sharpness of the message in the screen and the care of inking. Generally, screens with letters above 6 inches (15.2 centimeters) are handcut, while those smaller should be made from photostencils.

Stenciling. Stenciling is one of the fastest, cheapest, and most versatile methods of sign making. It has the flexibility of hand-painting, allows for extensive reproduction, and can be used for almost any kind of surface. All negative areas of a letterform must be connected to the outer edge of the character by the characteristic stencil "bridge."

Ink can be applied to the surface of the sign with a stenciling brush, spray paint, or roller. Hand rollers produce the most precise image and should be used on relatively smooth surfaces. Stencil brush application is the most time-consuming process and is not recommended for large quantities. It works well on rough surfaces such as concrete or burlap. Spray paint is the most commonly used method because the ink is applied quickly and dries fast.

Coatings

There are more sign finishes than there are sign materials. This section will not cover brand names of paints, varnishes, or expected coatings except for a few coatings for metal and wood signs that have proved particularly effective. In most cases, recommendations from the sign manufacturer should be sought.

Types. Paint technology consists of many different products employing many different vehicles and binders. Some of the most common are:

Alkyds. Alkyds are oil-modified resins; superior to phenolics; fast drying; exterior durability; good color retention except they tend to darken with age, because of their oil content; easy to apply; moderately priced.

Epoxy-Catalyzed. Two components, with limited pot life, catalyzed epoxy produces coating as hard as baked enamel; good solvent and chemical resistance; chalks rather freely under outdoor exposure.

Epoxy Esters. Epoxies modified with oil to dry by oxidation; not as hard as catalyzed epoxies; single component with unlimited pot life; chalks rather freely under outdoor exposure.

Latex Emulsion. Latex binders are synthetic materials which can be varied in hardness, flexibility, gloss development, and retention, etc. Common types of latex are styrene butadiene, polyvinylacetate (PVA), polyvinylchloride (PVC), acrylics and vinyl acetate-acrylics. Drying results from coalescence of latex particles as the water evaporates from the film; ease of application and freedom from solvent odor; ease of clean-up (soap and water); fast drying and recoating; minimal fire hazard with blister and peel resistance. Must be protected from freezing.

Coatings for Metal. There are several coatings for metal that have been proven especially effective in various parts of the country. Everyone talks about ways to protect steel (paint it, galvanize it, or seal it in plastic) or aluminum (paint it, anodize it, or seal it in plastic), but nobody has really done anything superpermanent or vandal-proof. The best available surfaces for long-lasting uses are the steel die-embossed or aluminum photoetched signs, but even they cannot resist the vandal's knife.

Thermosetting Acrylic Enamels. With a life expectancy of 12 to 15 years, thermosetting acrylic enamels are made from thermoplastic acrylic polymers that have been made thermosetting by "cross-linking" monomers in patented processes. A variety of colors are available, including metallics, in high-, medium-, or low-gloss finishes.

Polyurethanes. There are manufactured a wide variety of urethane coatings that are durable and heavy-duty for industrial applications. One is a polyurethane coating made from an aliphatic isocyanate prepolymer and a weather-resistant polyester tailored to provide a balance of crosslinking and end-to-end polymerization so that the final film has an exceptional combination of hardness and flexibility. It is available in a limited range of colors which can be blended to provide almost any desired color. It is a two-component product, with an 8-hour shelf life after mixing, which gives a high-gloss, colorfast finish. Care must be taken before application, and metal must be steam cleaned or sand-blasted and primed before the final coat. The product also works well on wood, masonry, or fiberglass. A 20-year life expectancy is not uncommon for this product, without chalking and loss of only a few degrees of gloss, and field tests have shown no color fading. Proper cleaning, down to the bare metal, is essential to a successful application, which is usually spraying.

Coatings for Plastic. Plastics require coatings which are modified to best adhere to their smooth surfaces.

Coatings for Wood. Many coatings for metal can also be applied to wood. Under a clear polyurethane coating they will last a very long time. Other polyurethanes are very good for wood and will not change the color or appearance of woods that are to be left natural looking. Generally, natural wood signs are best protected outdoors by a combination of pressurized preservation treatment with pentachlorophenol using liquefied petroleum gas as the primary solvent, adequate kiln drying, and use of a penetrating sealer for matte appearance, or a heavy solids-type finish such as polyurethane for a glossy appearance. Gymnasium finishing products are excellent for this purpose.

Varnishes. For all practical purposes, varnishes have been replaced by polyurethanes, although nothing can match the deep color luster that varnish can bring out in woods. Life expectancy is short, and weathering can cause checking and slight yellow within two years. Stains can be successfully used, especially epoxy stains or those covered with a urethane coating.

Proper fabrication and permanizing treatment of outdoor wooden signs is an art that has not been fully explored in this country. Eventual splitting of the wood is unavoidable because no wood is 100 percent dimensionally stable. This should be taken into account in the design of wooden structures.

Illumination

There are four basic types of illumination used for signs: incandescent, fluorescent, high-intensity discharge and reflective. Of course, there are two ways to use these types: externally and internally.

Types

Incandescent. Incandescent illumination uses common incandescent bulbs or quartz-iodine lamps. They light small areas with high intensity, their light output ranges from low to medium, their rendition of colors emphasizes reds and yellows, and they require no ballasts.

Fluorescent. Fluorescent illumination uses common fluorescent tubes in blue-to-warm colors. They light large areas with low intensity, their light output is fair to good (best with daylight-type lamp), their rendition of colors varies according to the color of the bulb, and they require ballasts. Care should be exercised in the selection of ballasts which are made for varying temperatures. Bulb sizes are generally available in lengths of 24, 48, 60, 72, 84, 96, 108, and 120 inches (61, 121.9, 152.4, 182.9, 213.4, 243.8, 274.3, and 304.8 centimeters).

High-Intensity Discharge. High-intensity discharge illumination uses mercury vapor lamps in cool to warm colors. Light is produced by an electric arc in mercury vapor. They light small areas with very high intensity, their light output is high, their rendition of colors is fair with normal tones taking on bluish and greenish casts, and they require ballasts.

Reflective. Reflective illumination depends upon an independent exterior light source controlled by the viewer, and not the designer.

Light Sources

Incandescent Lighting. Only practical for very small signs, incandescent lighting may be used for such special effects as flashing signs. The bulbs themselves may form the letter, or they may be arranged in a grid, with any combination of lightbulbs flashing to form simple letters or numbers.

The frame for this type of sign is usually a metal box with a sunshield glass front, mounted to a building. Within this box, each bulb is placed in its own black tubular frame to direct the light and prevent glare from adjacent bulbs.

Fluorescent Lighting. The most practical method for internally lit signs, fluorescent lighting requires a minimal electrical installation and comes in a wide variety of sizes. The tubes should not be placed more than 1 foot (.3 meters) apart and 4 or more inches (10.2 centimeters) away from the face of the sign to achieve an even light quality.

If the light source is excessively bright, "irradiation" or "halation" will cause the individual letters (if they are translucent against an opaque background) to merge with their neighbors, and the message will disappear as a blur of light. If the letters are opaque against a translucent background, halation will cause them to be eroded in thickness until they virtually disappear or lose much of the legibility for which they were designed. A white letter on a black background is more legible than any other arrangement due to an optical illusion called the "ona effect" which causes a white letter to appear larger. The degree of effect is directly related to letterspacing.

Large signs generally consist of several panels for quick accessibility when tubes need to be replaced. As these signs are illuminated from within and, therefore, as colors by night can only be perceived by light passing through them, translucent plastics or paints must be used. Otherwise, the colors will read correctly by day but as black by night.

Neon Lighting. Neon is generally used as the interior light source for channel letters. Intense colors can be obtained by using the same color in both neon tube and plastic face.

Exterior Illumination. An exterior light source provides the simplest and cheapest way to light a sign, in terms of both installation and maintenance. It is used to light large painted or printed signs, such as billboards, or signs made of various opaque materials such as metal, stone, or wood. Lighting techniques include spotlighting, floodlighting, backlighting, and utilization of ambient lighting. Light sources include mercury, quartz-iodine, fluorescent, and incandescent lights.

Lighting Techniques

Spotlights. Spotlights are the simplest kind of outside light sources and can be set up easily. They are strong, focused lights, used to light small areas from above, below, or side. Spotlights must be carefully placed to avoid reflections. Mercury, fluorescent, or incandescent lights are used.

Floodlights. Floodlights are used for uniform illumination of a large area. Light types are mercury, quartz-iodine, halogen-reflector, fluorescent, and—in some instances—also incandescent light. Both floodlights and spotlights must be adequately shielded from the eyes of the viewer, providing that they can also be protected from vandalism. This generally means putting the light sources up and out of reach, carefully shielding them against unwanted spill, and selecting a type of illumination that will not adversely affect the sign colors. Floodlighting can also be placed in ground trenches covered with a vandal-proof wire cage, but special care must be taken to properly shield the lamps from weather and ensure adequate drainage.

Backlighting. Silhouetting a sign can be done in several ways. Neon tubes, set into the back of an individual letter or sign, usually of fabricated sheet metal, will produce a glowing, repetitive outline of the letter or halo effect. Reflecting light off a wall, with the letterform or sign extending away from it, will create another silhouetting effect.

Ambient Light. The spill from existing light sources may offer sufficient illumination to make a sign legible. If so, there will be no need to provide additional lighting, thus reducing the initial and long-term costs of the sign system considerably. Designers planning to rely on this method for illuminating their signs should study carefully the matter of color contrast. Floodlight may also be used to boost the ambient light.

VARIETY IN FABRICATION

One of the fascinating things about architectural signing is the variety of results which can be obtained with relatively few materials. This is demonstrated by the alphabet and numbers reproduced here. The total number of basic materials used to fabricate all letters and numbers is only six: plastic, metal, wood, stone, glass, and concrete. But there are many possible combinations of materials, many available techniques for utilizing these materials, and many ways to illuminate and install the finished letter or sign. There are so many possible combinations that designers should not worry about being short of ideas.

Each letter in the alphabet shown here represents a different letterstyle. All were designed or selected to demonstrate how materials and techniques can enhance the special characteristics of the letterstyle. For example, the elegance and delicacy of the script N is reminiscent of fine, hand-engraved letters in gold or silver. The modern technique of Graphic Blast, combined with a modern plastic material, results in a precisely finished and durable letter, which would be nearly impossible to achieve using more traditional methods. Another example which requires a similar precision is the Q. Traditionally, silver-leafed letters on glass require hand painting and hand application of the leaf. For this example, the maroon line was applied using a *photographically reproduced* silk screen. It would be nearly impossible to achieve such perfect line work by hand. This is not to deny that hand work is still necessary. Hand work is involved in all these sample letters and numbers. But the right technique when properly used can speed up the fabrication process, reduce costs by saving time, and produce a superior end product.

The letter A is cut out of clear acrylic plastic (Plexiglas) sheet. By use of a gas torch, the edges are heated until molten and polished. Clear adhesive is used to bond the letter to the black Plexiglas background, which has a low-gloss finish, called F-10. Letterform designer: Herman Eidenbenz; sign fabricator: Ampersand Contract Signing Group, Pasadena, California.

This letter is cut out of ½-in. (12.7-mm) thick aluminum. The face is mirror polished and the sides are satin polished. A clear spray coating is used to protect the entire letter. The background panel is plywood covered with dark gray plastic laminate in low-gloss finish. The letter is attached to this background with concealed metal pins. Letterform designer: Hermann Zapf; sign fabricator: Cochrin-Izant, Los Angeles.

This C is cut out of ¼-in. (6.4-mm) thick Plexiglas sheet and spray painted. It is mounted with adhesive to a birch plywood panel which is spray painted with an egg-shell finish. Letterform designer: Michael Mills; sign fabricator: ABC Letter Art, Los Angeles.

This letter is cut out of 1½-in. (38.1-mm) thick Baltic birch plywood with a face veneer of American white oak. The edges of this plywood are given a clear lacquer finish to show off the solid birch veneer of which it is made. The panel used for mounting this letter is normal paint-grade birch plywood. Letterform designer: Herb Lubalin; sign fabricator: ABC Letter Art, Los Angeles.

This is a kind of tour de force of the sign painters' art. The illusion of depth is created by subtle graduations in shading and highlighting. Careful attention is given to the shadowing of the letter in relation to the background shading, enhancing the three-dimensional effect. Letterform designer: Warren Dayton; sign fabricator: Grant Follis, Pasadena, California.

Oiled Buckingham Virginia slate is the material used for this panel. An elegant F is carved into this stone by hand and then guilded with gold to make the letter stand out from its background. Letterform designer: John Benson; sign fabricator: John Stevens Shop, Newport, Rhode Island.

Representing a very old technique, this letter G is hand carved from 2½-in. (63.5-mm) thick redwood. The background is stained and the humorous little figure is colored using acrylic paints. Letterform designer: Stan Dann; sign fabricator: Stan Dann, Oakland, California.

This letter is fabricated from an alloy called "Zeloy." By polishing, a finish quite similar to polished chrome plating is achieved. The letter then receives a baked clear protective coating. The letter is blind fastened to a background of black Plexiglas that has a low-gloss, P-94 finish. Letterform designer: Herb Lubalin and Antonio Dispigna; sign fabricator: Environmental Signing Incorporated, Sepulveda, California.

This is an example of fabricated sheet metal construction. Made of 18 guage sheet steel, the joints of this letter are welded or soldered together. The material, construction, and finish of this letter are used widely for exterior signs involving nonilluminated letters of this size. A dark gray high-pressure plastic laminate with low-gloss finish is applied to the mounting panel. Letterform designer: Morris F. Benton; sign fabricator: Acme-Wiley Corporation, Elk Grove Village, Illinois.

The face of this double-stroke letter is fabricated of ⅛-in. (3.2-mm) thick red #2178 Plexiglas, and the sides are blue #2050 Plexiglas, with a polished finish. All joints are solvent welded. The letter is blind fastened to a typical painted birch plywood panel, which has an egg-shell painted finish. Letterform designer: Facsimile Fonts; sign fabricator: Ja-Rob Display and Manufacturing Company, Grand Rapids, Michigan.

For this letter a Black Tennessee Imperial granite panel with polished surface is blind fastened to a ⅛-in. (3.2-mm) aluminum sheet. With the use of a special technique called "Graphic Blast," the K is permanently processed into and slightly below the surface of the granite. Letterform designer: Stephenson Blake; sign fabricator: Best Manufacturing Company, Kansas City, Missouri.

Clear-heart redwood boards, mounted at a diagonal, make up the sign panel into which this letter is Graphic Blasted. Pigmented oil stains are used to stain both letters and background stripes in alternate colors. Letterform designer: Milton Glaser; sign fabricator: Best Manufacturing Company, Kansas City, Missouri.

This hand-carved wooden M is made of clear, kiln-dried northern white pine. It is soaked in linseed oil prior to having gold leaf hand-applied. Life expectancy is 30 to 40 years, exposed to weather. The background is walnut veneer with a hand-rubbed oil finish. Dark band is black smalt. Letterform designer: Tony Wenman; sign fabricator: Spanjer Brothers, Inc., Chicago.

A special plastic laminate called "engraving stock" is used for this sign panel. It is composed of two layers: white over black. Using the Graphic Blast process, the white layer is cut away, exposing the black. The plastic laminate is bonded to a plywood panel with painted edges. Letterform designer: Alan Peckolick; sign fabricator: Best Manufacturing Company, Kansas City, Missouri.

Utilizing a panel of ⅜-in. (9.5-mm) plate glass with beveled and polished edges, the letter O is applied to the front of the glass by the Graphic Blast process. The back surface of the glass is painted before attaching it to the painted plywood support panel to which it is blind fastened. Letterform designer: Collis Clements; sign fabricator: Best Manufacturing Company, Kansas City, Missouri.

The background of this letter is an aluminum plate which has a satin finish. Utilizing the Graphic Blast process, the letter P is reproduced into the surface and then paint-filled black. The plate is blind fastened to a supporting panel of painted plywood. Letterform designer: Herb Lubalin; sign fabricator: Best Manufacturing Company, Kansas City, Missouri.

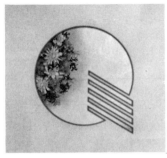

A thin maroon outline is silk screened on the back side of a panel of ¼-in. (6.4-mm) beveled plate glass. Then a sizing material is silk screened over the entire letter and silver leaf applied to the sizing. Finally the entire back side of the glass is painted, and it is blind fastened to the supporting plywood panel. Letterform designer: Rosemarie Tissi; sign fabricator: Padberg Graphics Company, St. Louis, Missouri.

This sign panel is made by mounting ⅛-in. (3.2-mm) thick white Plexiglas to a plywood support panel. The letter is cut out of chrome vinyl sheet that has contact adhesive backing and applied to the Plexiglas. Letterform designer: Herb Lubalin; sign fabricator: Berlian Signs, Incorporated, New York.

A panel of ⅛-in. (3.2-mm) thick aluminum that has a satin-polished, clear anodized finish is utilized for the background. An S shape is then cut out of ⅛-in. thick black Plexiglas so that it fits into the aluminum and is flush with the surface. They are then adhesive bonded to a plywood support panel. Letterform designer: Colin Brignall; sign fabricator: Ampersand Contract Signing Group, Pasadena, California.

The T is built up of two thick layers of acrylic plastic. Each layer is cut out and the edges are shaped. The layers are then polished and bonded together by the solvent welding technique. The letter is bonded to a thin polished acrylic panel, and the panel is adhesive bonded to the plywood support panel. Letterform designer: Alan Meeks; sign fabricator: Letterama, Incorporated, Plainview, New York.

Utilizing a process called "subsurface printing," this letter is silk screened on the rear face of 1/16-in. (1.6-mm) thick clear Plexiglas, which has a P-94, nonglare finish. The background paint color is then applied on the entire rear face of the Plexiglas and is blind fastened to the plywood support panel. Letterform designer: John Follis; sign fabricator: Architectural Signing Inc. and ASI Sign Systems Inc., Marina Del Rey, California.

This panel, with its recessed V, is cast of reinforced concrete. A wood form is built with a wood V attached to the inside of the form. Then the concrete mix is poured into the form and agitated to eliminate air bubbles. When the concrete is dry, the form is removed and the surface of the concrete is cleaned thoroughly. Letterform designer: Max Caflisch; sign fabricator: Golden State Precast Incorporated, Gardena, California.

This letter is another example of forming a letter by casting. In this case, epoxy resin is cast into a form and allowed to harden. After the letter is removed from the form, it is sanded, painted, and attached to the plywood background panel with concealed fasteners. Letterform designer: Milton Glaser; sign fabricator: Graphic Display, Sun Valley, California.

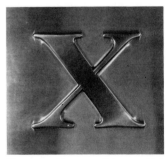

The natural bronze plate on which this letter is mounted has a satin finish achieved by machine sanding with a fine grit belt. The letter is cast in bronze from a wood pattern utilizing sand casting methods. A clear protective coating is applied to the bronze background to keep it from darkening by oxidation, and the letter is given a dark oxide finish. Letterform designer: Morris F. Benton and T. M. Cleland; sign fabricator: Ampersand Contract Signing Group, Pasadena, California.

The Y is a combination of silk screening, gold leafing, glass chipping, and mirroring. First, the lines are silk screened on the back of the glass and gold leafed over to complete the letter. The surrounding glass is then chipped away except for an area around the Y. Then the entire back is mirrored. Letterform designer: Silvestre; sign fabricator: Wed Enterprises, Glendale, California.

The background panel on which this letter is reproduced is fabricated of reinforced fiberglass. The Z is applied using a photo silk screen printing process, which reproduces the original art very accurately. A coat of clear linear polyurethane is sprayed over the letter to protect it. Letterform designer: Morris F. Benton; sign fabricator: Architectural Signing Inc. and ASI Sign Systems Inc., Marina Del Rey, California.

Plexiglas is used for the face of this numeral and sheet metal for the sides. Directly behind the numeral are several "runs," or loops of white neon tubing, used to illuminate it. The sign can, or housing, made of sheet metal, contains a transformer and other necessary electrical equipment for the neon. Numeral designer: Milton Glaser; sign fabricator: Ampersand Contract Signing Group, Pasadena, California.

The distinctive halo effect is achieved in the numeral 2 by using white neon tubes mounted within it. The numeral and sides of the box are made of sheet metal, but the face of the box is made of Formica, a high-pressure plastic laminate. Numeral designer: M. Miedinger; sign fabricator: Ampersand Contract Signing Group, Pasadena, California.

To make this sign, a hole the shape of the 3 is cut out of the violet-colored Plexiglas background. Clear Plexiglas is installed behind that opening, and then colored neon tubing is mounted inside the can, or housing, for illumination. Sides of the can are fabricated of sheet metal and then painted. Numeral designer: Stephenson Blake; sign fabricator: Jas. H. Matthews and Company, Pittsburgh, Pennsylvania.

This numeral is reproduced on the back side of Plexiglas using a color process called "Chromaline," which is highly resistant to fading. It is illuminated with fluorescent lamps mounted inside the sheet metal can, or housing. Numeral designer: J. Erbar; sign fabricator: Exhibit Group, Chicago, Elk Grove Village, Illinois.

Black Plexiglas is used to make the face of this sign, can, and metal for the sides. Exposed neon tubes, each filled with a different color of chemical gas, are bent to the shape of the 5. Electrical equipment is concealed inside the can. Numeral designer: John Follis; sign fabricator: Ampersand Contract Signing Group, Pasadena, California.

The face of this sign is composed of three different colors of Plexiglas. Using the solvent welding technique, all the acrylic parts are carefully fitted and then welded or glued together, with their surfaces flush. Internal lighting is fluorescent. Numeral designer: Graphic Concepts; sign fabricator: Donnelly Electric and Manufacturing Company Incorporated, Boston Massachusetts.

The panel of this sign is fabricated of aluminum with a satin finish. A white 7 is cut out of ⅛-in. (3.2-mm) thick Plexiglas and inlaid flush with the aluminum. Internal lighting is fluorescent. Numeral designer: Amsterdam Type Foundry; sign fabricator: West Side Neon Sign Corporation, Bronx, New York.

The appearance of clockwise motion in this 8 is achieved by the use of polarizing filters, a process called "Polarmotion." The color is reproduced by the chromalin process on a sheet of Plexiglas and laminated with the back of the polarizing material between another sheet of clear plex. Fluorescent lighting and all electrical equipment are concealed within the sign enclosure. Numeral designer: Michael Mills; sign fabricator: Exhibit Group, Chicago, Elk Grove Village, Illinois.

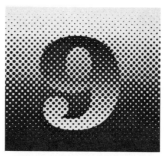

Artwork of the 9 is reproduced by the photo silk screen process in black on the surface of yellow ⅛-in. (3.2-mm) thick Plexiglas. The sign can is made of sheet metal, and internal light is provided by white fluorescent. Numeral designer: Christopher Lee; sign fabricator: Ja-Rob Display and Manufacturing Company, Grand Rapids, Michigan.

This numeral is mounted on a sign can, or housing, made of sheet metal. It contains fluorescent lamps and wiring to illuminate the numeral and its background. Sides, face, and background of the numeral are cut out of Plexiglas and welded together using an acrylic solvent. Numeral designer: Paul Renner; sign fabricator: QRS Corporation, Los Angeles.

13
Supervision

The definition of supervision which is most appropriate to sign fabrication is *oversee*. Design staff members responsible for supervision should be thoroughly familiar with every facet of the sign system. This *over* view allows them to *see* any errors as signs are fabricated.

Before the fabricator begins his work, it is helpful to meet with him for a detailed review of the working drawings and specifications and to talk over any anticipated problems. Even though the design staff has thoroughly prepared these documents, there are sometimes small details which need further clarification.

Every good fabricator follows an orderly process while translating information shown on the designer's working drawings and specifications into the final signs. The designer interacts with the fabricator at critical times during the process. Supervision occurs in three phases, with considerable overlapping: (1) checking submittals, (2) supervising fabrication, and (3) supervising installation.

CHECKING SUBMITTALS

The fabricator will usually begin making submittals a few weeks after being awarded the contract. Submittals are shop drawings, color samples, and other items requiring the designer's approval. Prepared by the fabricator, shop drawings are technical drawings from which his craftsmen build the signs. They include fully dimensioned construction details, information about materials, electrical equipment, fasteners, and so forth. All structural members shown on shop drawings have been calculated to satisfy code requirements. Inner construction details often shown in full size are adapted to the fabricator's specific production techniques, which may be unique to his shop.

It is common practice for shop drawings and other submittals to be sent a few at a time to the designer. Under normal conditions, he is expected to review and approve them in about ten days.

Checking Shop Drawings

The shop drawings should be checked for compliance with the design working drawings and specifications as follows:

1. All dimensions and details affecting the exterior appearance
2. Materials and colors noted on drawings to see if they are exactly as specified

3. Copy content, size, and placement (if copy layouts or lettering patterns are included with the shop drawing)
4. Electrical or mechanical equipment or hardware for compliance with the drawings and specifications

If minor items shown do not agree with working drawings, these should be correctly indicated on the shop drawing, which is then marked "approved as noted," dated, and a copy returned to the fabricator. If many or major corrections are needed, the drawing should be marked "not approved, resubmit"; in this case a phone call to the fabricator is usually needed to work out the problem.

Other Submittals

The fabricator may not submit full-size layouts (lettering patterns) of sign copy at the same time he submits shop drawings of a particular item. If, for example, because of time schedules basic sign construction takes place first, copy lettering may be applied weeks later. However, at the proper time the fabricator's copy submittals should be carefully checked against copy layouts shown on design documents as follows:

1. Copy placement on the sign panel
2. Spelling, capitalization, punctuation
3. Letter-, word-, and line spacing
4. Size, placement, and contour of any other visual item, such as arrows, numbers, or symbols

Color and material samples related to specific signs may be submitted at any time before signs are ready for painting and finishing. Paint colors are usually submitted in duplicate on samples of the actual material to be painted, using the paint material, methods of application, and sheen or gloss specified by the designer. Approval or disapproval is noted on the back of each sample by the designer, and one copy is retained for later use in checking the completed sign. A similar approval process is used for all other submittals.

Prototype Samples

The designer may request in the specifications that the successful bidder submit prototypes of certain signs which are to be fabricated in quantities. A prototype is normally a handmade model in full size, conforming exactly to the design shown on approved shop drawings. This prototype gives the designer an opportunity to test the feasibility of a design concept, material finish, or other visual details. A prototype may be used by a fabricator to demonstrate, for example, an assembly technique or support hardware. The needs for prototypes vary with each project, but in general they provide an excellent method of controlling the quality of the final sign. By checking the prototype carefully, the designer can see any detail that needs revising before quantities of the sign are produced.

SUPERVISING FABRICATION

The design supervisor visits the fabricator's shop periodically to check the progress of the work and to examine items before they are ready for the next step. Only about 10 or 15 percent of the design fee can be devoted to all phases of supervision, so it must be done quickly and efficiently. Supervision should be done by the staff person most familiar with the project. Some offices have one or two people doing all supervision, while others assign one member of each project team to this task. An analytical, critical turn of mind is an essential characteristic of a good supervisor, but this must be tempered with good judgment concerning acceptable levels of craftsmanship. Although standards of craftsmanship may be deteriorating generally, it is possible to obtain sign work of high or low quality. It seems increasingly important to have several standards for sign quality, which may tend to vary according to the time and budget available.

Approved Shop Drawings

Approved shop drawings, rather than design drawings, are the reference guide for checking signs as they are being fabricated. Shop drawings show *all* information including approved changes, and they supercede the design drawings. The supervisor must check each item against these drawings for substitution of materials or equipment and poor workmanship. Using a tape measure, he must check all sign dimensions, making note of any errors.

Quality Control

Personal judgment is involved in accepting or rejecting the craftsmanship of a particular sign. The judgment of a good supervisor is often based upon years of experience observing the work of many sign fabricators. The experienced supervisor knows the range of craftsmanship that is available and can easily judge what is acceptable for a particular job.

In Chapter 11 where the bidding process was described, the differences in quality of workmanship among various fabricators was discussed. At times the designer will have to supervise the work of a fabricator who makes signs of somewhat lower quality of finish than the designer normally considers acceptable. Careful finishing often requires hours of skilled labor, which is expensive; this cost-conscious fabricator may submit a lower bid based on less finishing time. He is not being unscrupulous, but bidding competitively. Other fabricators who specialize in exterior sign construction may make products which seldom require close examination; they build signs usually mounted 25 feet (7.5 meters) or more from the ground. However, when awarded contracts to make signs which are subject to eye-level examination, these fabricators have difficulty producing a more precisely finished product because their workers are not trained for this kind of careful work. If the supervisor is a perfectionist, he will have difficulty working with fabricators of this type, but he should make objective judgments and careful evaluations based on approved drawings and specifications.

Problems with Fabrication

Because of the almost limitless range of materials and techniques involved in sign construction, there are many possibilities for defects in workmanship or materials. The following should be corrected:

General

Colors, material, or hardware not matching approved samples.

Copy applications which do not follow approved alphabets, letterspacing, or lettering patterns.

Copy which is not parallel with edges of the sign panel or has other application defects.

Sign parts not made square, straight, or well-aligned.

Raised metal letters installed out of alignment with each other or out of plumb.

Color of fluorescent lamps or other light sources not as approved.

Exterior Wood Signs

Interior grade plywood used.

Plywood signs with edges unfilled and surfaces painted with interior grade paint materials.

Natural wood items glued with nonwaterproof glues.

Clear natural finishes which are not waterproof, merely water-resistant.

Wood parts below grade which are not treated to resist decay.

Wooden letters which do not follow approved patterns and specifications.

Fabricated Metal Signs

Routed letterforms which are done by hand. A template should be used to guide the router, for example, to reproduce the exact letterform.

Cast or fabricated metal letterforms which do not follow approved shop patterns or samples.

Spray-painted finishes that are uneven in gloss or have a bumpy surface, called "orange peel," due to improper application.

Machine or tool marks which show up after the finish is applied.

Plated finishes not as specified or of poor quality.

"Oil canning" or warped surfaces of metal sign enclosures.

Corners which do not fit neatly or which are not filled or finished smooth and flush.

Excessive number of crudely installed fasteners or exposed fasteners.

Access panels fitting poorly.

Substitutions of hardware or mechanical details.

Variations in surface brightness of illuminated signfaces caused by lamps being too widely spaced.

Plastic Signs

Materials which are the wrong color, thickness, or finish.

Rough edges or tool marks showing.

Adhesive joints not cleanly finished.

Open or improperly fitted joints.

SUPERVISING INSTALLATION

Sometime before signs are ready for installation, the fabricator or installer and designer should meet at the job site to mark exact sign locations. Although general locations of all sign items are shown on plans, the specific location of items must be verified on the job, as noted in Chapter 5, Design.

Interior Signs. Supervising the installation of nonilluminated signs in interior locations is usually a matter of coordinating the work with the fabricator or his installer. For repetitive signs, all of which have similar locations, such as office door signs, it is only necessary to supervise one typical installation of each sign type to verify that both the exact location and the method of attachment are correct.

When illuminated interior signs are to be installed, the project electrical contractor should be notified by the sign fabricator. During an earlier stage of construction he should have roughed in electrical service for these signs, and now he will work with the sign installer to make the final hook-up or electrical connection. Normally, the fabricator provides for electrical wiring within the sign, and the electrical contractor provides all wiring beyond the sign. The sign supervisor may coordinate this work or merely check the completed installation to see that the sign is functioning properly.

Exterior Signs. It is often necessary to review placement of exterior signs with both the general and sign contractors, particularly if signs are illuminated. If the project is newly constructed, electrical conduit should be installed well in advance of sign installation when other related electrical service is being installed. After final grading of the site has been completed, the location of each sign can be marked with a wooden stake showing the identifying sign item number.

Special Reinforcement. Certain exterior or interior sign items may be so heavy or difficult to install that special blocking or reinforcement must be built into the building to properly anchor the sign. The reinforcement should be indicated on sign drawings so that the general contractor can install it during construction of the building. Before signs are installed, the supervisor verifies the location of this reinforcement and coordinates the sign location to coincide with it.

Items to Check

Once all the preparatory work is complete, the designer can make periodic visits to the job, checking items as they are installed. Besides verifying that installation materials and methods being used are as specified, the designer must see that proper heights and locations are being maintained and that each item is set plumb or level. Some other things to look for are

Uppercase letters installed instead of lowercase, or vice versa.

Improper alignment of individually mounted pinned-out letters.

Chipped finishes.

Unpainted exposed fasteners.

Exposed or unsightly electrical connections.

Fabricator's labels displayed where not called for.

Improper cleaning of sign surfaces or surrounding wall areas.

Damage to surrounding wall or ceiling surfaces.

Final Inspection

Because of the great number of individual signs involved on the average job, it is usually necessary to make a written list of items to be corrected—what architects call a *punch list*. The schedule of items issued with working drawings can be adapted for use as a punch list; this should be filled out on the job and a copy sent to the fabricator, who will seldom argue about correcting defects. Many contracts between client and fabricator state that 10 percent of the contract sum is to be withheld until all corrections have been made.

WHAT ABOUT INCOMPETENT FABRICATORS?

At times, the designer must work with an incompetent fabricator who may have been awarded a government job simply because he was the low bidder. The designer did not recommend him, but must supervise his work nevertheless. Just as soon as it is apparent that the work is inadequate, the designer should review work to date with the client and recommend a stop work order. At times a subcontractor is at fault, in which case a new "sub" can often be found. However, at other times, all efforts to correct the problem may fail. Then a written recommendation to cancel the contract should be issued. Contracts between client and fabricator should have a cancellation clause, which outlines conditions governing cancellation.

EVALUATION AND FUTURE ADDITIONS

After the signing system for a project has been operating for several months, project managers will have feedback from employees, visitors, and tenants. Working under an extension to his original contract, the designer should be called back to evaluate any problems and make recommendations for necessary changes. Some changes are nearly inevitable because people do not always respond to signs in a predictable way. Signs the client may have deleted during planning may now be considered necessary. Other signs may be necessary to cope with internal changes in project operations. Whether the change merely involves a revision of an existing sign or the addition of a new one, the designer should be involved in all such decisions.

In addition to such short-term changes, institutions often need to develop a method of handling on-going signing problems. A project which includes leased tenant spaces must establish criteria for design control, as outlined below in the signing criteria manual. If a building manager needs to keep a system up to date, he can do so with the help of a sign ordering manual, also discussed below.

Another kind of future addition which involves the designer is signing for a new parking structure at a hospital. This should be handled as an entirely new project.

Signing Criteria Manual

The signing criteria manual, reproduced in full in the Appendix (with typical pages shown in Figure 102), sets forth criteria for the design and installation of tenant signing in a highrise bank building. The basic aims of the criteria are that

1. Each tenant will have adequate identification.
2. Each tenant will be allowed to display its corporate symbol, logotype, trademark, or name.
3. All signing in lobbies, corridors, or other public spaces will be consistent in appearance.
4. The design of signing on tenant floors will continue the high quality of graphic design established for nontenant areas.

To show how to implement those aims, examples of each signing element related to tenant signing are shown and/or described in detail in the manual.

Sign Ordering Manual

An example of a sign ordering manual, the one illustrated in full in the Appendix (with typical pages shown in Figure 102), was designed for the same bank building as in the above example. This manual refers directly to the designer's working drawings and is to be used by building management personnel. In this instance the sign fabricator who manu red the original signs is also responsible for supplying additional signs or parts. This will ensure consistency of quality and appearance between existing and new signs.

This manual cannot be produced until the designer's documents are completed. Because the manual is in effect an extension of those drawings, the manual drawings can be schematic, which saves time of adding dimensions, material notes, and details.

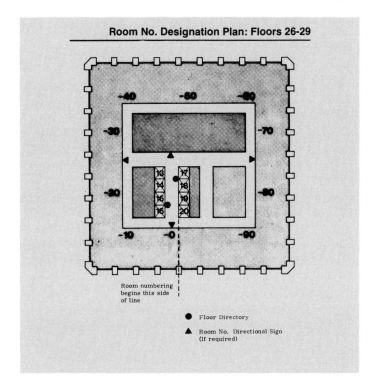

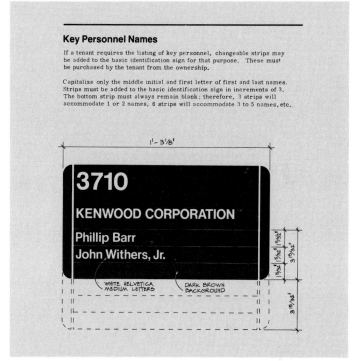

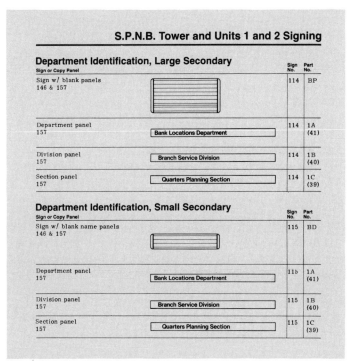

Figure 102. Two examples of the signing criteria manual are shown here at the top, and two from the sign ordering manual are below.

14
Compensation and Agreements

In the field of architectural signing and graphics, the designer faces a wide range of design problems and what can seem like a wild range of fees—from 5 percent to over 100 percent of construction costs. Architects handle a broad range of design problems for which they have established fee guidelines, based on years of professional experience. By contrast, signing and graphics is a new field, with each designer groping for a way to determine fees to fit his own needs. He must rely heavily on his own judgment, which is seldom backed up by many years of experience.

Several other factors add to the difficulty of establishing adequate fees. Some clients, having worked with architects, but being naive about signing fees, think the sign designer should be able to establish a fee as a percentage of project construction costs, as architects sometimes do. Many sign fabricators further muddy the waters by telling clients that they will do design "at no charge." They include in-house design costs as part of overhead costs. Over-zealous designers may bid low or buy a design project with the hope of doing more work for the same client. Or the inexperienced designer may estimate low on a project out of ignorance. Regardless of the reason, there is often a great range of fee bids on legitimate projects if bidding is open to all.

For one recent government signing project, fee bids ranged from $12,000 to $92,000, even though all designers were responding to the same written information from the government. Considering figures like these, it is not surprising that designers and clients alike have difficulty establishing overall budgets (including fees and fabrication costs) for signing programs.

Before talking to a designer, many clients guesstimate sign program budgets (covering design and fabrication), and often these are only one-quarter of what is really needed—perhaps just enough to cover design fees alone. Clients are shocked when a workable budget is finally presented to them.

Designers can do several things to create a general understanding about adequate fees. They can talk with other designers in their city or area who are doing work of similar quality and openly discuss fee problems. They can become members of the Society of Environmental Graphics Designers, an association of designers that is headquartered in Chicago, which is establishing professional standards for this field. Designers can refuse to bid against sign fabricators or others not providing full professional design services. They can encourage clients to select designers primarily on the basis of their ability, experience, and integrity, not on the basis of fees alone.

COMPENSATION

Compensation Varies with the Kind of Design Problem
Compensation is a broad term covering fees and reimbursement for out-of-pocket expenses which are directly related to the execution of design services.

Architectural and interior design fees are often based on square footage or computed as a percentage of construction costs of a project. Many clients expect the signing-graphics designer to establish his fees similarly. This should be avoided as the pitfall it is. Fees for designing a sign system depend on its complexity, which, in turn, relates to how a building functions, not on its size or cost. Fees for other graphic items depend on the specific nature of the problem. Several examples will illustrate the widely varying kinds of design problems graphic/signing designers may be involved with.

At one end of the scale is the design of a huge exterior sign for a Las Vegas casino. The designer can solve this problem by providing one full-color rendering without working drawings. His fee may range from 5 to 10 percent of the cost (perhaps $250,000) to build such a sign. On the opposite end of the scale are elaborate, three-dimensional graphic treatments of department store curtain walls designed to create a certain ambience for merchandise. Each of these graphics is unique, requiring many hours to design and perhaps necessitating the building of scale models or elaborate color renderings. These may require a fee exceeding 100 percent of fabrication costs.

Fees for Painted Wall Graphics. Estimating fees to design a two-dimensional painted wall graphic is much like estimating a poster or other printed graphic. So many hours should be allotted for concept sketches, preliminary color sketches, presentation drawings, and the final scaled drawing. Time should be included for selection of paint chips and supervision of the painter on the job. The range might be from $1,000 to $5,000 per item depending on the nature of the design.

Fees for Signing Systems. The large problem with estimating fees to design sign systems is that many clients want to know the total fee before signing a contract and even before the designer understands the full extent of the problem. The most experienced designer cannot know what fee is required for a large project until he has identified the different signing and graphic elements to be designed.

Sign Fees Based on Phase 1 Study. The most effective way of determining the number of sign types is to do a phase 1 study, as in Figure 25 on page 25 in Chapter 3, Organizing the Process. At the end of this study, all graphic elements are known and fees to design them can be determined. With some effort, the designer may convince clients to authorize this phase 1 study as a cost-plus expenditure, but a fixed fee is more normal.

Sign Fees Based on Educated Guesses. This is a much less effective way of determining the approximate number of sign types as the basis for fees. With this method the designer will use a combination of past experience, intuition, and personal judgment, but he should also spend time making a preliminary review of the problem before guesstimating fees.

Preliminary Review of Client's Signing Problem

Regardless of fee or contract arrangement, a preliminary review of the client's problem is a necessary orientation for the designer. He should talk with the client; inspect the site, buildings, and existing signing, if any; and review the architectural plans in some detail. This will provide preliminary information needed for writing an intelligent proposal and determining fees required for a phase 1 study, which might be outlined as in Figure 25.

Two fee arrangements which are most often used for phase 1 are cost-plus fee with an estimated maximum and fixed fee.

Cost-Plus Fee. The ideal fee arrangement for most design services is the cost-plus agreement; the designer charges for all direct costs, plus a percentage for overhead and profit. If the client is agreeable, the designer should proceed with a phase 1 study on this basis.

However, most clients prefer to know in advance how much they will be billed. A fixed fee or lump sum agreement is most often requested for phase 1.

Fixed Fee. After completing a preliminary review, the designer should have a good feel for the extent of the problem. But rather than using intuition or tossing a coin to arrive at a phase 1 fee, it is better to estimate workhours to complete each task listed in the outline above and then double the total. The phase 1 fee should be about 10 to 15 percent of the total design fee, ranging from $1,500 for a small sign system (with a total fee of $10,000) to $5,000 or $6,000 for a large one (with a total fee of $40,000).

Factors Affecting Fee Estimates for Remaining Services

When the phase 1 study is completed, the designer will have to determine fees for continuing services. It is to his advantage to submit a proposal covering only the next phase of services. Especially for new projects never before operational, the scope of services may change as work on phase 2 proceeds, requiring sign types to be added.

Whether quoting a fee covering phase 2 or phases 2 through 4, there are a number of factors to consider in determining fees.

Complexity of Project. If, for example, the project is a large hospital, with many interior corridors and separate departments, it will require a complex sign system. Because of the numerous points of decision, it will require many hours of planning even though in the end few different sign types are involved.

Sign Types. The quantity of sign types and their individual design characteristics are most important in estimating fees.

Each represents a unique item to be designed, documented, and coordinated, and each requires a different number of hours to complete. A major site sign identifying the project may require 10 hours for every one spent on a restroom sign. During phase 1 assign a difficulty factor to each sign type rather than treat all as taking an average number of hours.

Budget Money Available. At times the client requests a low-budget job and the designer must fit the solution to money available. Other clients may want a prestige job regardless of cost.

Design Criteria. Schematic designs presented during phase 1 should establish design criteria. If the designer plans to use standard, on-the-market sign panels, he can figure a lower fee. However, if he plans all sign elements to be custom-designed, the fee should be higher.

Extent of Services to Be Provided. If the client plans to provide supervision of installation, the phase 4 can be deleted from fee proposals.

Relationship to Past Experience. If the project under consideration is similar to one completed recently, the designer can often interpolate fee requirements from that experience and even utilize some part of the resultant designs.

Contingencies. Because of the variety of problems and the many unknowns, fee estimating is a very difficult part of the graphics/signing business. Even experienced designers are wary of underestimating; some advise to double the estimated time for an unusual creative problem. Others add a contingency of 10 to 50 percent depending upon the unknowns involved.

Another kind of contingency is the "escalator clause." As the term implies, this is a clause in the contract which allows for labor charges to keep up with inflation. Although the client may resist, the designer should ask for this on contracts in force for one year or more.

Considering Overhead and Profit

Regardless of whether the designer contracts for fixed fee or cost-plus services, he should establish a *factor* or multiplier to use in calculating billed-out rates for himself and all employees. Young design firms, with a studio in some loft space, will obviously have a lower overhead than a firm with posh offices in a high-rent district. *Overhead* is a broad term covering not only office operating expenses, but also employee fringe benefits and a percentage for profit. The factor should include the following:

Operating expenses such as rent, electricity, telephone, water, gas, materials, equipment, and maintenance

Taxes, insurance, social security

Employee benefits: health insurance, vacations, sick leave

Down time—time which is not billable

Profit and profit-sharing programs

Applying the Factor to Billing Rates. Every designer or design office will develop a different overhead factor depending upon its location, size of staff, employee benefits, and so on. But on the average a factor of 2.5 to 3.25 (which may be even higher in New York City) should be used as a multiplier of base salary to cover overhead and profit.

Billed-Out Rate. Some clients (especially federal and local governments) expect to limit the factor to 2.5. However they will allow the base salary to include fringe benefits. Two examples will clarify this:

1. If a junior designer is paid $5 per hour as a direct hourly rate and a factor of 2.75 is used, then the client is billed $13.75 per hour.
2. If the client allows a 2.5 factor times adjusted hourly compensation (including fringe benefits), then $5.75 × 2.5 or $14.37 per hour, is billed out.

Payment Schedules

For many designers who work under cost-plus agreements, it is common practice to bill the client on a monthly basis as the services are performed. Billing can be sent out monthly also under fixed-fee agreements. However, if the project is large or extends over a long period of time or if it is being designed for a governmental agency, it is often necessary to establish a *payment schedule*. This is arrived at by dividing the total fee into a certain number of increments and listing the dates on which each increment is to be paid. A typical schedule might look like this if the total fee is $25,000:

Phase 1	Payment due April 30	$3,750
Phase 2	Payment due June 30	$8,750
Phase 3	Payment due Aug. 30	$8,750
Phase 4	Payment due Sept. 30	$3,750

Governmental agencies seem to prefer payment schedules which divide the fee into equal increments, which is perhaps better suited to the way public monies are budgeted and allocated. Any schedule can be used so long as it is acceptable to both designer and client.

Each designer must use good judgment and past experience in evaluating all the foregoing when determining the exact fee. Based on many years experience with a variety of projects, one office uses a range of $500 to $1,000 per sign type to provide all services for phase 1 through phase 4 as listed in Figure 25.

Reimbursable Expenses

As part of compensation it is common practice to bill the client for out-of-pocket expenses directly related to his project. Items such as the following are appropriate:

Research materials

Prints, photos, reproductions

Art and graphic materials and supplies

Mockups of signs and architectural models

Delivery

Postage and long distance telephone calls

Travel expenses, mileage, and parking

Depending on the nature of the project, client attitudes, and the kind of contract agreement, clients may question the inclusion of certain items under reimbursables. A client may feel that charges for renderings, art materials, and similar expenses should be considered as part of the designer's normal operating expenses. But it is better to put them in the contract drafts so that they can be discussed openly as part of contract negotiations rather than be argued about later.

It is often advantageous to talk about fees with the client and review a preliminary draft of the contract agreement before submitting the final document for signing.

AGREEMENTS, FEE PROPOSALS, AND CONTRACT FORMS

To avoid misunderstandings with the client, fee arrangements must be clearly stated in writing. The kind of contract form used relates to the fee arrangement chosen for the project. Some types of contract agreements are reviewed here:

Fixed Fee (or Lump Sum) Proposal

Most clients want to know at the very beginning how much the total fee will be covering all services (planning, design, documentation, etc.). This is understandable because they want to know up front what the final costs will be for every element of the project in order to control overall project costs (Figure 103).

Terms and Conditions. For a fixed fee agreement, the section headed "Terms and Conditions" is a kind of catch all. It generally outlines separate responsibilities of client and designer and sets limits on the scope of services. The second and third items in this section concern sign wording and job coordination; both subjects have caused endless problems for some designers when responsibilities were not clearly defined.

Make Wording Explicit. If the designer prefers not to be involved in the problem of sign wording, the second item might read: "The client shall be solely responsible for developing the wording of all sign copy."

The third item, concerning coordination, could be stated differently as: "The client shall appoint one staff person as coordinator to provide information and final approvals." This can reduce the number of people whom the designer has to work with.

The two examples indicate the possible semantic difficulties involved with agreement wording, which can also have legal implications. On large projects, the designer may want to review the final contract with a lawyer.

Cost-Plus Proposal

By comparing Figure 104 with the fixed fee agreement it is apparent that the only significant difference is in the wording of the paragraph on fees. Also, there are detail differences in Terms and Conditions. Each agreement includes a place for the client signature so that if approved it can become a legal document.

All Services. To illustrate a different method of writing a cost-plus proposal, one from an architectural-engineering firm is shown in Figure 105. Note that the listing of services is divided into seven phases rather than the four shown in Figure 103. There is no separate Terms and Conditions heading, but client responsibilities are defined within the body of the proposal.

Insurance Provisions

On both private and governmental contracts it is often required that a section concerning public liability insurance be inserted; such a section might be worded as in Figure 106.

Governmental Contracts

Most governmental agencies issue their own contract documents rather than accept one issued by the designer. These documents are drawn or reviewed by some city, state, or federal attorney, and they are usually very thorough, lengthy documents. When negotiating such contracts, the designer usually is not in a good bargaining position; although he can question the terms and conditions under which he must perform, he can seldom change them.

Most often these contracts are for a fixed amount, or if cost-plus, they contain a not-to-exceed clause. It seems very difficult to negotiate an open-end cost-plus contract with any government agency regardless of the difficulties in pinning down the scope of services required. The designer must cover himself by making thorough estimates with a reasonable contingency factor. Then he should hope that everything he designs is approved the first time around.

The Use of Standard Printed Contracts

Designers who plan to design many small signing projects, all similar in nature, may wish to modify a standard contract and have it reproduced. Many professional design organizations such as the American Institute of Architects (AIA) and the National Society of Industrial Designers (NSID) provide their members with standard contracts which can be adapted, but they are often quite elaborate. Most corporate clients will immediately call in their attorney to go over the contract thoroughly if such a document is presented to them.

A simple letter of agreement, providing the terms are clearly stated, is more practical and less expensive to prepare in-house than having a more formal document prepared by a lawyer. Projects and clients vary greatly and it is difficult to have one contract which is flexible enough to cover all possibilities, so that the designer who tries to use printed contracts may end up with many different forms.

Mr. Richard D. Cannon
Contracting Officer
Veterans Administration Hospital
8400 East 4th Street
Metropolis, California

January 20, 1979

Project: 8950 V. A. Hospital, Metropolis
Subject: Proposal for Phase 2 & 3 Graphic Design Services

Dear Mr. Cannon:

In response to your letter of January 12, 1979, we submit this proposal for graphic design services related to the design of a comprehensive sign program for the hospital.

Specifically, this fee proposal covers Phase 2 (Design) & 3 (Working drawings and specifications) services as stated in our Outline of Services for the items shown in our Phase 1 Report of December 15, 1978.

Fees

Graphic Design Associates will provide these services on a fixed-fee basis for a fee of $35,000.

The work covered by this proposal will be billed at an hourly rate of $28/hr for the time spent during each month. All work will be billed by the 10th of each month and would be due and payable on or before the 20th of the following month. This sum shall include $3,200 for out-of-pocket expenses.

The proposed estimates of manhours required to develop a signing program for this project is based on past experience with other projects of similar scope.

The proposed hourly rate for personnel is based upon averages currently paid to staff and generally consistent with current rates paid in the graphic design field. However, it may be necessary to exceed the average rate shown for a unique designer.

Graphic Design Associates will maintain complete and adequate accounts, books and records on a generally recognized accounting basis and authorizes the client, or their agents, to inspect and audit all pertinent accounts, books and records in order to verify the amounts of expense for reimbursement.

Terms and Conditions

Revisions and Additions: This proposal covers only the services outlined. If the scope of work changes, approved revisions or additions will be charged for as an addition to the original contract.

The client and GDA shall mutually participate in development of all sign wording, with final approval provided by the client.

The client shall appoint a staff member to act as coordinator between the client and GDA.

The client shall provide GDA all necessary drawings and information regarding site conditions and codes which affect the signing.

This proposal does not include the cost of models, color renderings, or slide presentations which will be provided only at the request and approval of the client.

GDA is an equal opportunity employer abiding by the Provisions of Public Law 88-352.

The time required to perform our work is dependent upon the availability of the hospital's personnel and their ability to supply the required information within a reasonable period of time, and will be extended accordingly, if there are any delays.

Termination of contract: Assuming just cause either party reserves the right to terminate this agreement after giving ten (10) days written notice to the other. GDA shall be paid for services and reimbursables incurred under this contract up to the date of such termination, but not to exceed the agreed design fee.

The only design or coordination meetings which GDA shall be expected to attend are those meetings involving signing.

The designing of temporary signs is not included as part of this fee proposal.

Fabrication of signs, engineering of sign footings and foundations, and engineering within signs is by others.

If this agreement meets with your approval, please sign both copies and return the original to us. Upon receipt of the signed copy we will proceed with the work outlined.

For V A Hospital	For Graphic Design Associates
Date	Date

Figure 103. An example of a fixed fee proposal.

Mr. Andrew B. Rudy
St. Johns Hospital Medical Center
400 N. 24th Street
Tucson, AZ

March 2, 1979

Project: 2095 St. Johns Hospital Medical Center
Subject: Proposal for Phase I Graphic Design Services

Dear Mr. Rudy:

Graphic Design Associates proposes to provide Phase 1 services required for the development of an exterior and interior signing program for the St. Johns Hospital Medical Center in Tucson. The extent of these services is as shown on the Outline of Services. [See Figure 25, for example.]

The purpose of this Phase 1 work is to determine the basic design, location, function, and quantities of all signing elements to be designed and developed during subsequent phases of the work.

During Phase 1, we will coordinate our work with the hospital and review our work with the administration to be sure that the sign program will satisfy all operations, esthetic, and code requirements.

We will review the Master Plan now being prepared by the architect and shall develop a sign program for the existing facilities that will be responsive to the changes indicated by the plan.

Fees

Graphic Design Associates will provide these services on a cost-plus basis, that is 2.75 times employee compensation, for an estimated sum of $3,600. Itemized billings of fees and reimbursables will be submitted monthly and invoices submitted by the 10th of the month are due and payable by the 20th of the following month.

GDA will maintain complete and adequate accounts, books, and records on a generally recognized accounting basis and authorizes the client, or their agents, to inspect and audit all pertinent accounts, books, and records in order to verify the amounts of expense for reimbursement.

Reimbursables

In addition to fees Graphic Design Associates shall be reimbursed for all actual outside services or expenses related to the execution of this contract, plus 15 % to cover administrative costs. Such reimbursables include

the following: blueprints, vellums, and Xerox; photostats; film, photoprocessing, and printing; mileage and parking; typography; telephone and telegraph, postage; delivery charges; artistic and graphic materials and supplies; and out-of-pocket expenses directly connected with the execution of this work.

Terms and Conditions

The client shall appoint a coordinator on its staff who shall obtain information regarding special signing requirements and act as coordinator between the client and Graphic Design Associates.

The client shall provide Graphic Design Associates all necessary drawings and information regarding site or building conditions and codes which affect the signing.

This proposal does not include the cost of models, color renderings, or slide presentations which will be provided only at the request and approval of the client.

The designing of temporary signs is not included as part of this fee proposal.

Termination of contract: Assuming just cause either party reserves the right to terminate this agreement after giving ten (10) days written notice to the other. GDA shall be paid for services and reimbursables incurred under this contract up to the date of such termination, but not to exceed the agreed design fee.

Revisions and Additions: This proposal covers only the services outlined. If the scope of work changes, approved revisions or additions will be charged for on a cost-plus basis and as an addition to the original contract.

The client and GDA shall mutually participate in development of all sign wording, with final approval provided by the client.

If this agreement meets with your approval, please sign both copies and return the original to us. Upon receipt of the signed copy we will proceed with the work outlined.

_____   _____
For St. Johns Hospital   For Graphic Design Associates
Medical Center

_____   _____
Date   Date

Figure 104. A sample cost-plus proposal.

March 10, 1979

Michigan Hospital
2046 E. Olympia Blvd.
Tree Lane, Michigan

Attention: Ms. Sue Wellborn
Senior Interior Designer

Dear Ms. Wellborn:

In line with your request for our Professional Services, we propose to perform such services in connection with the development of a comprehensive exterior signage program for the Michigan Hospital, Tree Lane, Michigan.

The objective of these services is to develop a complete exterior signage system that is responsive to site conditions, building architecture, interior conditions, and signage as well as the desired hospital image.

Our services will be performed as outlined below:

1. *Planning*
   The planning phase defines the scope of work, consultant and owner responsibilities, budget and maintenance considerations.

2. *Programing*
   Programing establishes the design parameters resulting in a written statement for the owner's approval.

3. *Preliminary Design*
   Preliminary design investigates the component options that comprise the system. Specific items are now developed based on programing criteria.

4. *Design*
   Design becomes the final determination of items under investigation in preliminary design.

5. *Documentation*
   Documentation will take the form of a printed copy of a user's manual that will be utilized for initial imple-

mentation as well as subsequent additions or changes to the system.

6. *Award*
   The consultant will assist owner in the review of bids. Approval of shop drawings, mockups, and samples as well as construction observation will be the responsibility of the consultant.

7. *Operation*
   Operation is continuing implementation. Consultant responsibilities include periodic review of installation.

The development of the exterior program will include the following types of information:

1. Directional (including trail blazers)
2. Informational
3. Regulatory
4. Identificational

Work will include identification of those buildings identified in your letter of February 18, 1979, requesting this proposal. All signage as required for parking lots, directional information, regulatory roadway information will be confined to the general physical area as bounded by those buildings. Signage requirements for the medical science complex and its related educational facilities, as well as the educational and residential facilities located at the southeast part of the complex is not considered part of this proposal.

We estimate our fee to provide all services as indi-

Figure 105. A typical cost-plus proposal of an architectural-engineering firm.

cated to fall in the range of $12,500 to $14,000. This is based on a fee of 2.75 times our direct personnel expense for all manhours worked, plus the cost of overtime premiums. Direct personnel expense includes the hourly rate of employee and mandatory and customary benefits such as taxes, insurance, health, holiday and vacations, pensions, and similar benefits. In the case of a salaried employee, the hourly rate shall be determined by dividing the salaried employee's annual salary by 2080.

In addition, the owner shall reimburse the graphic/signage designer as follows: actual cost of travel and subsistence outside the Detroit metropolitan area as incurred in the performance of the graphic/signage designer services or authorized by the owner; long distance and toll telephone calls; telegrams; reproduction of drawings, specifications, and other documents incurred for the project or requested by the owner, except those for the materials, models, construction, mockups, perspectives or renderings, brochures and special reproductions incurred for the graphic/signage designer's own use; special presentation and materials, models, construction, mockups, perspectives or renderings, brochures and special reproductions incurred for the project or as requested by the owner; postage and handling and other similar items; fees paid for securing approvals of authorities having jurisdiction over this project; fees of special consultants for the other than normal design, architectural, mechanical and electrical engineering if authorized by the owner in advance.

We estimate these out-of-pocket expenses to be approximately $2,000. Where the owner requests changes or additional services, the time required to perform such services will be defined and separated by a change memorandum (CM) to give the owner a separate accounting of those costs which are in addition to the estimated cost of other graphic/signage designer services. Approval of CMs by the owner is required prior to commencement of the work by the graphic/signage designer.

It is understood that while consultation and interviews will take place at all levels within the hospital, the graphic/signage designer will consider only one individual as the designated authority and representative of the hospital pertaining to the acquisition of information needed for the program and approval to do work and work satisfactorily completed.

We look forward to the opportunity to present to the hospital our capabilities for completion of work as described in this proposal and to the opportunity to work with you in the development of a unified exterior visual identification and communication system for employees, visitors, and patients.

Your acceptance of this proposal can be indicated by signing in the space provided below and returning one signed copy for our files. Upon acceptance of this proposal, we would anticipate a start date of June 1, 1979.

If you have any questions concerning this proposal or request additional information, please contact Mr. John R. Cooke.

Very truly yours,

Donald J. Mathis
DJM/ARS:ns

Accepted By:

Title:

Date:

INSURANCE

Commencing with the performance of our services here-under and continuing during the term of this agreement, we shall provide and maintain insurance policies in full force and effect with responsible carriers of the following type and amount:

Workmen's Compensation

Workmen's Compensation and Employer's Liability Insurance which shall comply with the statutory requirements of the State of California and any other state in which services are being performed and shall apply to all persons employed by us.

Comprehensive Liability Insurance

Comprehensive General Liability Insurance, of not less than Five Hundred Thousand Dollars ($500,000) for death or bodily injury to one person and One Million Five Hundred Thousand Dollars ($1,500,000) for death or injury to more than one person and property damage, or both combined, in any one occurrence.

Automobile, bodily injury liability coverage of not less than One Hundred Thousand Dollars ($100,000) each person, Three Hundred Thousand Dollars ($300,000) each occurrence, and property damage liability Twenty-five Thousand Dollars ($25,000) each occurrence, covering one corporate automobile and nonownership liability.

You shall be listed as an additional assured under the above policies and said policies shall provide that they cannot be cancelled without ten (10) days' prior written notice to you. We agree to furnish evidence satisfactory to you that the said policies are in full force and effect.

We agree to fully protect, indemnify, and hold harmless and defend you, your officers, agents and employees from and against any and all loss, cost, damage, injury, liability, claims, liens, demands, taxes, penalties, interest, or causes of action of every nature whatsoever, including, but not limited to your and our offices, agents employees and/or property in any manner arising out of or incident to or in connection with our services under this agreement and resulting from (1) any negligent act or omission or willful misconduct of us or our officers, agents, or employees; (2) any negligent act or omission of you or your officers, agents, or employees arising out of conditions existing on your property known as Pacific Terrace Convention Center or the facilities, materials, and equipment located thereon, causing injury to or death of our officers, agents, or employees, or loss or damage to our facilities, materials, and equipment, except for such liability resulting from or caused by the personal participation of you or your officers, agents, or employees in an affirmative act of negligence.

We agree to perform the consulting services hereunder as an independent contractor and not as your employee, and all persons employed by us in connection with such services shall be our employees and not your employees.

Figure 106. Statement of public liability insurance that is often required in both government and public contracts.

Security Pacific Plaza

Multi-Tenant Floor Signing Criteria

Introduction

It is the intention of Security Pacific Plaza to provide an environment
of the highest quality both for those who work in the building and for
business visitors. The planning, architecture, interiors and landscaping
all reflect this concern for a well-designed atmosphere in which to work.

Consistent with this approach, the ownership of Security Pacific Plaza
has paid particular attention to the design of all signing elements on, in
and around the project. Although individually designed, each sign has
been carefully considered in relation to the architecture and in relation
to the total graphic design program of Security Pacific Plaza. In order
to implement these considerations throughout the building, the project
Graphic Design Consultants, John Follis & Associates, have developed
signing criteria for multi-tenant floors.

Properly adhered to, this criteria will work to the advantage of both the
tenant and ownership in the following ways:

1. Each tenant will have equal and adequate identification.
2. Each tenant will be allowed to display its corporate symbol, trademark
    or logotype.
3. All signing in public lobbies, corridors and other public spaces will
    have a consistent appearance.
4. Multi-tenant floor signing will continue the high level of graphic
    design found throughout the Security Pacific Plaza.

Tower Directory

Each tenant of Security Pacific Plaza may display information on the building directory located on the Plaza Level. Changeable directory strips with suite number, company name and division listing, where appropriate, will be provided for each tenant.

To insure uniform identification of all tenants the Graphic Design Consultants have established that all strips will be black background with white Helvetica Medium type of uniform size. All listings will capitalize the first letter of words keeping the remaining letters lower case. Listings in all capitals (upper case) will not be permitted. No individual colors, corporate trademarks or logotypes will be used on this directory.

All listings will be alphabetical and include company names, and as required, division, services description and key personnel.

Company Listings

3250	Rutgers, Schelling & Walters
	Attorneys at Law

Key Personnel Listings

Key personnel may be listed separately or under company name. When listed separately, they will appear last name first.

2960	Major Distribution, Inc.
3000	Malt, John R., Jr.
3700	Midmark Books

When key personnel are listed under the company name, they will appear first name first.

1300	The Lind Corporation
	John L. Gregg, Jr.

Room Numbers

When all listings under a company name have the same room or floor number, the room number will be listed once only, opposite the company name.

1300	The Lind Corporation
	John L. Gregg, Jr.
	Walter Park

If individuals in a company have individual room numbers, the numbers will appear beside each name.

	Malkey & Associates
2750	John J. Arno
2810	Ford T. Colbalt

Multi-Tenant Floor Directory

Security Pacific Plaza will provide a floor directory in the elevator lobby of each multi-tenant floor. It will display the floor number, directional arrows and a listing of each tenant on the floor with suite number and company name and, as required, division or services description. Space will not permit the inclusion of key personnel names. All companies will be listed in numerical order by room numbers.

The Graphic Design Consultants have specified that the changeable strips in these directories will be dark brown background with white Helvetica Medium type of uniform size. Company names will be all capital letters while division names will capitalize the first letter of words only, the remaining letters being lower case. No individual colors, corporate trademarks or logotypes will be permitted.

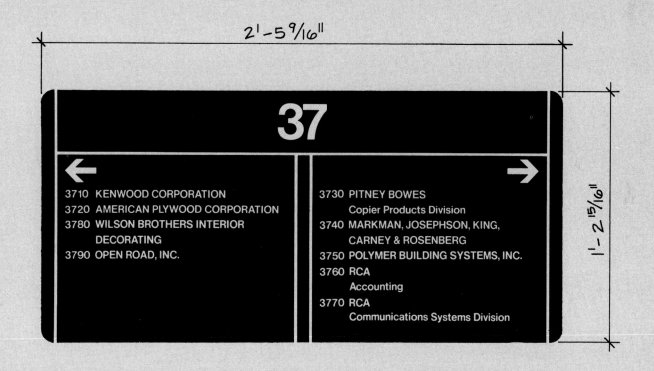

2'-5 9/16"

1'-2 15/16"

37

←
3710 KENWOOD CORPORATION
3720 AMERICAN PLYWOOD CORPORATION
3780 WILSON BROTHERS INTERIOR
     DECORATING
3790 OPEN ROAD, INC.

→
3730 PITNEY BOWES
     Copier Products Division
3740 MARKMAN, JOSEPHSON, KING,
     CARNEY & ROSENBERG
3750 POLYMER BUILDING SYSTEMS, INC.
3760 RCA
     Accounting
3770 RCA
     Communications Systems Division

Directional Signs

Security Pacific Plaza will provide directional signs within the Multi-tenant corridors as needed.   They will present only room numbers and directional arrows.   No other directional signs will be allowed.

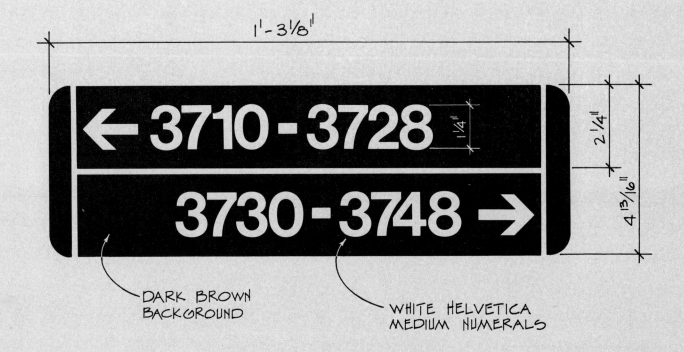

DARK BROWN
BACKGROUND

WHITE HELVETICA
MEDIUM NUMERALS

Building Utility Signs

Security Pacific Plaza will provide all institutional code and required signs within the public areas. These will include identification signs for restrooms, fire extingushers, sprinkler control valves and stairwells.

Tenant Identification Signs

Basic Identification Signs

Security Pacific Plaza will provide each tenant with a basic identification sign for the entrance to his area. It will display room number and corporate name. Division name and/or description of services will be added as required. Corporate names will be listed in all capital letters and description of services will capitalize the first letter of words only.

The length of all signs will remain constant at 1' - 3 1/8" with the height varying according to the amount of information displayed. The sign for a one line corporate name with no additional information will be 4 1/2" in height.

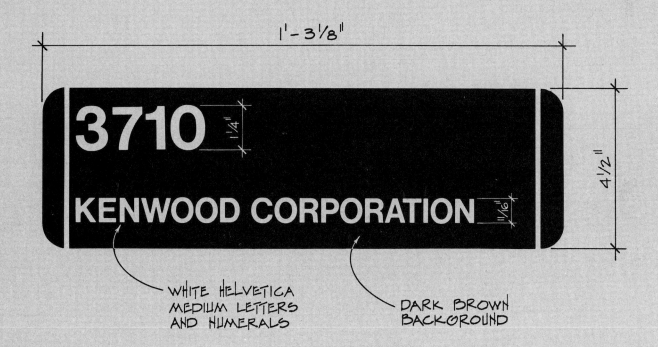

If the corporate name, etc., requires 2 or 3 lines of copy, the sign height will be increased to 6 3/4"

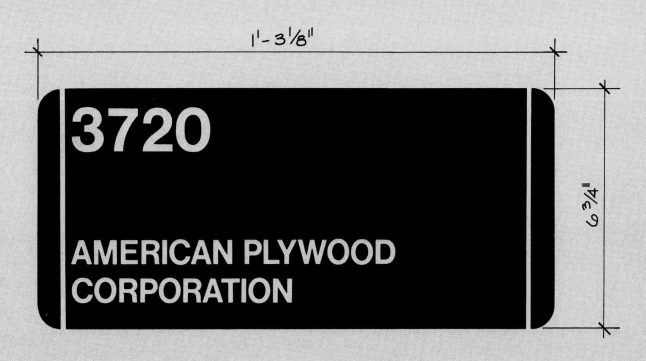

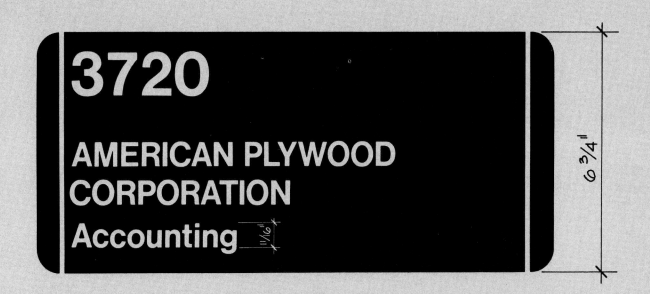

The sign height will be 8 7/8" for 4 or 5 lines of copy. In the event
that even more lines of copy are required the height will be increased
by 2 1/8" increments.

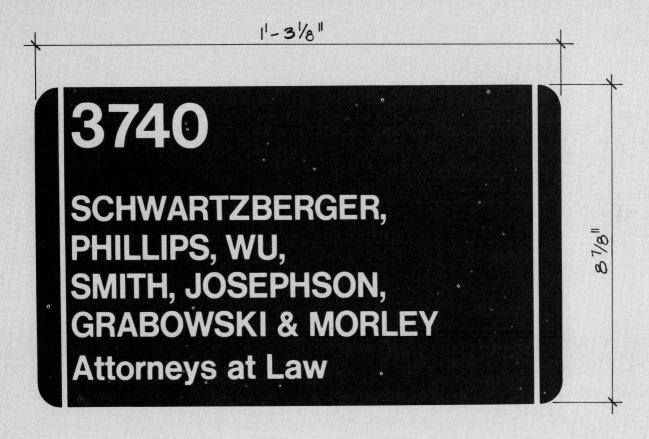

Key Personnel Names

If a tenant requires the listing of key personnel, changeable strips may be added to the basic identification sign for that purpose. These must be purchased by the tenant from the ownership.

Capitalize only the middle initial and first letter of first and last names. Strips must be added to the basic identification sign in increments of 3. The bottom strip must always remain blank; therefore, 3 strips will accommodate 1 or 2 names, 6 strips will accommodate 3 to 5 names, etc.

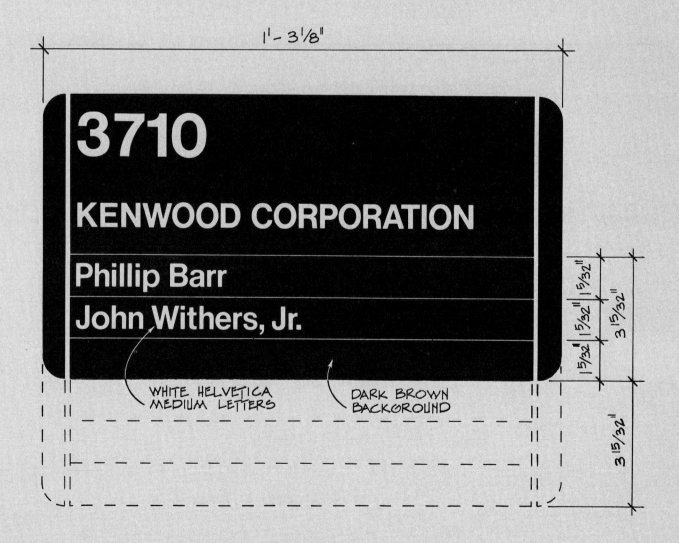

Corporate Identity Signs

Tenants wishing to display their corporate trademark or logotype may do so on a 9" high x 1" - 3 1/8" wide separate sign panel mounted above identification signs.   These signs must be fabricated and installed at the tenants expense following specifications included in this criteria.

Trademarks or logotypes only may be used on this sign.   No promotional copy or slogans are allowed.   The color and layout of this sign will be determined by the tenant.   The ownership and Graphic Design Consultants will review all designs for conformation with specifications.

Tenants with a logotype which clearly states the company name
may prefer not to repeat the name on the identification panel below.

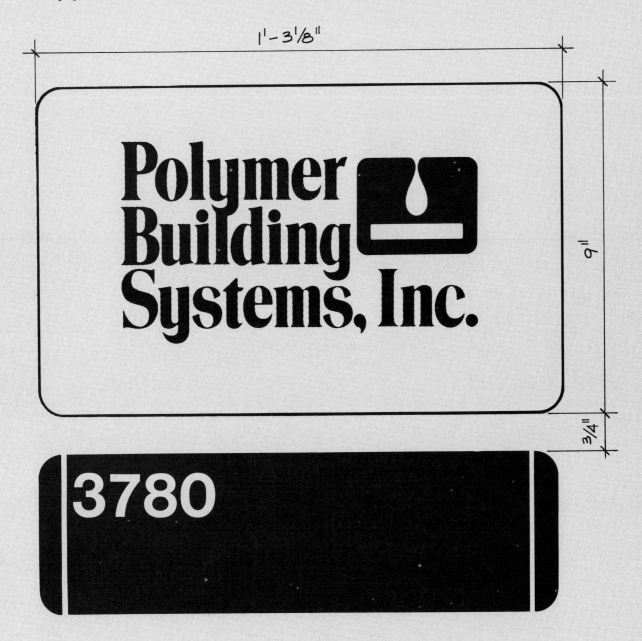

These signs may be made of any reasonable sign material, however, the
graphics on the signs must be or appear to be integral with the panel.
That is, no applied, cut-out or stick-on graphics may be used. Acceptable
processes include: silk-screen, casting, photo etching, engraving, etc.

JF&A

John Follis and Associates
2124 West Venice Boulevard
Los Angeles, California 90006
Telephone (213) 735-1283

All ideas, designs, arrangements and plans indicated or represented by this drawing are owned by, and property of John Follis and Associates and were created, evolved and developed for use upon, and in connection with the specified project. None of such ideas, designs, arrangements or plans shall be used by or disclosed to any person, firm or corporation for any purpose whatsoever without the written permission of John Follis and Associates. Written dimensions on these drawings shall have precedence over scaled dimensions. Contractors shall verify and be responsible for all dimensions and conditions on the job and this office must be notified of any variations from the dimensions and conditions shown by these drawings. Shop details must be submitted to this office for approval before proceeding with fabrication.

Security Pacific
Plaza

date 9-6-74
project 142
drawn K.F.
check
rev.

196

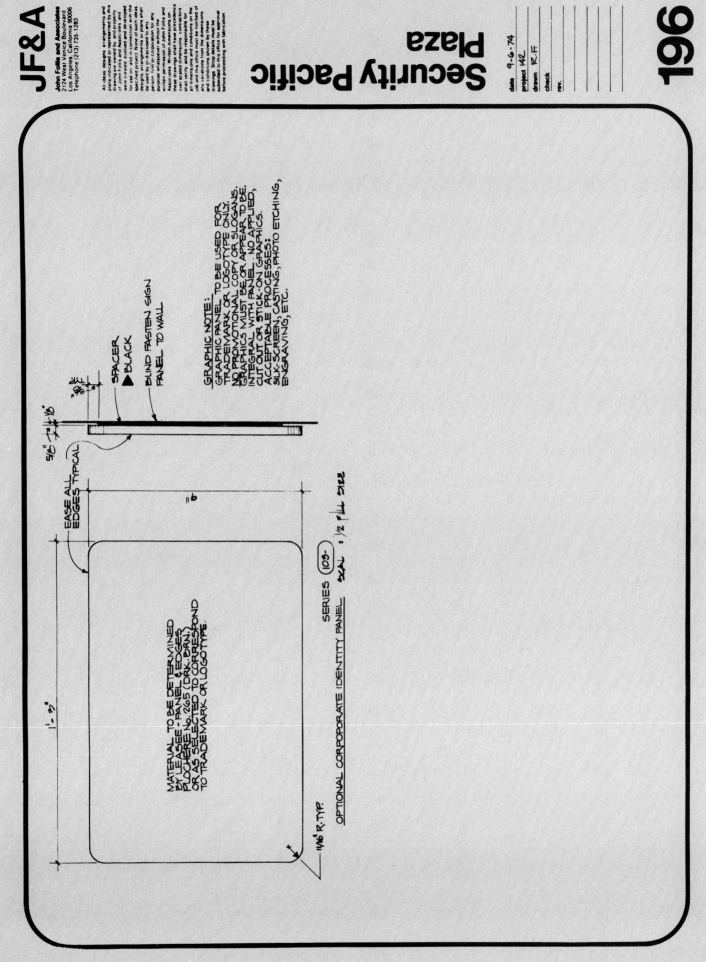

SPACER
▲ BLACK
BLIND FASTEN SIGN
PANEL TO WALL

GRAPHIC NOTE:
GRAPHIC PANEL TO BE USED FOR
TRADEMARK OR LOGOTYPE ONLY.
NO PROMOTIONAL COPY OR SLOGANS.
GRAPHICS MUST BE, OR APPEAR TO BE,
INTEGRAL WITH PANEL. NO APPLIED,
CUT-OUT OR STICK-ON GRAPHICS.
ACCEPTABLE PROCESSES:
SILK-SCREEN, CASTING, PHOTO ETCHING,
ENGRAVING, ETC.

EASE ALL
EDGES TYPICAL

MATERIAL TO BE DETERMINED
BY LESSEE - PANEL & EDGES
PLOCHERE No. 265 (DRK. BRN.)
OR AS SELECTED TO CORRESPOND
TO TRADEMARK OR LOGOTYPE.

SERIES 105-
SCALE : 1/2 FULL SIZE

OPTIONAL CORPORATE IDENTITY PANEL

Mounting Locations for Tenant Identification Signs

Security Pacific Plaza will install all basic tenant identification signs on the wall adjacent to the door on the doorknob side.

Corporate identity signs will be mounted by tenant directly above the identification signs.

The same location requirements apply to glass areas next to entry doors. All signs mounted on glass require identically sized panels mounted on the inside of the glass. Panels are not to be mounted on doors except in extreme cases. Permission from the Office of the Building is required. Specific mounting instructions and detail drawings are available from the Office of the Building.

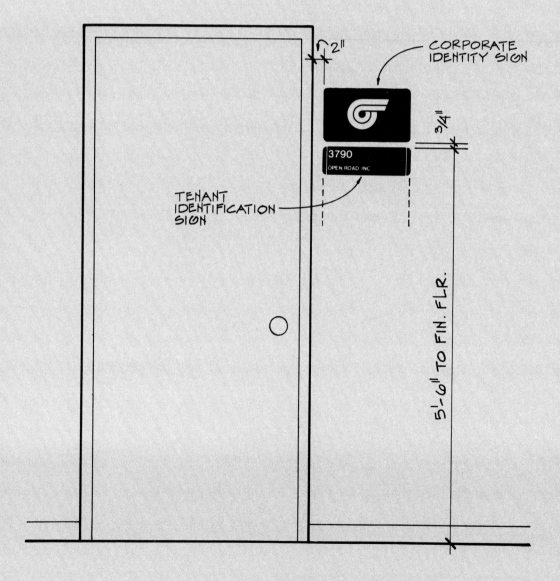

Tenant Internal Signs

Each tenant is responsible for all signing needed within his own specific area.

The following signs have been designed by the Graphic Design Consultants for use within tenant areas but are recommendations only. These signs are designed to coordinate tenant internal signing with building signing in order to create a total cohesive system. The recommendations include 3 sign types designed to cover the basic needs of most tenants.

1.   Desk name plates.
2.   Door signs for identifying departments or individuals or for presenting informative and/or restrictive information.
3.   Signs suspended from the ceiling that may be used to identify departments or for directional information.

Detail drawings for design and fabrication of each sign type are attached. It is suggested that the signs be fabricated by Architectural Signing, Inc., Vomar Products, Inc., or equal.

JF&A

John Follis and Associates
2124 West Venice Boulevard
Los Angeles California 90006
Telephone (213) 735-1283

Security Pacific Plaza

197

date 9-6-74
project 142
drawn R.F.
check
rev.

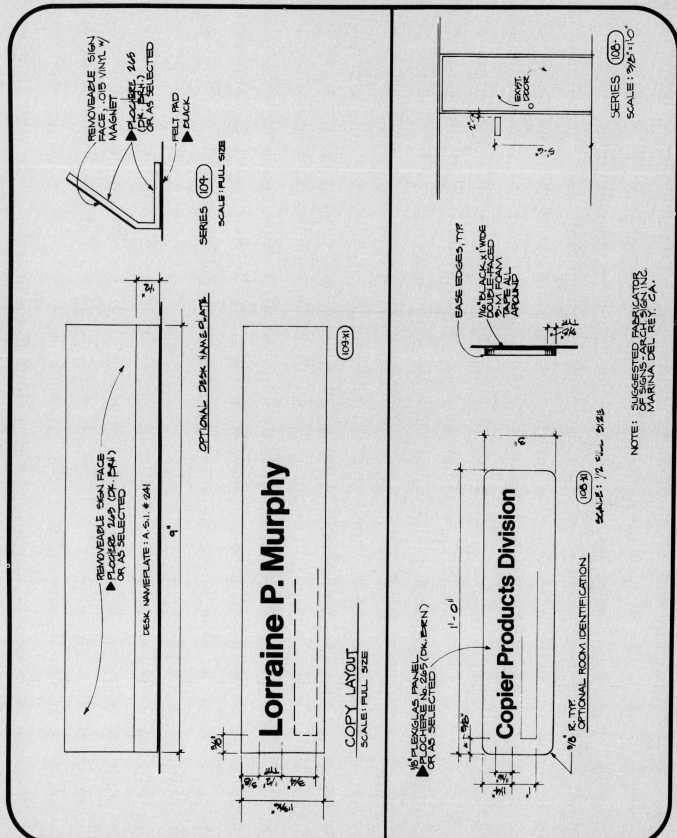

REMOVEABLE SIGN FACE, .015 VINYL W/ MAGNET

PLOCHERE 265 (DK. BRN.) OR AS SELECTED

FELT PAD

BLACK

SERIES 104-
SCALE: FULL SIZE

REMOVEABLE SIGN FACE
PLOCHERE 265 (DK. BRN.) OR AS SELECTED

DESK NAMEPLATE: A.S.I. #241

OPTIONAL DESK NAMEPLATE

Lorraine P. Murphy

COPY LAYOUT
SCALE: FULL SIZE

(109-XI)

EXIST. DOOR

SERIES 108-
SCALE: 3/8" = 1'-0"

EASE EDGES, TYP.

1/16" BLACK x 1" WIDE DOUBLE-FACED 3-M FOAM TAPE ALL AROUND

(108-XI)
SCALE: 1/2 FULL SIZE

1/8" PLEXIGLAS PANEL
PLOCHERE No. 265 (DK. BRN.) OR AS SELECTED

Copier Products Division

OPTIONAL ROOM IDENTIFICATION

NOTE: SUGGESTED FABRICATOR OF SIGNS-ARCH SIGN INC. MARINA DEL REY, CA.

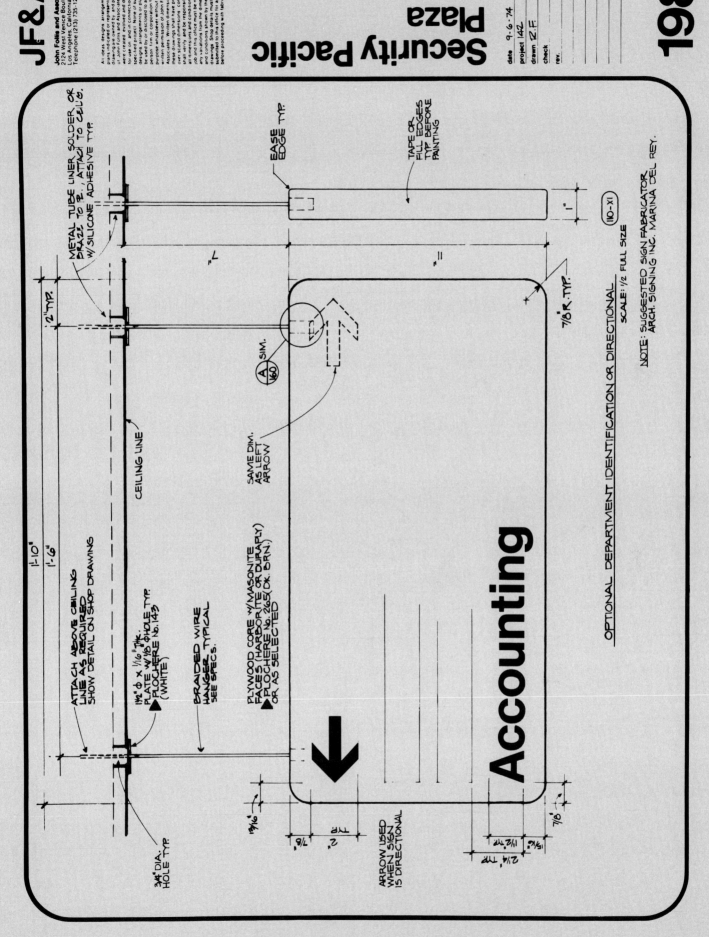

Room No. Designation Plan: Floors 26-29

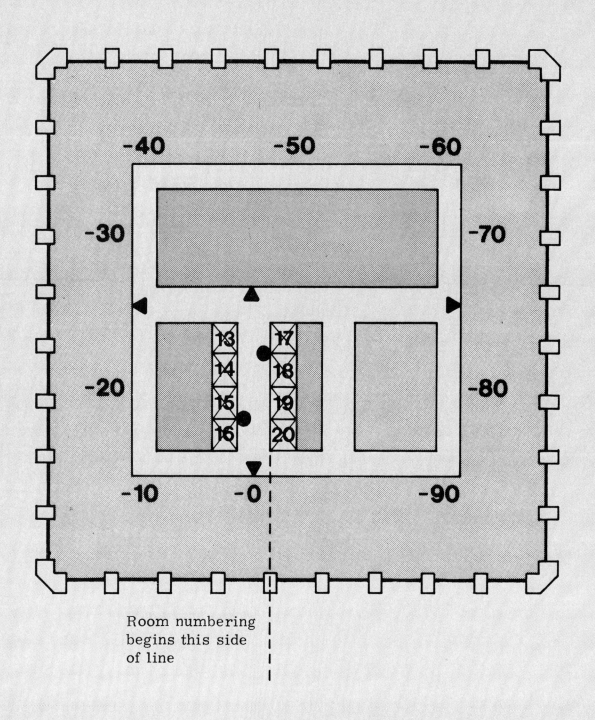

Room numbering
begins this side
of line

● Floor Directory

▲ Room No. Directional Sign
(If required)

Room No. Designation Plan: Floors 35-38

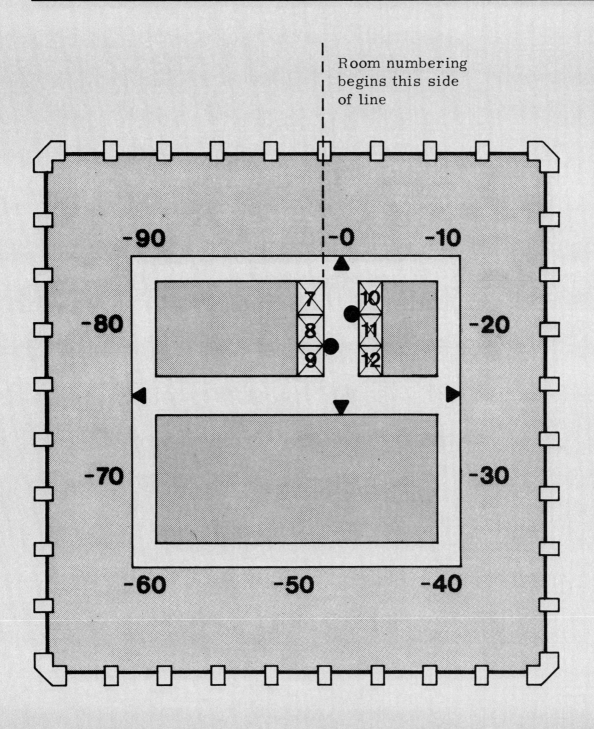

Room numbering begins this side of line

● Floor Directory

▲ Room No. Directional Sign
(If required)

Room No. Designation Plan: Floors 46-52

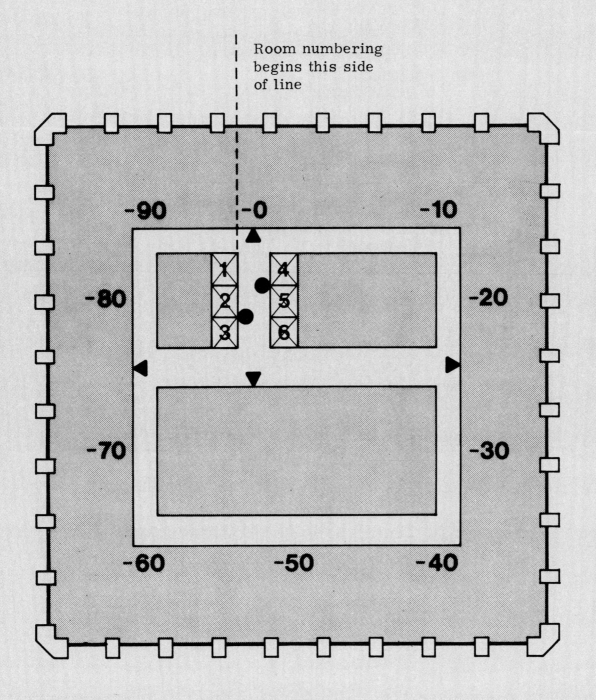

Room numbering
begins this side
of line

-90   -0   -10

-80   -20

-70   -30

-60   -50   -40

● Floor Directory

▲ Room No. Directional Sign
(If required)

Security Pacific Plaza

Sign Ordering Instructions

Instructions for Ordering Signs

This booklet will give all necessary information for ordering "systems" signs for Security Pacific Plaza.

The sign systems covered are as follows:
Directory for entire project on Plaza Level (Page 2)
Directory for Concourse occupants on Concourse Level (Page 2)
Signing for Concourse Bank and banking facilities in crossover floor lounges (Page 3)
Signing for all S. P. N. B. occupied spaces (Pages 4-8)
Signing for all Multi-tenant Tower public areas (Pages 9-11)

Explanation

Sign or Copy Panel		Sign No.	Part No.
Typical panel, two-line 157	**Administration &** **Industrial Development Section**	117	2C (39)

For each tenant directory strip, sign or name panel a title is given and if required special instructions. Underneath the title are page numbers that refer to John Follis & Associates drawings that were originally issued for the fabrication of the signs. New signs ordered will be in accordance with these drawings, all shop drawings and corresponding specifications.

For visual reference a drawing is included with sample copy.
These drawings are not to scale.

The "Sign No." column gives the identifying number of each basic sign series and when used with the Part No. exactly identifies the item being ordered.

The "Part No." column gives the number of a particular part of a sign. In addition, for all copy panels that identify a company, department, individual, etc., a number is given in parenthesis. This number is the maximum number of characters and spaces per line. For some signs a double-sized strip is available for copy that is too long for a single strip.

The sign company has a copy of this book and is responsible for supplying the sign as ordered with the Sign and Part No's. They are responsible for the layout of the copy, punctuation and capitalization, letter and word spacing and colors.

Architectural Signing Inc.
4082 Glencoe Ave.
Marina del Rey, Ca 90291
213-821-8094   Rep: Hanley Bloom

Ship & bill to:

Pacific Southwest Realty Co.
Attn: Office of the Building 29-2
P.O. Box 2097 Terminal Annex
Los Angeles, California 90051

Date of order 0/0/00   Ordered by xxxxx   Order no. 0
Date required 0/0/00   Approved by xxxxx   Page 1 of 1

Unit no.	Sign no.	Part no.	Qty.	ASI	Room no.∗	Copy	Floor no.	Tenant
1	117	2C	2			Administration &	35	S. P. N. B.
2						Industrial Development Section		
3								
4								
5								
6								
7								
8								
9								
10								
11								
12								
13								
14								
15								
16								
17								
18								
19								
20								

Special instructions:

For use by Architectural Signing, Inc. (ASI) only:

Qty.	Description	Unit	Ext.
Qty.	Description	Unit	Ext.
Date received		Typeset	Die-cut
Approved by		Proof	Check

∗ Room no. only applicable to directories 18, 20 and 101

S.P.N.B. Section

Strip		Sign No.	Part No.
Department identification 30, 37 & 40	**1100** **AUDIT DEPARTMENT**	18	S1 (20)
Division identification 30, 37 & 40	**Central & Mid-City Div.**	18	S2 (23)
Individual, listed separately 30, 37 & 40	**1300** Malt, John R., Jr.	18	S5 (25)

Tower Tenant Section

Strip		Sign No.	Part No.
Company 30, 38 & 40	**3250** **Rutgers, Schelling & Walters** **Attorneys at Law**	18	T2
Individuals, listed under a company 30, 38 & 40	**2810** Margaret J. Richter	18	T3
Individual & Title, listed under a company 30, 38 & 40	Gerhard Schmidt-Peterson, Asst. Corporate Tr. Officer & Secty.	18	T4
Individual, listed separately 30, 38 & 40	**1300** Malt, John R., Jr.	18	T5

Concourse Section

Strip		Sign No.	Part No.
Store identification 30, 38 & 40	**Hallmark Books and Cards**	18	C2 (23)

Strip		Sign No.	Part No.
Store identification 35, 40	**12** **Hallmark Books and Cards**	20	6 (32)

Desk Bar

Sign or Copy Panel

Sign or Copy Panel		Sign No.	Part No.
Name/Title sign w/o name panels 20		10	NP
Hours information sign w/ upper name panel 24	Hours	10	H
Department sign w/o name panels 22		11	NP
Name panel Note: Same panel used for signs 10, 11 & 131	**Byron M. Caveny**	10	1 (30)
Title panel, one or two-line 20	**Assistant Manager**	10	2 (30)
Time copy panel Note: Same panel used for signs 11 & 151 24	**Monday thru Thursday** 10 am to 3 pm **Friday** 10 am to 6 pm	10	3
Title panel, blank		10	4
Dept. panel, one or two line Special instructions: Indicate if the panel should have FDIC symbol 22	**New Accounts** **FDIC**	11	2 (30)

Hours Information, Wall

Sign

Sign		Sign No.	Part No.
Sign w/ upper name panel 24 & 25	Hours	151	HP

Floor Directory

Sign or Copy Panel		Sign No.	Part No.
Sign w/ blank name panels special instructions: Indicate floor number. Two signs/flr. 144 & 155	**14** ← →	112	BP
Dept. name panel, one-line Special instructions: Two/flr. 155	Bank Locations Department	112	1A (37)
Division name panel, one-line Special instructions: Two/flr. 155	Branch Service Division	112	1B (36)
Section name panel, one-line Special instructions: Two/flr. 155	Quarters Planning Section	112	1C (35)
Typical name panel, two-line Special instructions: Two/flr. 155 *Copy flush left Indicate A, B, or C	Administration & Industrial Development Section	112	2* (*)

Department Identification, Primary

Sign or Copy Panel		Sign No.	Part No.
Sign w/ blank name panels 145 & 156		113	BP
Department name panel, one-line 156	Bank Locations Department	113	1A (41)
Division name panel 156	Branch Service Division	113	1B (40)
Section name panel 156	Quarters Planning Section	113	1C (39)

S.P.N.B. Tower and Units 1 and 2 Signing

Department Identification, Large Secondary

Sign or Copy Panel		Sign No.	Part No.
Sign w/ blank panels 146 & 157		114	BP
Department panel 157	Bank Locations Department	114	1A (41)
Division panel 157	Branch Service Division	114	1B (40)
Section panel 157	Quarters Planning Section	114	1C (39)

Department Identification, Small Secondary

Sign or Copy Panel		Sign No.	Part No.
Sign w/ blank name panels 146 & 157		115	BD
Department panel 157	Bank Locations Department	115	1A (41)
Division panel 157	Branch Service Division	115	1B (40)
Section panel 157	Quarters Planning Section	115	1C (39)

Directional, Wall

Sign or Copy Panel		Sign No.	Part No.
Sign w/ arrow panel and blank name panels Special instructions: Indicate left, right or up arrow 147 & 157		117	BP
Department panel, one-line 151	Bank Locations Department	117	1A (41)
Division panel, one-line 157	Branch Service Division	117	1B (40)
Section panel, one-line 157	Quarters Planning Section	117	1C (39)
Typical panel, two-line 157 *Copy flush left Indicate A, B, or C	Administration & Industrial Development Section	117	2* (*)

Directional, Ceiling

Sign or Copy Panel		Sign No.	Part No.
Sign w/ arrow panel and blank name panels Special instructions: Indicate left, right or up arrow 148 & 158		118	BP
Department panel 158	Bank Locations Department	118	1A (41)
Division panel 158	Branch Service Division	118	1B (40)
Section panel 158	Quarters Planning Section	118	1C (39)
Full panel 158	←Elevator	118	2

Clock Identification

Sign or Copy Panel		Sign No.	Part No.
Sign w/o copy panel 149		131	NP
Zone panel 149	New York	131	1
Time identification panel, reversible 149	Standard Daylight Savings	131	2

Room Identification w/Reversible Panel

Sign or Copy Panel		Sign No.	Part No.
Sign w/o copy panels 149		151	NP
Room identification panel 149	Conference Room	151	1
Enter information panel, reversible Note: Back side is blank 149	Occupied	151	2

Corporate Identity Panel

Sign		Sign No.	Part No.
Two signs per floor, to be ordered with 112 143	SECURITY PACIFIC NATIONAL BANK	111	1

Room Identification

Sign		Sign No.	Part No.
Sign, one or two-lines of copy 150	Authorized Personnel Only	116	1

S.P.N.B. Tower and Units 1 and 2 Signing

Fire Extinguisher Identification

Sign		Sign No.	Part No.
Sign 150	Fire Extinguisher	132	1

Core Room Identification

Sign		Sign No.	Part No.
Sign Note: To be used on dark laminated doors only. For light colored wood doors use Sign 99 on page 12. 42	**Sprinkler Control Valve**	133	1
Sign 42	**Men**	133	2
Sign 42	**Women**	133	3

Maximum Occupancy Information

Sign		Sign No.	Part No.
Sign Note: Indicate room function & maximum occupancy nos. 150	This room or area is approved for the following use: **Dining Room** The maximum number of occupants shall not exceed: **163** City of Los Angeles Municipal Code	134	1

Floor Directory

Sign or Copy Panel		Sign No.	Part No.
Sign w/blank name panel Special instructions: Indicate floor number. Two sign/floor 192 & 203	**14** ← →	101	BP
Company panel, one-line Special instructions: Two/flr. 203	3710 KENWOOD CORPORATION	101	1A (30)
Department panel, one-line Special instructions: Two/flr. 203	Accounting	101	1B (35)
Typical panel, two-line Special instructions: Two/flr. 203 *Copy flush left indicate A or B	3740 MARKMAN, JOSEPHSON, KING, CARNEY & ROSENBERG	101	2* (*)

Room Number Directional

Sign or Copy Panel		Sign No.	Part No.
Sign w/o copy panels 193		102	NP
Left arrow panel 193	← 3710-3728	102	L (8)
Right arrow panel 193	3730-3748 →	102	K (8)
Blank panel		102	B

Tenant Identification, Small

Sign or Copy Panel		Sign No.	Part No.
Sign w/o copy panel 194 & 204		104	NP
Room No. & one-line company or Room No. alone panel 204	**3710** KENWOOD CORPORATION	104	1 (19)

Tenant Identification, Medium

Sign or Copy Panel		Sign No.	Part No.
Sign w/o copy panel 194 & 204		105	NP
Two or three line company panel 204	**3720** AMERICAN PLYWOOD CORPORATION Accounting	105	1 (19)

Tenant Identification, Large

Sign or Copy Panel		Sign No.	Part No.
Sign w/o copy panel 194 & 204		106	NP
Four or five line company panel 204	**3740** SCHWARTZBERGER, PHILLIPS, WU, SMITH, JOSEPHSON, GRABOWSKI & MORLEY Attorneys at Law	106	1 (19)

Individual Identification

Sign or Copy Panel		Sign No.	Part No.
Sign w/o name panels Special instructions: Indicate Tenant ident. panel (104, 105 or 106) & total quantity of name panels. 194, 195 & 204		107	NP
Individual name panel 204	Lorraine P. Murphy	107	1 (25)

Fire Extinguisher Identification

Sign		Sign No.	Part No.
Sign Note: To be used on painted cabinets only. For vinyl covered cabinets use Sign 132, page 9. 42	**Fire Extinguisher**	100	1

Core Room Identification

Sign		Sign No.	Part No.
Sign Note: To be used on light colored wood doors only. For dark laminated doors use Sign 133 on page 9. 42	**Sprinkler Control Valve**	99	1
Sign 42	**Men**	99	2
Sign 42	**Women**	99	3

Glossary

Acrylic. Widely used for signing, this plastic is available in colored or clear sheets or shapes which can be heat-formed. Common trade name, Plexiglas.

Ambient light. The existing or spill light in the environment.

Architectural graphics. Graphic design devices which are primarily decorative in nature such as wall graphics, flags, and banners, not including signs, directories, or graphic devices which communicate information.

Ascender: That part of a letter extending above the body of the letter, as in: b, d, f, h, k, l, t.

Blocking. Wood or metal backup material used to facilitate the wall installation of heavy signs.

Ceiling-mounted signs. Signs supported by a ceiling, whether directly attached to or hanging from it.

Channel letter. A three-dimensional letter of metal or plastic with an open back or front for neon lighting.

Code. The body of laws, ordinances, or legal restrictions imposed by a governing body to control the use of signs.

Copy. See Message.

Corporate logotype. The graphic design of the name of a corporation or institution which identifies that entity.

Corporate symbol. The graphic device or mark which a corporation or institution uses to identify itself.

Descender. That part of a letter extending below the body of the letter, as in: g, j, p, q, y.

Die-cut vinyl letters. A machine is used to cut out letters using an edge-bent rule of sharpened steel.

Double-faced sign. Signs with a message or copy on both front and back.

Family of signs. Signs which share common design characteristics such as shape or color.

Fiberglass. A plastic made from polyester resins reinforced with chopped glass fibers. See also Chapter 12.

Figure-ground. Psychological term related to perception of a pattern and its background, where the foreground-background relationships may be reversible.

Finished art. Art used in the process of fabricating signs or wall graphics.

Flush mounted. Signs or letters mounted tight to a surface rather than spaced away from it.

Foam tape (or adhesive foam tape). Name given to various vinyl or urethane foam tapes with self-adhesive backing.

Framing-projector. Special lighting fixture designed to confine light to a specific shape or area.

Galvanize. To plate metal with a zinc coating as a protection against rust.

Halo effect (or halation). A halo or overglow around lighted plastic letters caused by overly strong internal lighting.

Hard-edge(d) graphics. Painted graphic designs of flat areas of color which meet to form a line or hard edge.

High-pressure laminate. A thin laminated sheet of plastic with a melamine surface. Trade names: Formica, Textolite.

Hot stamping. A process of pressing the copy (message) into a plastic sign by using heated metal letters.

Let-in. Refers to creating a wall recess or mortise to receive a sign panel or plaque.

Letterforms. The shapes that the letters form.

Letter style. All the letters and numerals of one alphabet of the same design. Also typeface or alphabet.

Lexan. Trade name for shatterproof, transparent sheet plastic (polycarbonate), made by General Electric. Used as a protective covering over graphics instead of glass or acrylic.

Magnetic signs. Removable signs or copy strips utilizing a very thin layer of magnetized metal.

Message. All items on the sign face, such as letters, arrows, symbols. Also referred to as copy, wording, or legend.

Negative area. The space surrounding letterforms.

Photoetching. The photochemical process of reproducing a sign message on a metal plaque or plate.

Photo positive. A photographic image on paper, film, or glass which reproduces the original copy.

Photo negative. Reverse of the positive.

Pinned-out letters. (Also pinned, blind pinned, or pegged out.) Letters which are held out from the wall using pins or pegs.

Polyurethane coating. See Chapter 12.

Porcelain enamel. A glass-like coating for metal signs, which is fused to the surface using high temperatures.

Prespaced letters. Refers to letters (normally of vinyl) which have been prespaced on a removable tape by the manufacturer.

Primary alphabet. The alphabet most extensively used for a project's sign system.

Punch list. A list of errors or omissions in the sign fabricator's work requiring corrections.

Routing. Any process of cutting into or through a material to reproduce letter forms.

Router-engraving. A machine process of reproducing a sign message in plastic or metal with a high-speed router burr or rotating cutter.

Sans serif. Pertaining to those Gothic-type faces without the short cross line or "trick" at the ends of the main strokes in Roman letters.

Secondary alphabet. A second or less important alphabet used in a signing system for signs of minor importance or for contrast.

Seed lamps. Very tiny (seed-like) incandescent lamps.

Sign can or enclosure. The cabinet or body of three-dimensional signs, particularly of internally lighted signs.

Signface. Surface on which message or copy is placed.

Sign symbol. The graphic device which stands for a concept or object. A symbol may be a pictogram, pictograph, glyph, or geometric or abstract shape.

Sign type. A group of signs which are identical in size and shape but differ in copy message.

Silicone adhesive. A silicone rubber glue widely used for the installation of signs.

Silk screen printing or screen process. A method of printing in which paint is forced through a special screen to print on any material.

Soft-edge(d) graphics. Painted graphics involving modeled forms or areas of blended color with soft edges.

Wall-mounted signs. Any method of attaching a sign to a wall.

"Wall-washers." Built-in lighting fixtures used to illuminate walls evenly.

Selected Readings

Birren, Faber. *Light, Color, and Environment*. New York: Van Nostrand, Reinhold, 1969.

Boston Redevelopment Authority. *City Signs and Lights*. Boston: MIT Press, 1973.

Carr, Richard. "The Legibility of Signs." *Print Magazine,* November/December 1969.

Cooley, R.H. *Complete Metal Working Manual*. New York ARCO.

Crosby/Fletcher/Forbes. *A Sign Systems Manual*. London: Studio Vista, 1970.

Ewald, William R., Jr., and Daniel R. Mandelker. *Street Graphics*. Washington, D.C.: American Society of Landscape Architects Foundation, 1971.

Fox, Martin, ed. *Print Casebooks: The Best in Environmental Graphics*. R.C. Publications, Inc., Washington, D.C.

Furstenberg, Arno Ford. *Architectural Signing Handbook*. Marina Del Rey, Calif. ASI Sign Systems, 1978.

Gibson, J.J. *The Perception of the Visual World*. Boston: Houghton-Mifflin, 1950.

Glass, Jim, ed. *Environmental Graphics Sourcebook,* Part One. Chicago: Society of Environmental Graphics Designers.

Herdig, Walter, ed. *Archigraphia*. Zurich, Switzerland: The Graphis Press.

Holland, Morris K. *Psychology: An Introduction to Human Behavior*. Lexington, Mass.: Heath and Co., 1978.

Itten, Johannes. *The Elements of Color*. New York: Van Nostrand, Reinhold, 1970.

Kepes, Gyorgy, ed. *Education of Vision*. New York: George Braziller, 1965.

———. *Sign, Image, Symbol*. New York: George Braziller, 1966.

Malay, Rod. *Graphic Communication: Urban Complex*. Ottawa, Canada: Community Planning Association of Canada.

Margolies, John, ed. *Design Review: Industrial Design 22nd Annual*. New York: Whitney Library of Design, 1976.

Mead, Margaret, and Rudolf Modley. "Communication among All People, Everywhere," *Natural History* 77, no. 7 (August/September 1968), pp. 56–63.

Sutton, James. *Signs in Action*. London: Studio Vista and New York: Reinhold, 1965.

Walker, John R. *Modern Metal Working*. South Holland, Ill.: Goodheart-Willcox.

Index

Italic numbers refer to illustrations of a particular work, or an architect or designer's project, or the location of an illustrated work.